# CRIME SQUAD

# CRIME SQUAD

LIFE AND DEATH ON LONDON'S FRONT LINE

MIKE PANNETT AND KRIS HOLLINGTON

THISTLE
PUBLISHING

First published in 2016 by:

Thistle Publishing
36 Great Smith Street
London
SW1P 3BU

www.thistlepublishing.co.uk

It is important to ensure that the secrets and histories of some of the individuals encountered through my work (witnesses, police officers engaged in sensitive work and informers, all of whom have good reason to fear retribution) are not set out in a manner that would enable people to recognize them. To be true to both requirements, the authors have, with the exception of names that are in the public domain, protected the identities of these people by changing names and altering some background details. The reader should be left in no doubt that every case is real, however. Those cases which are a matter of public record are reported in their original detail.

*Dedication*

*Every day police officers around the country say goodbye to friends and family; close their front door behind them and set off for work. Too many of those officers have never returned home to their loved ones. The Roll of Honour and Remembrance lists more than 4,000 names of UK police officers killed in the line of duty. Whether you patrol an inner city or a rural beat, danger can be obvious or appear when you least expect it. This book is dedicated to the men and women – past, present and future – of the thin blue line who everyday leave their homes prepared to put themselves in danger for our safety.*

*With this in mind, a portion of the sale from every book sold will go to Care of Police Survivors (COPS), a UK registered charity dedicated to helping the families of police officers who have lost their lives whilst on duty. It aims to ensure that surviving family members have all the help they need to cope with such a tragedy and that they remain part of the police family.*

*Please see the COPS website ukcops.org for more information, to volunteer or to donate.*

# ACKNOWLEDGEMENTS

The authors would like to thank the family of Police Constable Patrick Dunne as well as all those who read and gave feedback on the book, along with our agent and publisher, Andrew Lownie and David Haviland for their tireless support.

Mike would also like to thank Yorkshire Tea and Grand Central Railways for all their support, for getting him up in the morning and for keeping him moving throughout the day!

yorkshiretea.co.uk

grandcentral.com

# PREFACE

DETECTIVE SUPERINTENDENT JOHN
JONES, SOUTH WEST LONDON MAJOR
INVESTIGATION POOL (RTD).

Crime Squad provides an accurate and fascinating picture of police work at the sharp end in the violent streets of South West London a quarter of a century ago. From weary hours spent on uncomfortable perches high in the rooftops watching the activities of drug dealers and street robbers, to moments of real danger when bullets buzzed past one's head, it brings alive the day-to-day lives of the police officers whose lives are dedicated to protecting our lives and safety.

Much of the book is devoted to setting down the investigation into the brutal murder of a likeable rogue, William Danso, and that of P.C. Patrick Dunne. Patrick was everyone's ideal community copper. Intelligent, caring and industrious; his last act in life, trying to protect the safety of others, was symptomatic of his character.

I was a policeman for 35 years, nearly all of that time as a career detective, and was involved in the investigation of many brutal and violent crimes, including murders, rapes, armed robberies, cases of torture, child abuse and many more. None of them touched me as much as the murder of Patrick. The deliberate murder of a police officer is an attack on society. When celebrated by the miscreants, it almost defies belief.

This book does not make for comfortable reading. It is in fact a very real horror story. Grit your teeth and read it. Patrick, and others who have fallen in our service deserve it.

# PART ONE

F riday evening and I'm crouched on a stinking tenth-floor stairwell, deep inside Battersea's vast and notorious Winstanley Estate, home to gangs, guns and drugs.

It's November 1989 and I'm a keen, newly-arrived 23-year-old probationer constable, desperate to prove myself and this is my chance, my first ever drugs raid.

Even though it's supposed to be an easy job, my heart's pounding like a pair of trainers in a tumble dryer.

Having grown up in rural North Yorkshire, I've only ever been in a tower block once before in my life (the police training college at Hendon), and never so high up.

This area's not only top of London's crime tables; the local criminals are smashing records for car thefts and street robberies for the whole of Europe.

From my vantage point in the stairwell I peer across the landing and examine the target door. Behind it is suspected cannabis dealer Clinton Smith. The most remarkable thing about him is that he is 70-years-old.

\*\*\*

A week or so earlier, I'd just left the nick on my solo foot patrol when I glanced up to see a white lad in his early 20s looking at me nervously from across the street. He broke eye contact in the way only the guilty can and so I stopped him.

"Excuse me sir," I said, blocking his way, and taking hold of his wrists so he couldn't do a runner. "Why are you so nervous?"

"Nervous, me? I'm not nervous, I-"

His eyes were glazed and puffy.

"I'm going to search you, ok? Don't move."

I went through his pockets and amongst keys, bits of paper and some loose change, was a tiny piece of cannabis, wrapped in cling film.

"Oh god, please don't arrest me," he said. "I've had a caution before. I'm a postman with two kids, I can't lose my job."

"Tell me where you got it from, I'll dispose of this and we'll say no more about it."

He considered this for a few seconds. "Ok. It's an old guy on the top floor of a block in the Winstanley."

I took the man's details and dropped the little piece of cannabis down the drain.

"In future, if I search you again and find so much as a crumb of cannabis, I will arrest you."

The postie sloped off gratefully and I returned the short distance to base, our grand Victorian redbrick building, which was but a truncheon's toss from the Thames and Battersea Park.

I found Pete, red faced (the result of a hangover) his clip-on tie missing and his shirt un-tucked, enveloped by pipe smoke at his desk in a small, dark office behind the canteen on the second floor. Pete had served 28 years as a PC, the last six of which had been as the LIO (Local Intelligence Officer).

Pete, whose white beard, glasses, pipe and unkempt appearance made him look like a wise but absent-minded old wizard, was surrounded by library drawers which were packed full of thousands of index cards for suspects that went back forty years.

"Alright Pete?"

"What is it Constable Pannett?"

As the new boy and a probationer PC, I was at the bottom of the rung in Battersea and still had a lot to do to win the trust and respect of my fellow officers.

"Do we have anything on a possible septuagenarian cannabis dealer in the Winstanley estate?"

I explained my encounter with the postie as Pete's fingers skipped skilfully through the mass of yellowing index cards. He stopped and pulled out a card.

"Yes, we have something, not much though. Some similar reports. But if you want a warrant you're going to need more evidence than a street-side confession from a stoned postie who would say anything to avoid losing his job."

He passed me the card.

"Thanks Pete, I'll check it out."

"Fill your boots, Constable Pannett."

***

The Winstanley: a huge council estate built in fits and starts between 1956 and 1972, overlooked by three monstrous 20-storey towers surrounded by 25 low-rise blocks, which, for a lad recently arrived from North Yorkshire, added up to a confusing concrete warren full of dark and dead-end alleys. Along with the adjacent council blocks on nearby streets, it was home to 10,000 people, and sat to the immediate north of Clapham Junction, the busiest railway station in Europe, with more than 2,000 trains rattling below residents' windows every day.

This station attracted street robbers who stole from commuters and tourists at knifepoint before blowing their booty on drugs, readily available from flats across the estate, or from the Wellington Pub, a squat sixties building of dark bricks and concrete where no police officer dared show his face, unless accompanied by a battalion from the riot squad.

The estate was also a short sprint from the busy high street, full of gastropubs and boutiques thronging with the borough's wealthier residents who lived in luxury apartments and renovated Victorian town houses, and who drove the expensive cars so beloved by the thieves of Winstanley.

As a lad who'd grown up in the Yorkshire countryside where everyone knew and looked out for each other, I was still in shock from the lack of community. Law-abiding residents felt helpless, as though criminals were holding them hostage. Every day we dealt with two or three robberies and/or burglaries. Sometimes, especially in the case of the elderly, burglars struck in broad daylight, often kicking the doors in while residents were still in their homes. Treasured personal possessions were sold for peanuts or swapped for small amounts of drugs.

I'd been to one flat that had been completely emptied of every last piece of furniture, along with its new doors and windows, when the owner, a young woman with two children had gone to spend a couple of days with her sick mother. She'd just finishing furnishing the flat after the council gave her a grant.

"I had sod-all as it was," she said, "And they've even taken that."

Taking down a 70-year-old cannabis dealer didn't sound like it was going to make much of an impression on our terrible crime figures but I had to start somewhere. Besides, it was unpleasant for residents to walk past kids smoking cannabis in the communal areas.

I went in plain clothes first thing in the morning, a time when any self-respecting drug dealer would still be in bed. At night the atmosphere changed and lookouts announced the arrival of any stranger (i.e., cops or possible prey).

After getting the keys to the emergency stairwell from the caretaker who'd just done his rounds and picked up the detritus of the night's drug taking (syringes scattered around the swings in the children's play area), I went up with my best mate and fellow eager-beaver probationer Mark, a 28-year-old, black-haired Cornish lad who'd won the 'Baton of Honour' at police training college.

We spent the day watching the long corridor from behind the fire door and counted fifteen people who were prepared to climb the ten flights of stairs (the broken lifts had been awaiting repair for more than a week) to score their cannabis.

I then found out the name of the person paying the bills at the address and spoke to Brian aka 'Bry', a senior PC with fifteen years of service who was about to join the CID, and who knew the Winstanley better than anyone else at the station.

"Good work Pannett, let's talk to Phil about putting together a job."

Sergeant Phil was an old sweat with 28 years' service. Phil was of the 'been there, done that and worn the T-shirt' type. He was unflappable, no matter what mess was dumped in his lap.

"Well, it's not worth much, really, is it?" he muttered, keeping his cigarette clamped between his lips.

"It'd be good experience for Pannett, sarge," Bry said, "And a drug dealer is a drug dealer, no matter how small-time he might be."

Phil squinted at me through his cigarette smoke.

"Alright Pannett. Put the job together. But don't fuck it up, alright?"

***

Even though it's 7pm on a Friday night I'm not expecting a lot of people to be inside, or much in the way of resistance. I'm more worried about Winston; that he'll drop dead of a heart attack when I kick in his door, which, as far as we can tell, is only secured with a simple latch lock. As it's supposed to be an easy one, I've been given the honour of leading the charge; I can't wait to get it over with.

I look around. We're all in plainclothes, doing our best not to be rumbled, although in true amateur undercover cop fashion, we're all clean shaven and dressed in freshly-pressed jeans, so we're not going to fool anyone.

Along with Bry and Mark, two other officers are behind me on the stairwell. Timbo, a 6"4' ex-Royal Marine and Johnny, a hyperactive officer whose ambition is to one day drive the Area Car (Area Car drivers are trained in advanced driving and tactical pursuit and are the Met's fast responders, i.e., experienced cops able to deal with any job; they were gods to us probies). Another two officers are waiting down below, in case Clinton decides to chuck the evidence out of his window, and to keep an eye on our unmarked van, and in case the local gangs decide to nick it, petrol bomb it or give it a new paint job.

The others look suitably bored and I try to play along, as if this is no big deal.

I'm shaking from the adrenaline so force myself to take slow, deep breaths. My mouth is dry and my hands are sweaty. I can't wait until this job is over, so that I have one raid under my belt.

"You alright Pannett?" Bry asks.

"I'm fine."

"Only you look like you've eaten a rotten egg."

I look at the landing. All quiet. And then across the estate. It's dark but the glow from the lights of Winstanley is turning the night clouds orange. I'm an outdoors country lad, used to the dales and moors of Yorkshire. This concrete jungle is something else.

I look back down the line. Mark, white-faced, looks exactly like how I feel.

Even Bry, perhaps picking up on our nerves looks uncertain when I say: "Ready?"

Four heads nod.

"Ok, follow me!"

I charge out of the fire escape, along the landing and turn to face the plain black door. I take a step back, heart pounding at the thought that I'm about to crash headfirst into the unknown, but with no time left to dwell, I raise my size ten boot and, with as much weight as I can, leap towards the door, aiming for the Yale lock. To my relief, it implodes, flying back into the wall with an almighty crash, and comes off its hinges as I push past it and into the dark hallway that stretches before me. I see the door to my left and burst through it and into a bedroom, yelling: "Police!"

The light is on and the room is full of acrid smoke.

A young black man is standing in front of me. He's tall, thin, sinewy and wild-eyed, and he's pointing a double-barrelled sawn-off shotgun at my head.

# CHAPTER ONE

# YORKIE COMES TO TOWN

One year earlier, Sunday 28 November 1988.

I looked through the glass at Mum and Dad, waving me off from the small platform of our hometown station and then glanced down at the seat next to me. Someone had left behind a copy of *The Sun* newspaper. I pressed it against the window so Mum and Dad could see the front page. The headline read: *Police Cadets in Sex Drugs and Rock and Roll Scandal* and there was a photo of some young lady officers laughing as they showed their stocking-stops. Mum and Dad's expressions froze in shock. I grinned and gave them the thumbs-up as the train pulled away.

Dad was a scientist who worked with fibre optics and my brother and two sisters were all academics. My brother went on to become quartermaster of the Thames, responsible for all shipping on the river. I was the black sheep. Academia held no interest for me; I was the outdoors type (we lived deep in the Yorkshire countryside) and loved to talk to anyone and everyone about girls, motorbikes and York City FC.

After school I'd joined the Territorial Army (First Battalion, Yorkshire Volunteers, the barracks backed onto York City's home pitch and you could watch the Tuesday night footy for free). I specialised in Signals, which I loved, and was the runner up out of 180 men when we were tested for overall performance (I was pipped by the Sergeant Major's son, funny that). I then went from job to job (vacuum cleaner salesman to farm labourer) and worked selling car parts from a Ford garage (I can still remember some of the seven-figure serial numbers for different parts) before I decided I was going to join the police.

I applied to join North Yorkshire and sat the multi-choice exam. I was a bit worried about my performance until I noticed there was an intelligent university boy sitting to my immediate left and, well, I passed everything. Then I learned they wouldn't take me because I was short-sighted and wore glasses. I told them I could shoot a gnat's nut off at fifty paces but they weren't having it.

The only force that didn't mind (apart from Devon and Cornwall, way too far away from home) was London's Metropolitan Police, aka the Met. Apparently, after two years, you could transfer and any force would then take you, glasses or no.

When the Met accepted my application, I was 24-years-old, driving a van, delivering engine parts all over Yorkshire. I loved the scenery but it wasn't well paid and it certainly wasn't a challenge. If I wanted to move on, I had to leave all this behind for the big city.

\*\*\*

I'd never been to London and so was quite nervous when I stepped out of the train at Kings Cross; I'd never seen so many people in one place. They were rushing around, like some emergency was taking place; I seemed to travel at half their speed. The first person to talk to me was a tall lady who was standing with a friend on the station concourse. She stopped me by placing a hand on my chest. She was attractive, in her 20s and was holding an unlit cigarette, which she waved at me hopefully.

"Got a light, luv?" she said.

"Yeah, sure," I replied, fishing out my lighter.

The young lady and her friend then propositioned me, for a price, an offer which, blushing, I politely declined. My next encounter was with an illegal minicab driver who offered to take me to Hendon for a fiver.

I opted instead for the tube, which was in its own way no less daunting. The Met had warned all us young recruits that pickpockets and street robbers were targeting naive students heading for the college, so I was on high alert as I descended into the bowels of London.

I'd only seen one black person before in my life, a friend of mine who was in the TA with me and whom everyone referred to as 'Black Ronnie.' We'd become quite matey after working together at a terrible job cleaning bricks (Ronnie went on to become an RAF navigator). Now there were loads of black people everywhere I looked and I couldn't help but stare, fascinated at everyone and everything.

There was standing room only on the crowded tube train. I smiled at the other people around me, like any Yorkshire lad would, and said: "Busy isn't it?" to a man I found myself a touch too close to. He gave me a tight-lipped smile in response and turned away. No one was making eye contact and no one was talking, which left me totally flummoxed. Why weren't people talking to one another? I stood in uncomfortable silence as the train rattled its way north and the crowds gradually thinned out until I stepped off, above ground, in Hendon.

I found my way to the college and then had no trouble locating the Peel Bar, marvelling at the dozens of people that were already there (the Met was on a recruitment drive and 170 people were in my group). Blokes outnumbered the ladies by at least five-to-one. I'd been expecting the place to be overwhelmed by Cockneys, but there were people from all over, even all the way from Wales and Scotland. I eventually made myself known to the administration and was presented with a key.

"Ninth floor," the woman told me, handing me an A4 paper with a long list of do's and don'ts. The ninth floor! I'd never been in a tower block before in my life.

The room was cell-like, with a sink, which doubled as a urinal. There was an old fashioned chest of drawers. I opened the top draw. A bible was inside. I looked out through the thin, drafty window and saw the underground trains rattling by, the city lights and heard the unceasing ocean-like roar of traffic. The wind rattled the window; it felt as though the building was swaying with the weather. I lit a fag and sat down at the desk. Someone had carved a message into the surface: 'Good luck you're going to need it!' and I wondered what the hell I'd done.

*** 

We had twenty weeks of intensive training. I was fit thanks to the TA and had no fear of the physical tests. We needed to be in top physical condition and had to be able to run one-and-a-half-miles in under twelve minutes; a piece of cake, as were the trials involving sit-ups, push-ups, press-ups and standing jumps. But when it came to studying, I was terrified. I'd left school with no qualifications and succeeding at exams was to me, as likely as getting hit by a snowball in the Sahara. Fail two exams at Hendon and you were done.

But I was lucky. Two academics – Graham, a muscular rugby player from Durham, who came from a family of miners, and Mark, a good-looking, dark-haired posh boy from Surrey – were in my class and bunked on the same floor as me. They took me under their wing

"The trick is to avoid the bar at all costs," Mark said, "Until we've studied for at least three hours and had a run."

"Then we can have a quick pint," Graham said.

"Or three," I added hopefully.

"And then to bed."

Mark and Graham taught me how to study, and the use of cue cards as memory aids. We spent hours working each night and even questioned each other first thing in the morning (after Graham, an expert trumpet player, had woken us at the crack of dawn by playing First Call) when we were in our floor's three baths, all in a row, separated by thin partitions.

Our first exam was on a Monday morning with the result handed out that night in the classrooms (classes were eight hours a day, Monday to Friday). I was terrified and my hands were shaking by the time the results were delivered but was totally delighted when I realised I'd passed. I may not have been near the top like Graham and Mark (who once managed to score 100%) but this was enough to make me realise that I could learn just as well as the university types; it was all down to application and enthusiasm. I learned everything verbatim and can still recall every word of the Theft Act as it was when I learned it then. And because I was actually interested in the law, I started to do well, sometimes coming third, behind Graham and Mark.

Although they were academically gifted, Graham and Mark were a couple of years younger than me and didn't have much in the way of real-world experience, and were lacking in the common sense department, so I was able to teach them a bit about this. Together we formed a bond and stuck together, and took everything to do with our studies seriously – although we cut loose at weekends. We were being paid a salary and had no expenses, so we could afford to party and once even ended up in Stringfellows.

My 'common sense' sometimes got me into trouble, however. Our first ever role-play was on a London bus. The trainer asked for volunteers.

"Go on Yorkie," Mark said so, unable to resist a challenge, I stepped up. We were on the top deck. The instructor asked me to get him off the bus.

"Begin," he commanded.

"Excuse me sir," I said, "Would you mind stepping off the bus?"

He grabbed hold of the pole and refused to budge, despite my pleas.

"Come on sir, get yourself off the bus."

He still refused, and turned his back to me. I found myself uncharacteristically flustered. How should a copper go about this? Inspiration hit. I withdrew my truncheon and raised it above my head.

"IF YOU DON'T FU-!"

"STOP!" the trainer screamed. "Stop the role play! Good god man, if someone doesn't do what you want you can't whack them!"

I was still so naïve about how a police officer should act. We were of course expected to behave responsibly even when off duty. It slowly dawned that, as I would have the power to take away someone's liberty, I had to be professional at all times.

The instructors were enthusiastic and really cared about their work. The majority were still serving cops but a few had been injured on duty and had been forced to retreat to the classroom, a reminder of the dangers we would be facing once out in the 'real world' trying to arrest 'real criminals'.

There was lot of horseplay among us, some pushing and shoving, finding out the pecking order but people who were overly aggressive tended to disappear. Seven students were sacked after they got into a drunken brawl in a KFC (they became known as the Kentucky Seven) and I was surprised at how many people dropped out as time progressed. It was tough, however, you could be "back-classed" a month for failing an exam and if you failed again then you were out, no ifs or buts.

We were given many physical tests, from jumping off the high board in the Olympic-sized pool, to boxing tournaments with rival classes. I enjoyed all the physical stuff and was quite loud, bolshy and earned a reputation as the toughest trainee in the college. I found out I wasn't *quite* the toughest during a boxing tournament held towards the end of the academic year when, after donning gloves along with head and mouthguards I turned around to see the biggest, nastiest bloke I'd ever encountered in my short life. He gave me a murderous look as he pounded his gloves together. He was a former bouncer (and turned out to be one of those aggressive students who were weeded out before graduation). He smacked me in the head for two minutes and fifty seconds while Graham and Mark yelled at me to run for my life. I tried, and ran around and around the ring, forcing him to chase me, pounding my head, for so long that he grew really tired and finally, seeing a moment where he let his guard down, I snuck in a punch, causing him to slip in his own sweat and he hit the canvas like a lead weight. I leapt in the air claiming victory to the triumphant roar of my colleagues.

Our graduation celebrations were held at the Heathrow Park Hotel, with Commissioner Paul Condon and his wife in attendance. Lots of newly-graduated coppers were doing spots on stage – Graham played his trumpet, for example. As 'Yorkie' I was known for being a bit of a clown, so, after a bit of chanting from friends (and a lot of alcohol), in a hired white tuxedo, I climbed onstage and did an impression of a mating pig – and was quickly pulled off. Commissioner Condon's wife was not enjoying my act and this impression almost cost me my career. Mark, on the other hand, was presented with the Baton of Honour, the prize awarded to the most outstanding student. We were so hung over that along with Mark and Graham, I missed the bus booked to take us all back to Hendon for the passing out parade. We spent a fortune on a taxi and arrived with a minute to spare, luckily our colleagues saved us by polishing our shoes so we ran out, heads still spinning, to salute Sir Paul in the nick of time.

I was 24 and couldn't be prouder that I'd been accepted into the Met. When I put the uniform on it felt like a protective shield (this belief would be corrected in due course). Then it was to the noticeboard to see where we'd been posted. We'd all heard horror stories about policing central London, as well as rough areas like Tottenham, Brixton and Kilburn. As the crowds of cops craned over one other to get a look at the noticeboard, I noticed some blokes laughing at one of their mates who'd been posted to Brixton. I was hoping for something leafy in north London, Enfield or Barnet, easier to get home to Yorkshire on the weekends. But no.

I was heading south of the river.

# CHAPTER TWO

# FROM HENDON TO HELL

Battersea (the area from Nine Elms to Wandsworth west to east and from the Thames to Clapham Common north to south) was top of the crime table for all the wrong reasons. Street robberies, drug dealing and car thefts were off the scale. Apart from this, all anyone would tell me was it was a really bad patch to end up.

I had a week off after Hendon and spent it in a state of mixed emotion – between wanting to get stuck in and high anxiety about what I'd got myself into. I still had very little practical experience of life in London, let alone working as a police officer in one of its most challenging boroughs.

My home was a police section house, essentially a boarding house for police officers. The ladies who ran it were like surrogate mothers and took good care of us by preparing slap-up dinners.

When I arrived at the station for my first day – a huge Victorian brick building just over Battersea Bridge, overlooking the park – I spotted a photo-shoot taking place in the multi-storey carpark just opposite. Nothing wrong with that I suppose, except that the woman being photographed was naked. Not entirely sure whether any decency laws were being broken, I decided better not be late on my first day and, after a brief gander, carried on to the station.

I was joining with four other probationers including – to my delight – Mark. After we picked up our uniform, handcuffs and truncheon, we went to the canteen. We had to watch where we sat. There was an Old Sweats table that was strictly off-limits. Woe-betide any probationer foolish enough to even think of sitting there. You didn't speak to the Old Sweats until spoken to.

Area Car Drivers, the guys who drove the fast cars, responding to crimes-in-progress, were Gods to us. Even constables who'd finished their probation wouldn't get anywhere near their table, let alone be able to strike up a conversation with them or be trusted enough to listen in on their conversations.

It was busy and everybody stared at us through untrusting eyes. Nobody wanted to talk to us in case one of us was a mole put in by Complaints. This was a tough area and things hadn't always been done by the book, so to speak.

Plus, Battersea nick had just been through the horror of the Clapham Rail disaster. A packed passenger train had crashed into the rear of another train stopped at a signal, and then an empty train, travelling in the other direction, smashed into the debris lying across the tracks. Thirty-five people died and nearly five hundred were injured, so the mood was sombre.

We'd only just sat down with our teas when someone yelled: "Dave's called for urgent assistance, Winstanley!" and everyone charged out of the station.

It was scary to see it for real. Paul, a PC with 25 years' service, and our guide, along with Chris, a sergeant with 20 years' service, stopped us from following.

"Training school's all very well," Paul, a gruff, tough, dark-haired man, said, "But reality is a bit bloody different. Come on, we'll give you the guided tour."

As we left I glanced across the now empty canteen, hazy with cigarette smoke, half-eaten meals on the tables and wondered whether I would ever make it to the senior officers' table. It was then that I also noticed a huge fridge standing against the far wall. It was away from the serving area and looked totally out of place. I meant to ask Paul and Chris about it but quickly forgot as we boarded an old riot bus for the grand tour and they began a running commentary on where so-and-so got murdered, stabbed or shot; where drugs were dealt (I didn't even know what drugs looked like); which pubs were dangerous; stories about car thefts, fights and chases. I soon felt like we were driving through a warzone. Groups of lads hanging out on corners just went quiet and stared as we passed by.

"Stay switched on at all times," Paul said. "You get in a fight, don't go down, stay on your feet otherwise they'll kick you to pieces."

"Right Pannett, tell me what street are we on?" Chris asked me.

I shook my head. "No idea, sorry."

Chris leaned over and looked me straight in the eye. "If I ever have to fucking ask you again ... If you don't know where you are, how are you going to ask for urgent assistance?"

I always paid attention to where I was after that.

Paul and Chris knew what we were thinking and how to handle us. I felt like I was in good hands but terrified about messing up at the same time.

"You feel like outsiders now," Paul told us, "And you are. Also, you don't have a clue. Trust me on that one. You might have your laws memorised and done your little role-plays but you have to give it time out here. Don't rush into anything. My advice, and you should really pay attention to this, is to listen to everybody who is more experienced than you, but stay independently-minded. Make your own way in life and you'll do alright."

After that, Mark and I, along with some other probationers, were taken on a day-trip down the Thames in the Commissioner's Launch. The Commissioner's Launch was essentially a Thames Police Boat that transported Metropolitan Police commissioners and Thames Division superintendents as well as members of the Royal Family, visiting MPs and probationer PCs like me. I felt like royalty as we cruised through the middle of the greatest city in the world.

The boat was named after magistrate Patrick Colquhoun, one of the founders of the Thames River Police in 1798, formed to tackle theft and looting from ships anchored in the Pool of London. The Patrick Colquhoun is no longer part of the police service but the John Harriott (named after the Thames Police's other founder) was recommissioned to carry commuters from Chelsea Harbour into Central London, and is still operational at the time of writing.

Our destination was the Black Museum (now known as the Crime Museum after some black police officers complained) in Room 101 at New Scotland Yard. Created in 1874 by Inspector Neame after an 1869 law permitted the police to retain prisoners' property for 'instructional purposes', it's not open to the general public and nor should it ever be (although plans are rumoured to be afoot). It's inaccessible with good reason. The exhibits are grim beyond belief and are designed to give bright young police officers a reality-check. In other words, the Black Museum is a warning not to trust anyone not wearing a police uniform; to never let your guard down.

"Some people faint when they come in here," the museum's curator told us with a friendly smile as we stepped behind the door and entered a room that looked like it belonged to the Victorian age. "Even experienced constables sometimes find it a bit too much."

After an exhibit of disguised weapons and fake and real guns we passed by serial killer Dennis Nilsen's cooker (he boiled the flesh of his victims), John 'Acid Bath' Haig's apron, various weapons with real bloodstains and the ricin pellet that killed Georgi Markov after a secret agent had stabbed his leg with a modified umbrella in 1978. We saw the so-called "From Hell" letter supposedly written by Jack the Ripper and the noose that hanged Ruth Ellis in 1955, the last woman to be executed in the UK.

We finally stopped at a recent display. It was of some riot shields from the Broadwater Farm Riots of 1985. They'd been melted by petrol bombs and pierced by bullets. Finally, there was a section about Met officers killed in the line of duty, and on display was the clothing of PC Keith Blakelock, stabbed to death by youths during the Broadwater Farm riots; the stab marks had been highlighted so you could see just how many there were.

By the time we'd seen all the Black Museum had to offer, we returned to the Commissioner's Launch in a somewhat subdued mood, fully aware that doing your job could cost you your life.

***

We spent several weeks with PC Paul and Sergeant Chris and they did their best to drum in every practical part of policing they don't tell you about in training school. They were the first people to mention the Yardies, gangs of crazed drug dealers from Jamaica, and to point out a young man who was South London born and bred called Gary Nelson who was into protection rackets and heading fast up the criminal ranks.

"He's one to watch," Paul said ominously. "Dangerous but he's got a brain in him, that one."

Finally, it was time for me to step out on my own. I was Whisky Alpha 150 and walking out that first day was extremely surreal. I felt like anything could happen and I wondered whether I would be up to the challenge. And then it came. My first arrest. A young lad had had a bit too much to drink and was kicking off, picking fights outside a pub just off the high street. I spotted the "Oh shit!" expression on his face when he saw me and I knew then he was going to be as good as gold. My uniform did all the work for me. I put on the handcuffs and called in the Sherpa van to come and collect him.

As a probie (probationer), I got sent to deal with all the crap jobs, shoplifters and sudden deaths. It was all about learning the job of course but, being a naive Yorkshire lad, I found some aspects of my job really difficult. My first dead body was in a tower block. It had been there for a good few days and the smell filled the landing. Where were his friends and family, his neighbours? Did no one care? It was so different from Yorkshire where it seemed everyone kept an eye on the older neighbours.

Mark and I were called to backup other officers when pub fights got out of hand, especially on Friday and Saturday nights in Chelsea and Fulham which, if nothing else, was a bonding experience. When Mark and I arrived at our first pub riot, it looked as if a bomb had gone off. The cops were outnumbered four-to-one by football hooligans in full riot mode and PC Timbo, an ex royal marine, 6"4" of pure muscle, waved cheerfully at us as we arrived and beckoned us to get stuck in, before picking up a rioter (who stupidly, blinded by beer, had decided to pick a fight with the normally gentle giant) and sending him swiftly and firmly to the ground. Timbo was recently married and always policed with a smile. He had loads of compassion for victims and was, therefore, ruthless when it came to street robbers. He did us the occasional honour of joining us on the probies' table in the canteen. I spent most of this particular fight running from one side of the pub to other to help various colleagues cuff their prisoners, dodging punches and kicks as I went.

I was looking for where I should go next when I heard: "Could you possibly give me a hand old chap?" come from somewhere behind me. This was Triston Fairweather aka 'Trist', and he looked just like his name sounded, like an RAF pilot from the Biggles era. A university toff in his late 20's from the Home Counties, his family owned a National-Trust-sized country mansion and saw Trist's love of policing as a phase he was going through (Trist already had seven years in when I joined). He played on his public school boy image to impress the ladies, but he was a tough cop who adored his job. When he asked for my help he was throwing a huge skinheaded man with homemade tattoos up against a wall, and was struggling to hold his hands to get the cuffs on.

That done, I was amazed to see a petite WPC in the thick of the action. This was Mandy Fox aka 'Foxy', one of only two girl PCs at Battersea. Foxy had eight years' service and was a no-nonsense biker girl. She was proof that women could handle themselves just as well as any man when it came to policing a pub riot and had wiped the smiles off more than one hooligan's face with a well-placed truncheon (not to forget her judo skills).

Eventually, the riot, which had started, as these things always tended to do, for no good reason other than someone had taken offence at the expression on someone else's face, was brought under control, the prisoners were in the Sherpa vans bound for the sobering reality-check of being booked in by the duty sergeant Phil, a totally unflappable old sweat with almost thirty years' service, followed by a night in a police cell, which in turn would be followed by a court date.

Being in the police was like having a huge extended family. Although us probies were kept at arm's length by the more experienced coppers, it was very much a case of all for one and one for all, and this was brought home to me when, as part of a random check, I stopped a car close to Clapham Common and I wasn't sure about a legal technicality and so called it in. The driver was a man in his 20s and had been understanding about the delay and my checking, so not wanting to keep him waiting any longer than necessary, I said: "Control could I have some quick assistance?"

The radio went quiet and I told the driver: "Won't keep you long now."

About thirty seconds later I heard several police sirens heading our way. I was curious as I hadn't heard anything urgent come over the radio. And then I saw the Area Car, followed by a patrol van and then one of the local pandas. And then I saw Darren aka 'Doctor Death', sprinting towards me from a side street where he'd been on foot patrol. Tall, pale, thin and sly as a fox, Darren looked like the Grim Reaper. He had eight years' service and fancied himself as a bit of a ladies' man. He loved to surf, owned a camper van and sometimes slept in the thing after a night out on the town. He was also, to my amazement, into fly-fishing. He was always used for plain clothes observation as he didn't look anything like a copper.

His truncheon was already drawn as he approached and he yelled "What is it Pannett!? You alright mate? Is it this wanker? What's he done?"

And then I had a sudden sinking feeling that I was about to make myself extremely unpopular. In essence I'd asked the police operator for "urgent assistance" an expression that meant a police officer's life was in imminent danger and this had meant she had scrambled the entire nick to come to my rescue.

A minute later my worst fears were confirmed as I was surrounded by every vehicle from the police nick, sirens on, road-blocks up, coppers with mouths still chewing the remains of bacon and egg rolls they'd left cooling on the canteen tables. Soon Clapham was gridlocked, and the poor driver at the centre of it all, who newly-arriving police officers kept insulting and trying to arrest, was practically in tears.

And then I felt a very solid finger poking me in my back. It was Patters, the senior beat cop, an old, roll-up-smoking, cockney sweat in his mid-40s, divorced and with over twenty years' service.

"You fucking useless twat," he spat, getting right into my face, "Fucking sort your life out," he added, before turning his back and bad-mouthing me to anyone in the vicinity.

"He has a point," another voice said. I turned to see Timbo leaning out of the window of a van he'd commandeered to rush to my aid. "People sometimes hurt themselves running to help," he said, starting the engine, "Better learn from this Mike, OK?"

A few minutes later, I was on my own again and sent the dazed driver on his way. I was gutted. I had a lot to do if I was going to redeem myself for this gaffe.

*** 

A few days later, I thought I'd cracked it. Pete stayed seating, looking at me as I breathlessly explained.

"Just from a stop and search, thought they were looking dodgy and sure enough." I gestured triumphantly at the object between us on the desk – a kilo of hash – the heavy, oily brown derivative of marijuana.

Pete unwrapped the clingfilm and had a close look. He then looked at me curiously.

"Is this a wind-up Pannett?"

"No, of course not."

"Where are the prisoners?"

"In the custody suite."

Pete put down his pipe and went to have a look for himself. Sure enough, there were two young West Indian men looking extremely pissed off as they awaited booking in. Pete strolled back to the desk and looked at the large lump of dope in front of him. I was practically levitating with excitement.

"Better test it then, hadn't we then Pannett?" Pete said, scratching his beard.

"Eh?"

I watched, incredulous as Pete broke of a chunk, put it in his mouth and chewed. "Mmm. S'good stuff."

It was molasses cake.

Despite having a mountain to climb in terms of experience, I wasn't lacking in enthusiasm. I teamed up with Mark and we stalked the streets, targeting the street robbers who liked to hang out at Macdonald's, and patrolled the estates at night, looking for gang members up to no good. Local people were happy to talk to us and impressed upon us the urgency with which we needed to tackle gangs, weapons and drugs. They wanted to like the police, they said, but we simply weren't doing enough to make a difference on a day-to-day level. We'd missed and then ignored the rise in drug use and now all the associated crime, especially street robbery, was out of control.

We were both passionate about what we thought were the best solutions – I wanted to go after the drug dealers and Mark argued that we needed to tackle the street robbers. If we made it impossible for robbers to operate in Battersea then the hard drug dealers would lose money and would dissipate. I argued that we should go after the drug dealers first and make it impossible for them to sell their wares in Battersea and then all the associated crime would fall.

"It's too late for that," Mark argued, "They're too secure, too hidden, we'll never catch them. At least we can go after street robbers, by definition they're visible to us."

It was late at night and the station was quiet, so we'd taken our argument into the luxury of the senior officer's canteen. We were both extremely competitive and at some point our discussion grew overheated and one of us shoved the other and moments later we were fighting and rolling around on the floor when Inspector Barry walked in on us.

Barry was in his mid-30s and married with two kids. He had taken a shine to Mark and me, encouraging our enthusiasm. Once Barry had pulled us apart made us shake hands, Mark and I never argued again, we were the best of friends from that day.

And then came my first real cannabis discovery via the postie. This, I thought, was a chance to target a drug dealer in their den. Ok, Clinton was in his 70s, and only sold cannabis but everyone has to start somewhere. The last thing I was expecting was to be confronted by a young man aiming a shotgun at my head.

*** 

Everything went blurry for a moment. I was so full of adrenaline I thought I was going to pass out. I heard screams behind me, someone shouted "GUN!"

"I bloody know!" I thought, not realising someone had found more guns at the other end of the flat.

The man was stick-thin and despite the cold, and despite the fact he was dressed in nothing but vest and shorts, was glistening with sweat. I had to fight to tear my eyes away from the double barrels and look him in the eye, which were partly concealed by long dreadlocks. They were like saucers, almost entirely overtaken by huge pupils. It had just been a few seconds but right then, it felt like time slowed, I'd never been more alert to the need to stay alive and I felt like this could go either way. No doubt, this young man was going through his own thought process, weighing up the pros and cons of several courses of action, the key one of which had to be to shoot or not to shoot. Normally not short of words, I knew I had to find something to say to try and help him come to the right decision. After all, shooting a copper meant spending the rest of your life in prison with no hope of getting out – or at least that's what I thought and I hoped he would think so too.

"Look, I'm police mate, don't shoot," I pleaded, "Put down the gun, ok?"

His eyes flashed for a moment with realisation, and he turned, tossing the gun out of the open window. The moment it left his hands, I charged, knocking him to the ground. He fought back but I held him as he writhed, wriggled and kicked.

Outside, the PCs' eyes popped when they saw the shotgun hit the ground and they – with incredible bravery – ran straight in to help just as the young gunman was about to wriggle free of my grip. Between the three of us we got this lad under control and cuffed.

"I've never seen someone fight like that before," one of the PC's said.

"Me neither," I replied with emphatic breathlessness. I was a mess. My jumper was ripped, my glasses were broken, my nose was bleeding and I felt as though I'd been kicked in the ribs by a horse.

I spotted a small metal pipe, along with some pale-brown crumbs loosely contained in a cellophane wrap, sitting on a coffee table covered in burn marks, scratches and stains. We had a closer look.

"What is this stuff?" I asked. What I knew about drugs could be written on the back of a postage stamp but even the clued-up officers weren't sure.

Meanwhile, the rest of the team had been through the flat. Seventy-year-old Clinton was in the kitchen, fag on, calm as anything, as the team proudly showed me a loaded crossbow and another shotgun, also loaded, propped against the wall. On the table was an ounce of cannabis.

The young man turned out to be a drug dealer on the run from some rivals. Clinton had decided to let him hideout the night before our raid, so us catching him along with the weapons stash was just dumb luck (although I felt that perhaps Clinton didn't feel as though he could say no to a man who walked the streets of Battersea with a shotgun hidden under his coat).

It took us some time to sort everything out and get Clinton and the shotgun kid booked into the nick but eventually, in the small hours, the raiding party was ready for a debrief in the canteen.

Patters was waiting for us on the old sweats' table. My heart sank at the sight, as he hadn't yet forgiven for my mistaken call for urgent assistance and I was convinced he never would. I braced myself, expecting him to give me hell about sending officers into danger and not conducting proper surveillance of the flat we were about to raid.

Patters got up, looked at me for a moment and, not saying a word, he walked over to the mysterious fridge and opened the door. Every shelf was filled to the brim with cans of beer. He removed two, and came up to me, fag on, squinting through the smoke. He put the can on the table in front of me.

"Good job that, Pannett. Bet you're feeling a bit lucky tonight."

This was the second time Patters had ever spoken to me. Although neither he nor I made a big deal of it, he'd made it clear: I could be trusted.

# CHAPTER THREE

# DEATH ON THE RIVER

Coming on duty during parade one Saturday night in August, Inspector Barry silently checked our appearance and our gear (even checking that our notebooks were neatly up to date) before having a word with Sergeant Phil who came up to me and said: "You need to polish your shoes Pannett."

I looked across the room at Pete who was sitting at his desk, searching through innumerable index cards. He caught my eye and frowned back at me enquiringly. He was smoking his pipe, his beard was scraggly and coloured yellow from nicotine, his tie was off and his shirt, with an undefinable yellow stain on its front, was hanging out of trousers that had been polished to a thin shine from so much sitting.

But you never questioned an order.

Minutes later, shoes buffed, I hit the streets with Timbo and we endured the usual drunken chaos of a Saturday night which climaxed at 1.30am when we were called to attend one of our regular domestics, a pair of alcoholics who lived in a Peabody estate on the Black Prince Road in Vauxhall. I was appalled by the sheer number of domestic disagreements we were called to and wondered why all these people stayed together if they were so unhappy. Not to mention the number of alcohol-generated crimes we seemed to spend 90% of our time cleaning up, from sons who'd smashed up the family home, to paralytic women who'd collapsed on the street and had been molested by drunken men.

The door was thrown back a second after I knocked and I took an involuntary step backwards as Sandra, the abused wife, yelled at us to go away.

"Bloody nosey neighbours calling the police when it's no business of theirs!"

The fact that her face was covered in blood made me think that the neighbours' decision had been a good one. Sandra, who was white and in her thirties, looked like she was bleeding to death from what turned out to be a minor head wound, the exact circumstances of which we would never find out about because she didn't want to press charges against her husband. She loved "the bastard" as she described him, and the blood was the result of "a fall" because she had had too many snakebite-and-blacks (a lethal cocktail consisting of 50% cider and 50% lager, with a dash of blackcurrant to lend it that edge of sophistication).

Timbo had been glaring at the husband the whole time, who was hiding in the shadows at the other end of the hall while his wife did all the talking and defended him. The man was, like all bullies, an utter coward.

We were interrupted by a call over the mainset: "MP: Pleasure cruiser crashed into Canon Street Railway Bridge, people in water units to deal." That meant it was all hands to assist. Being so late, there was no traffic and, after Timbo hit the blues and twos and stamped on the gas, our Panda car flew over the Elephant and Castle and up Newington Causeway via Borough to the railway bridge and we arrived to find we were one of the first responders to arrive at the scene of the Marchioness disaster.

Such is the nature of policing that a pair of fresh-faced police officers, one barely out of training school, can be called to deal with a major disaster.

The party on board the Marchioness had only just begun when the tragedy happened. The passengers, most of whom were in their twenties, were celebrating the 26th birthday of banker Antonio de Vasconcellos. People were just starting to dance when the pleasure boat lurched and then pushed down into the water before turning on her side. The screaming intensified as the lights went out and the boat started to sink.

The fact that the dredger Bowbell's anchor had torn through the upper decks of the Marchioness made it possible for some people on these decks to quickly escape the sinking boat and swim to shore, by which time the Marchioness had vanished from view. Those left in the water found themselves being dragged upstream by the powerful currents which, as the river was an hour from high tide, were at their strongest, and people who had managed to cling onto lifebuoys found themselves being swept west as the tide continued to rise. Eyewitnesses, including the landlord of a riverside pub who'd run out to help, and many survivors who were already ashore, spotted dozens of people in the water.

We were woefully ill-equipped to deal with an event of this scale. We could see the huge 1,800-tonne dredger (a boat that sucks up sediment to keep waterways navigable) stuck under the bridge. The crew of another pleasure cruiser, the Hurlingham, had thrown life buoys into the Thames and were trying to pluck survivors out of the water – seven people were clutching to one lifebuoy – before they were swept upstream by the strong currents.

Those members of the crew of the Marchioness who'd managed to escape had no idea how many people were on board, so we had no idea how many people were still in the water.

The Marchioness was by this time already at the bottom of the Thames with 24 people trapped in its hull.

Eyewitnesses, including the many survivors who were already ashore, told us dozens of people were in the water but had been dragged upstream, so we raced as far as Battersea Bridge to try and catch up with them. We skidded to a halt on the Chelsea Embankment, grabbed the powerful Dragon Lights we kept in the boot and shone them on the water, looking for people to rescue, as a fireboat crew arrived and threw dozens of life jackets into the river.

With the lights on we could see people being pulled upriver at high speed, twisting in strong eddies before being dragged under by the current. We were on the banks but too far away to pull anyone in.

"What do we do Timbo?" I shouted, in a panic of helplessness. "What the fuck do we do?"

My sense of helplessness was matched by the rest of the emergency services, we just couldn't find the people who so desperately needed our help.

The fire brigade arrived and we helped them set up lights to spot and rescue people who were trying to swim ashore. I then ran with Timbo down to the riverbank where some large boats were moored. Timbo spotted a small launch tied to one of the boats. The owner came out as we crashed aboard.

"We're commandeering your launch!" Timbo roared and we leapt aboard the small motorboat, ignoring the man's protests, and shot out into the Thames. I held the light as Timbo steered the tiny boat, which bucked in the choppy waters.

"Over there!" I'd seen a head break the surface and Timbo steered the boat towards my light but by the time we were there it had vanished. I shone my torch frantically over the water; I kept seeing shadows passing by, but we just couldn't keep pace with the river or keep track of the people in the darkness. We yelled until we were hoarse for people to make a sound so we would be able to find them in the dark. I felt sick with horror and frustration; it was utterly, utterly horrible. And then the motor died. Out of fuel! We were dragged along by the current; helpless, Timbo called the station, we were picked up and returned to the scene.

It had been just half-an-hour since we arrived but it felt like we'd been there all night already. I stopped in horror when we came across the first batch of body bags; there were at least twenty.

Bodies were still being found the next day, miles downriver and even though extra cops from Battersea were drafted in to join the search teams, it still took several days before every body had been recovered. One of the last to be found was recovered close to HMS Belfast. The exact figures were uncertain for a while as there was no passenger manifest but it was eventually established that 51 people of the 131 people on board the Marchioness lost their lives. Twenty-four were recovered from inside the hull. 27 were recovered from the river. The average age of the victims was just 22.

The majority of the survivors had been on the upper decks at the time of the collision and had been lucky enough to be able to swim to the riverbanks within ten minutes; any longer then they would have been overtaken by exhaustion and hypothermia and then dragged under by the currents of the fast-rising tide.

Debriefing after something like this was vital. We sat in the canteen, emptied the fridge, which everyone called the 'wobbler' and talked. It was a comfort to be able to offload, to talk about what we'd seen and to go over why the accident had happened, all part of coming to terms with it, accepting that it had happened, we had done our best and there was no use beating ourselves up over it. Poor Trist found it especially hard to deal with; he had been put on the body identification team and found the job almost too much to bear.

"They're so young," he said, "There was a beautiful young girl, her whole life ahead of her and now..."

Among the dead were Antonio de Vasconcellos, his older brother Domingos and Francesca Dallaglio, the older sister of future England rugby captain, Lawrence.

It was impossible to imagine how the family and friends, not to mention the survivors must have felt. My feelings of helplessness were only compounded by seeing the unavoidable newspaper and TV coverage. One survivor later said he spent a month going to the funerals of his friends. A mother of another victim said she kept thinking her child was out there somewhere but she was unable to reach him. She hadn't been able to sleep or eat since the tragedy and I couldn't blame her. Their deaths were totally avoidable. They had been robbed of the long, successful and happy lives that were ahead of them.

It was only revealed some years after the Marchioness Disaster that – as part of identification procedures – it was standard practice for coroners to order the removal of the hands of the deceased after a mass disaster so they could be sent to the Forensic Science Laboratory for printing (due to the lengthy immersion in water, they could only be fingerprinted at FSL), a grisly task for the fingerprint officers. Of the 25 individuals who had their hands removed, only three were identified through the use of fingerprints, the rest of the identifications being made through dental records. Some of the hands were removed even after this positive identification had been made. In a number of cases the hands were not returned to the body before the body was released to the family. Policy and procedure have long since changed, thank goodness, but this was small comfort to the families who had to come to terms with this controversial decision. One of the parents, speaking of her son, said: "He was a brilliant musician. It's unbearable to think they cut his hand off, but nothing was said about it."

Westminster Coroner Dr Paul Knapman was strongly criticized by Lord Justice Clarke in his 2001 report into the circumstances surrounding the collision. That this report came about at all was thanks to the Marchioness Action Group, formed by relatives of victims and survivors, who had to fight for a full inquest and public enquiry, which came over a decade after the disaster. The recommendations in Lord Justice Clark's report into the Identification of Victims Following a Major Transportation Accident have had a highly significant impact on the way in which individuals are treated following disasters. Without the commitment of the Marchioness survivors and bereaved, the public enquiry would not have taken place and Lord Justice Clark's recommendations – which have influenced policing for the better – would not have been made. Those of us whose lives have been unaffected by disaster owe them a debt of gratitude. They have helped to make the river a safer place. The inquiry also found that the Metropolitan Police were "ill-prepared" and had no contingency plan for such an event and, thanks to the Marchioness Action Group, four lifeboat stations were installed on the River Thames by the Royal National Lifeboat Institution in 2002. New laws on being in charge of vessels under the influence of alcohol were also introduced.

No one was ever prosecuted for what was regarded as an unlawful killing of these 51 young people. After two trials in which the juries could not agree on a verdict, the captain of the Bowbelle was acquitted of failing to keep a proper look out. Evidence had shown that he had drunk five pints of lager the afternoon prior to the collision.

***

That night had started like any other but, as is the way with policing, and as I was learning, no two nights are the same. The sun was coming up by the time minicabs were summoned to take us home to sleep it off, to regroup, to prepare ourselves for whatever unexpected challenges the next day would bring.

# Chapter Four

# BLUE BLOOD

No one really knew why we were in the middle of such a massive rise in crime. Car thefts were the highest in Europe and, not far behind, were thefts of bicycles. King of the bike thieves was someone we called, for obvious reasons, 'Mick the Bike'. Mick was fast and prolific, sometimes stealing six bikes in one day. When Mark and I approached Inspector Barry with a proactive plan to catch Mick in the act by luring him with the temptation of a prize catch, he was a tad skeptical.

"Sounds like a lot of trouble for a bike thief," he said, "And you're risking entrapment."

We had to be careful not to make it too easy for Mick. If we left a £1,000 mountain bike secured to a railing with dental floss then it could be argued that such a target would tempt even a normally law-abiding, non-bike thieving citizen to pinch it. Although entrapment is not a defence, it can lead to a case never making it to court.

"But guv," Mark said, "By our reckoning, Mick's stolen upwards of two hundred grand's worth of bicycles," which was perhaps a slight exaggeration.

"And we'll secure the bait properly, so there won't be an entrapment issue."

After checking with the Crown Prosecution Service, the police's lawyers, Inspector Barry agreed. After all, Mick had generated a hell of a lot of crimes and upset hundreds of Battersea residents. He warned us not to endanger the public and to make sure every step was taken to ensure his arrest was carried out safely. We gave Inspector Barry our word and set about laying our trap.

We had a brand new, extremely expensive white Saracen mountain bike in our evidence room (it had been recovered from another bike thief but no one had come forward to claim it), so we took that and, using a proper chain lock, secured it to a cycle parking stand right next to Battersea Park, a popular haunt of Mick's. We then parked ourselves in an unmarked van in a side street with a view of the bike and settled down to wait for Mick to take the bait.

We didn't know what Mick looked like exactly, we just knew he was highly efficient; he attacked bikes secured by chains (as opposed to the more secure D-locks, which some people found too heavy or didn't like to affix to their bike) using – we supposed – a pair of 30-inch bolt cutters. We weren't sure whether he arrived in a van or car and threw them in, or simply rode off on the bike, but we assumed he used a vehicle just because it must be hard to cycle with 30-inch bolt cutters down your trousers.

We had barely settled in the van when I noticed a young man roll up to one of the bike stands on an old-fashioned ladies' bike. I watched as he parked it up, not thinking anything of him in particular, and secured it with a flimsy looking lock. Well, he didn't have to worry about Mick the Bike, I thought, with an old rust heap like that.

Mark passed me a tea in a flask cup and I opened the lid and took a sip and when I looked back up again our bike was gone!

"Mark! The bike!"

"Where is it?"

The young man had nabbed it. His method was to roll up on an old rust heap and cycle away on his target bike, bolt-cutters and all, to his van, which he usually parked a mile away. Simple!

Tea went out the window as we fired up the van and took off after him. Our plan had been to nab Mick in the act but he was so quick, we were in danger of major embarrassment. Mick soon realised that he was being chased by two determined-looking young men in a white van, so he ditched the bolt cutters and turned up the speed. And boy, could he ride. Mike's legs were soon ablur as he whizzed down the road, bunny-hopping speed bumps, the first one of which took Mark – who was driving – by surprise and every one of our four wheels lifted off the ground for a brief second, causing the suspension to make a godawful noise as we bounced on after our thief. By this time I'd had the presence of mind to call it in, and this was one of those moments when one is reminded and eternally grateful for the fact that the police is the biggest gang in London and, despite what many people think, you're never that far from a police officer. I prayed that someone would be able to intercept Mick, who had by now cut away from Prince of Wales Drive and was now on Battersea Park Road, zipping in and out of traffic, nearing the Doddington Estate, where the only way we could continue to pursue him was on foot and I didn't rate our chances, although we were both determined not to give up, especially as the railway tracks of Clapham Junction meant he couldn't escape to the south, so maybe, with reinforcements, we'd be lucky.

And then Mick turned into a pedestrianised area, just by the library next to the estate.

"Take the next left!" I yelled at Mark who swung the van into Austin Road and then took the very next left, a 90-degree turn into a tiny road that brought us into the estate, just in time to see Mick expertly ride down the library steps, dodging a little old lady who was struggling up them with her shopping, before pedalling like fury along the pavement of a road with a dead end which led straight into the estate, through which we would not be able to follow and with Strasbourg Road on the other side, well, by the time we got out of our van to continue the chase on foot, it'd be too late. We skidded to a halt at the entrance to the central pedestrianised area of the estate and watched as Mick whizzed across, knowing he had us beaten and he turned to look in triumph – and that's when he ran into PC Dave Davis who rolled into view on a BMW K100LT motorcycle. Mark and I both winced as Mick struck Dave's front wheel, leaving the bike behind as he somersaulted through the air, landing on his back, winded and wheezing, allowing us to grab the bicycle thief. Once he was in a fit state to be moved, he came quietly.

We found ten bikes in his flat, along with more cutting equipment than your average steelworker and about £3,000 in cash. Mark and I were cocks of the walk that day and let the hearty congratulations from the team go to our heads.

A few hours later, with Mick booked in, lawyered up, interviewed and bailed, I was called, along with PC Bry, to deal with some trespassers. Brian aka Bry, whose real name was Brian, had fifteen years' service and walked the homebeat on the Winstanley, the toughest beat in Battersea. He'd taken me under his wing and had suggested that this beat might be mine one day (he was planning to become a CID detective), an idea that simultaneously delighted and terrified me. Bry knew and tried to get along with the community better than anyone. He also loved practical jokes and taking the Mick out of the probies.

The trespassers turned out to be two girls in their 20s sitting on a wall. I wasn't sure what offence had taken place exactly when Patters rolled up in the Area Car, fag on.

"Right Mike," he said. "Lock 'em up. They shouldn't be there."

I couldn't really see an offence but I wasn't about to argue with Patters. I remembered from training school that you could arrest someone for being "unlawfully on enclosed premises," so I just got on with it and explained to the girls, almost apologetically that they had been trespassing and that I was going to have to arrest them. They took this news surprisingly well and were as good as gold as I arranged for transport to take us to the nick. Once we'd climbed out of the van and walked into the station one of the girls said suddenly, pointing to me: "He touched me up when we was in the van."

"No I didn't," I protested, "No way, I didn't do anything!"

"He did," said her friend, "The creep fondled her when we was in the van. I saw him."

"What? No way! Come on, guys, you can't believe this nonsense."

Sergeant Phil was at the booking desk. He was married with three kids. An old sweat with 28 years' he was of the 'been there, done that and worn the t-shirt' type. He fixed me in his stare and said: "Are you sure Mike? She's a good-looking lass. It happens from time-to-time, power goes to your head and you think, 'a quick fondle, no one's going to mind, are they?' Perks of the job and all that."

"What? Are you mad?" I yelped, really starting to panic now.

The Inspector Barry arrived and asked what was going on. Bry and Phil filled him in while I continued to protest my innocence while the girls continued to insist I'd fondled one of them. Barry came up to me and said: "She wants to make it official Mike, so we're going to have to do this properly."

It wasn't until I was dressed in a white paper rape suit and demanding a solicitor that Bry finally collapsed in laughter and I realised, with bowel-wobbling relief that I was the victim of an initiation wind-up, designed to make sure I didn't get too big-headed about my recent successes (the girls were WPC's from Wandsworth).

"You got off lightly Mike," Pete told me later. "I've been here long enough to see a whole host of terrible pranks. Other PC's have had 'bodies' leap out at them in the morgue. One poor lad was called to a 'cardboard box steaming and emitting radiation,' and was sent into Clapham Common wearing a hazmat suit. I'll never forget the fear in his voice over the radio when he picked up the smoking box and asked: 'Where should I bring it guv?'

"Classic that one," Patters added, "We told him to hang on to it and keep people away until the blokes from Porton Down arrived. He was there for an hour before we put him out of his misery."

I was learning that cops have a weird sense of humour. The longer you're in the job, the stranger and darker it gets. Pranks remained rare (they tended to be planned well in advance) and we spent far more time together bonding over a beer or three in the canteen. Sometimes, in the warmer months, we'd get changed at shift's end, empty the wobbler and have a picnic in Battersea Park. We worked and lived together, went on booze-cruises and on day trips to Brighton for a beach barbecue. I soon came to realise that as a police officer, you were a member of a huge family and, just like your family, you can't choose your colleagues, but you're all bonded by blood. In the case of the police, the blood was blue.

# PART TWO

I t's the day after my 'initiation' and I'm on foot patrol with Foxy. It's 5am, the May sun is just coming up and we're really, really bored.

We pass a playground. I'm overcome by urge to jump on the swings. I look at Foxy and smile; she guesses, and the next thing I know we're flying through the air, swinging back and forth, laughing like a pair of eight-year-olds. Eventually we slow and light up, smoking as we coast slowly back and forth.

It's one of those extremely rare times when everything is at peace, even here in the Winstanley, and the only sound we hear is the birds' dawn chorus; I could almost hear the opening flute of Grieg's Peer Gynt suite wafting over London.

The peace is suddenly shattered by the sound of much glass being broken, steel crashing to the floor and the all-too-familiar noise of someone kicking a door in. We chuck our fags, jump from the swings and run towards the sound, calling the job in on the radio as we go.

It's the local chemists' and we're probably the last thing the two young thieves are expecting to see at 5am in an otherwise deserted Battersea. We give chase, delighted to have something to do, as they leg it out of the chemist and away, booty in sweaty little hands. I notice that one of the young men is carrying an axe, which he must have used to smash his way in.

They are black, in their early 20s and in good shape; they give us a good run but I dig in, relying on the old police officer's adage that all you need to do to catch your fleeing prey is to match their pace, wait until they have to slow to navigate some kind of obstruction and then charge at full pelt. Sure enough, they come to a kind of kissing gate at the entrance to an underground walkway, designed to stop people hurtling through the tunnel on bicycles and motor-scooters. The first lad expertly vaults and barely loses any speed, but lad no.2 is carrying the axe and doesn't have enough hands to hop the gate cleanly, so I turn up my speed and charge into him and he drops the axe as we fall; he nevertheless proceeds to 'resist arrest' most vehemently and punches land on me before I even know which way's up.

"I got this!" I yell, sounding more confident than I was as Foxy hurtles past, after lad no.1.

She returns a couple of minutes later. I am sitting on lad no.2's back.

"He got away," she says as we pull him to his feet.

"No worries, one will lead us to the other, I'm sure."

"I'm not sayin' nuffink."

And peace falls over the Winstanley once more.

# CHAPTER FIVE

# THE HANDBAGS AND THE SCUMBAGS

**P**ete the collator took one disdainful look at lad no. 2 and strolled over to a filing cabinet, puffing on his pipe, flicked though a row of index cards and pulled one out.

"Here we are," he said, "Paul Demarcos. Lives on the Winstanley with his mum, nice lady, Lorraine. Given her quite a bit of trouble over the years haven't you Paul, aka Little P?"

"No comment."

"Indeed," Pete said.

"Thanks Pete, we'll be off then."

"Don't you want the name of his friend?"

"How could you possibly..."

"Well, according to my index," Pete said, squinting at the card, "It says here that Little P's chief partner in crime is Ricky Philpott, also from the Winstanley."

He went back to the filing cabinet, pulled out another card.

"There he is. Nice description of him too."

"Thanks Pete, that's amazing."

"Anytime Mike."

I smiled at the use of the first name. I was no longer 'Constable Pannett'.

Little P gave us a long list of "No comments," during the interview. We let him cool his heels and went straight back to the estate for a good look around. Foxy found a holdall containing the stash in the communal bin. It was full of methadone.

Then it was off to South Western Magistrates court to apply for a search warrant for Ricky's address. We hit it the following morning. Well, when I say hit, I knocked politely at 9am sharp. It was his mum's flat and I didn't want to upset her by kicking her door down and charging through her house at the crack of dawn. I hoped and had a feeling that she might be on our side and would agree that Ricky needed to learn a harsh lesson.

Having said that, she did not look at all pleased when she opened the door and saw two uniformed coppers smiling back at her.

"Mrs Philpott?"

"Ms. What is it?"

She looked like she was dressed for work and ready to leave.

"We'd like to talk to Ricky."

"What's he done now?" she asked as she adjusted her earrings and then reached for her handbag.

"May we come in?"

Ms Philpott stood back, sighing as we stepped into the hallway.

"Let me guess, he's been thieving?"

"A pharmacy. We have his friend, Phil in custody, a bag full of stolen methadone which, we believe is covered in Ricky's prints."

"Help yourselves, he's in bed asleep. Don't go gentle on him. I have to go to work so make sure you close the door behind you. I don't know; I've given up trying to control that boy. Ever since his father left, he's been a nightmare. There was a time ..."

I felt sorry for Ms Philpott. "Maybe if he's forced to take responsibility for his actions."

"Don't forget to shut the door will you?"

And she was gone.

I looked at Foxy. "Let's give him a wake up call to remember, shall we?"

Foxy nodded. We crept oh-so-quietly into Ricky's room. He was fast aslumber, duvet pulled up high; he was practically sucking his thumb. I crept up until I was right beside him while Foxy took hold of the end of the duvet.

I mouthed "On three," Foxy nodded and oh-so-quietly, I said: "One, two, three."

Foxy yanked the duvet cover back.

"RICKY PHILPOTT YOU ARE UNDER ARREST, ANYTHING YOU SAY WILL BE TAKEN IN EVIDENCE-"

I'd never thought levitation possible but Ricky leapt into the air from a lying position and struggled to catch his breath as I continued to read him the riot act and then ordered him to get dressed.

# CHAPTER SIX

# TAKING OVER

Policing is all about people. We sometimes lose sight of that these days, particularly when it comes to media debates, which always seem to be about statistics and cutbacks, which is right and proper to a degree, but we sometimes forget that to be effective as police officers, we have to know the community in which we operate. It's the only way to get ahead of the criminals that blight the lives of law-abiding people, people who would do more to support the police if they believed we could be effective. We had lost a lot of trust in the communities of Battersea. Bry had done an awful lot to try and rebuild that trust and the community liked and respected him but, with crime going through the roof, it was an uphill battle to get people onside.

With this in mind, I paid a visit to the burgled chemist. It sat in a short row of shops, a newsagent's, mini-supermarket/off licence, a bookies and a small greasy spoon cafe. The window and door were both boarded up. The doorframe was more or less intact but the glass was gone and the steel shutter that covered the shop window was twisted and bent, and wouldn't wind all the way to the top.

There was a beautiful young black girl in her twenties behind the counter. I entered carrying two cups of tea and passed one to her.

"Didn't know if you took sugar, so brought two in case," I said, and introduced myself.

"Thanks for the tea, that's very sweet," she said before telling me her name was Sandra.

"How are you coping?" I asked, gesturing at the door.

"Oh that! That's nothing, I've worked here since I left school and we've been robbed plenty of times, a couple of times at knifepoint."

"Really?"

"Sure, it's like we're the go-to place if some good-for-nothings want to make some quick cash. I don't know who buys it all, there's so much around already. I mean you'd think the prices would be so low no one needs to steal methadone these days. It's really a second-rate substance; as a recreational drug, I mean."

"I know plenty of locals who would prefer to run a mile uphill rather than have a friendly chat with a cop."

"Not me. No way. I'm not afraid of drug dealers. I grew up with them. I don't know who they are or where they are now, so don't go getting any ideas, but to me they're just the kids I knew from school. Besides, I've just been robbed. It's pretty obvious the cops are going to stop by, so we're good to talk."

"So where are all these dealers, then? The estate always looks empty whenever I'm around."

"Yeah well, spotters are going to see you guys coming a mile off. You don't see dealers out on the streets, they just appear when they're needed, or sell from blindspots from which they can drop and run, or from stash houses. They've been doing this long enough to know how to fool the police. You guys really don't have a clue. No offence."

"None taken. I wish there was more we could do. I wish we could do better."

Sandra was really lovely, and it was great talking to her but I knew my time was up once our tea was drunk. I tapped the empty cup on the counter. "Well, I'd better be off. Promise me you'll call and ask for me if you have any more trouble."

"I will."

Sandra would turn out to be one of the most important people I ever met in my career, but for the time being, I went on cultivating local sources, learning under Bry's wing as he took me on his patrols around the Winstanley.

It was true that the estate always seemed deserted whenever we rolled up. One or two people might be about, but the estate had an uninhabited air, as if the mess of low-rise and high-rise flats, the rows of little maisonettes and town houses ensconced in a concrete warren filled with more dead ends than Wandsworth Cemetery had suddenly been abandoned.

"Drug deals that take place in the open tend to be pre-arranged," Bry said, "But I reckon most deals take place when buyers travel in to a particular address, which is kept supplied by large gangs who arrange the transport of drugs like cannabis and heroin."

He nodded at the sounds of trains clattering in and out of Clapham Junction.

"Two thousand trains a day and people come from all over London and beyond to score at the Winstanley, even from as far as Essex. It's probably the most popular estate in London. It's all tied up in here. Youth gangs deal at street level. They're quick, hard to prosecute if we do manage to catch them, they know these streets and alleyways like the backs of their hands and stash the gear in bushes, bins, lampposts and walls with loosened bricks."

"Can't we at least raid the houses that are selling? Or catch the gangs when they bring the drugs in?"

"It's a question of knowledge and motivation. The houses change all the time, unless they get really lazy, and the fact of life on this estate is that they can see us coming a mile off, so all evidence is gone by the time we arrive. Plus we don't have specialist drug squads. If we don't have a drugs squad then how can we have a drugs problem? The powers that be don't want drugs in the newspapers every day. It makes them look bad."

"It's not right, Bry," I said, not sure what else to say. "There must be a way we can make a difference."

"Well, we're making a difference right now, just by walking through the estate. But change doesn't come easy. I love history and I was always struck by a quote from Charles Booth. You know who he was?"

"No, never heard of him."

"He was a wealthy Victorian social reformer who spent a lot of time in Battersea. He was concerned about the effects of poverty in London, along with his cousin Beatrice Potter. At the end of the nineteenth century he produced colour-coded poverty maps of parts of inner London, showing street-by-street how much of it lived below the 'poverty line.' He was the first person to use that phrase. At the bottom, coloured black, was the 'lowest class, vicious, semi-criminal,' then dark blue for 'very poor, casual, chronic want,' and gradually it went up to 'fairly comfortable' which was beige, then red for 'middle class, well-to-do' and finally gold for the 'upper middle and upper classes.'"

"And what did he find?"

"That 35% of Londoners were living below the poverty line. But what I always remember is what he wrote about Battersea: 'side-by-side, the newly prosperous with the old wealthy conditions of life; new, as well as old poverty.'

"This problem is not new but we've been able to cope until drugs got here, which made the problem of poverty far, far worse, and the need to act more urgent than ever. At the moment, all we can do as PBOs (Permanent Beat Officers) is keep our wits about us, do the best we can for the community and never park our cars within brick-dropping range of one of the high rise blocks."

I later looked up the work of Charles Booth and what he had to say about Battersea was utterly fascinating to me as a young Yorkshire lad turned copper on the streets of London, which still seemed to me to be like a foreign country.

Booth described how the railway was a defining feature of Battersea even then, before going on to describe how rich and poor lived side by side: "There are here, side by side, the newly prosperous with the old wealthy... new, as well as old poverty; new, as well as old slums; while, pervading all and spreading everywhere in its thousands, is the ordinary London working-class population, which must, after all, claim our greatest concern."

It was just the same today; the extraordinarily wealthy living within a half-brick's throw of some of the least well-off people in the country. And the key to a successful community of working class were strong community leaders, who were, in Booth's day, philanthropists. One such philanthropist was Mrs Despard. Boom wrote about her in one of his reports: "Mrs. Despard, a very noble-minded Roman Catholic lady, gives her life to... the young; and the people recognise her self-devotion... her home is their club... "You hurt me," cried a big strong fellow, but he did not resist when she took him by the arm in the cause of order. She laments the stunted growth of the lads and the early age at which they become their own masters. They are allowed to smoke in the club... it is felt that to forbid smoking would be unwise. There is a Sunday 'conference' [but] the work is ostensibly more social than religious in character, and there is no trace of the propagandist spirit... Mrs. Despard never proselytises, and the representative of the Church of England himself says that if some do adopt her religion it is from admiration of her character."

And at the heart of the community in Battersea was the Providence House Community Centre, which had been going for nearly thirty years. Originally a run-down chapel with a flooded basement, it was transformed in the 1970s into a purpose-built community centre which was, by the end of the 1980s, also a bit run-down.

"Providence House may not look like much," Bry said, "But it's a gem that's done more for this community than almost anything or anyone else over the last thirty years. Its doors are open to all colours and creeds and it has taken in young people over the last three decades and changed their lives for the better. If this doesn't symbolise hope in a tough climate, then I don't know what does."

Bry introduced me to one of the centre's managers 'Dave', who explained how the estates, intended to transform slums into centrally-heated homes with hot water had accidentally worsened the environment for children. Dave was black, in his mid-forties and spoke with a quiet authority that belied a strong passionate undercurrent.

"Wherever you are in the world, kids need somewhere to exist which isn't school or home; somewhere they can call their own. The estate took away their territory: the streets. It killed open spaces with dead-end alleys and corridors, and filled open spaces with concrete with too few play areas that are way too small to share."

Before the regeneration of the sixties, people's front doors opened onto pavements, a shared road and play area, spaces in which they could run safely and socialise. Families had back-yards for hens and pigeons. Neighbours had the space to open their doors and chat, or argue – and clear the air. Now their doors opened onto narrow areas that belonged to no one, that no one wanted to claim. The streets had been rubbed out and with that went the sense of belonging and responsibility.

"There was nothing for kids in this area when this place first opened its doors," Dave said. "The young volunteers who worked here came from the community and were at the heart of making the centre work. You could come and just hang out, shelter from the rain, or you could learn a skill like carpentry, improve your English, take part in sports, cookery, learn about the media and arts. We eventually started taking people out of London on trips to a farm in Devon. Almost none of the kids had left London before and the countryside blew their minds and opened their eyes to new possibilities.

"We always seem to be on the verge of closing down for lack of money," he said. "But somehow the community manages to pull together to persuade the council to keep us funded for a few more months."

"Our job would be a lot harder without you," Bry said. "The kids here have energy and they want to put it somewhere. If they're left with nothing but the estate to run around in, then there's a real danger they'll be drawn into crime."

"It's all down to our kids," he replied. "To keep the youth work going we needed to being young people in as leaders, for discipline and security. Plenty of young people in the Winstanley, and across London, want to belong to something good like this and are smart and have talents that the more traditional society has failed to spot and nurture. Some of our volunteers have become official staff and are employed by the local authority. And if the local authority had seen these kids when they first walked in they would have refused point-blank to have anything to do with them. Everyone should feel like they can come here but clearly some people feel marginalised and don't come, and we need to do something more to bring them in. People need to feel as though they belong to something. That they have a place in which they fit, and that helps people find themselves, gives them a sense of purpose, and when you belong somewhere, you are the part owner, part responsible because it's yours, it's something precious.

"Drugs have turned what was for us a struggle into an uphill battle. I mean, cannabis was always around, alcohol too, but there's been a change, there's aggressiveness in the air. People still need places like this but it's become harder to bring young people inside. Something else has a bigger pull for these kids, whether it's the false promise of money, of getting rich quick for those motivated enough to become dealers or down to the high of these new drugs that creates an addiction, I don't know, but it's definitely getting worse. You guys need to step up and do something because we can't solve all of our young community's problems, not by any stretch."

Today, Providence House no longer receives money from the local authority and youth services have seen cuts of between 20% and 70% across the UK since austerity measures kicked in in 2010. And then came the riots of 2011. Kids, once marginalised who'd found homes in our community centres were suddenly told the one thing they loved was no longer theirs and were turned out into the streets. After they've seen things like MP's excessive claims or the open, criminal greed of some bankers, which went completely unpunished, then when the chance comes to take something for nothing during a riot, then some will be tempted. The fact that we have lost so many community centres has not only made policing more difficult because we've lost an important conduit to communication, it's also become more difficult because more kids, tempted to become involved in crime, have no respect or trust for anyone in authority.

"If you don't mind me asking," I said, "What keeps you here?"

"The kids," Dave replied. "The sense that the job isn't done. I only planned to work here for a year or two when I first arrived but there came a point when I realised that I was meant to be here."

Bry also introduced me to local people, many of whom refused to report burglaries, muggings and other crimes because they didn't see the point, they thought it was a waste of our time and theirs. I nearly had tears in my eyes after talking to an elderly lady who'd lived in Battersea for forty years as she told me how, since moving to the Winstanley she virtually felt a prisoner in her own home – and even that didn't feel safe; she'd been burgled twice in six months.

Another man, a former drug addict, described how his home had been taken over by drug dealers and used as a base for the dealers to sell their wares; in return the addict was fed drugs to keep him quiet and so he couldn't protest as his home steadily fell apart in front of him, until it was time for the dealers to move on and abandon him to withdrawal.

"The message seems to have spread all across London," one young mum told us. "People from all over know if they come here, they will be able to score drugs and many of these people are criminals and bring more crime with them. I hate having to push my baby past kids smoking hash in the communal areas. And as for leaving home at night, forget it, never on my own anyway. It feels like it's just too high risk."

"If you want peace and quiet, you have to mind your own business," a local man who worked as a plumber's mate told me. "There are certain parts I won't go near at night."

"It's hard after seeing all this," Bry said, "To believe that a tiny minority of this community, about 0.1% of people are responsible for 99% of the crime."

I was determined to bloody well find them and take them off the streets. People needed to know that if they came to Battersea to buy or sell drugs, we were going to bloody well arrest them.

This was easier said than done, of course.

When the rocks we'd recovered after my drugs raid came back from the lab, the report said they were cocaine with a few additives. It was only when Pete made a few calls that we got some proper feedback from a drugs squad who worked in the Kings Cross area. We were right in the middle of London's first crack boom and didn't know it.

This was why street robberies, shoplifting, bicycle thefts and car crime had gone through the roof on our patch. Addicts were stealing anything they could sell so they could stay high.

My probation was ending. Sergeant Phil took me to one side in the canteen. "I've been watching you Pannett. You're good with people. You work hard and people respect you. Bry's been taken on by the CID and he's recommended that you take over his permanent beat."

"The Winstanley?"

"That's the one."

"I'd be honoured, sarge."

I'd be the youngest in service officer in the Met with my own permanent beat. This would give me great freedom to gather intel, to get to know the local people, and find out who we should be going after. It also came with great responsibility and great danger of course, but I was up for the fight.

"We're trusting you with this, Pannett," Phil said as he got up to leave, "Don't fuck it up."

# Chapter Seven

# ATTACKING THE BLOCK

It was after midnight and Mark and I were crouching in the dark, hiding behind the steel doors right at the top of the fire escape of one of Winstanley's towerblocks. Behind us were the block's water tanks and, even though it was summer, the temperature dropped massively at night, making us wish we'd brought our thermals. We shivered quietly, waiting for our targets, not daring to make a sound. And then we heard footsteps and muttering voices echoing through the twelve-storey stairwell. I put my finger to my lips; Mark nodded as we got to our feet, oh-so-quietly, and then crouching, I peered out of the keyhole.

Two young lads were on the landing one flight down. They were in their late teens or possibly their early twenties, one black, one white. They were both extremely focussed on what they were doing and continued to mutter to one another as they took a seat on the steps and started to go about their business, which was smoking the crack they'd just bought.

I'd discovered, from residents and caretakers, how the stairwells of the towerblocks had been taken over by drug users. It was bad enough for residents to have to use the stairs because the lifts had stopped working, but many were scared to go out at night and have to walk past (or step over) drug users, some of whom were aggressive and abusive (especially when high), and some of whom were street robbers. And then in the morning, their detritus would be all around (sometimes needles but mostly cans converted into pipes) as would the stink of dried urine and high-strength lager (among many other types of spilled booze) that had made its way down flight after flight of stairs and, a surprising number of times according to the caretaker of one particular block (a robust lady in her early forties), human faeces.

This was as good a place as any to start my own small war against the drug dealers.

Mark and I had been given carte blanche in terms of overtime to deal with the Winstanley. Inspector Barry appreciated our youthful enthusiasm and knew we had the energy to go with it. If we could do anything to make a difference, then all the overtime we were being paid (strictly limited these days) was worth it. And we really needed the extra time. Policing is a job that requires patience, a hell of a lot of waiting around in cold and damp locations, trying to figure out what the criminals are up to, and where one might be best positioned to catch them in the act. Mark and I went on to rack up a hundred hours in overtime in just one month; most of it spent lurking near the water tanks of the various tower blocks and processing our many prisoners. It was dangerous work, no question, and we spent a large part of the time spent waiting, filled with apprehension of what would happen when we made the arrests. After all, it was just the two of us at the top of a towerblock in the heart of gangland. If we got into trouble, it was up to us to deal with it because even if we yelled 'urgent assistance,' it would take some time for back-up to reach us at the top of the block.

After checking the keyhole and seeing the two lads, who were on the landing, their backs to us, one flight down, were smoking up, I turned and nodded to Mark, who moved close to the door. I slowly turned the round handle (which I'd greased earlier), looked at Mark and nodded, one, two and THREE!

"POLICE DON'T MOVE! YOU'RE UNDER ARREST!"

To get to them quickly (some of these lads were extremely quick on their feet and if you gave them half a chance you'd be chasing them around the estate all night), Mark and I leapt from practically the top step just as the two lads turned. They must have thought they were hallucinating, two cops in full uniform flying down the stairs from nowhere, screaming kamikaze-style; they cowered as we crashed into them, grabbing and cuffing them before they could even think about reacting.

Now came the really important part. As anyone will tell you, I like to talk. And I like to talk to the people I've arrested. Once the fight is over, there's no point clamming up or just yelling at your suspects to 'confess'. The other big part of policing, apart from watching and waiting, is intelligence, and the best place to go for intelligence was to the criminals themselves.

I always treated the people I arrested with respect and talked to them in a friendly way. I wanted them to open up, to tell me anything, even the most random thought from a criminal can be useful to a copper working a beat. I was perhaps more motivated than most because so often I felt like I fish out of water in Battersea, it was so different from Yorkshire that it constantly took me by surprise, from stepping into a posh penthouse flat that had been burgled and almost stepping straight into an unexpected swimming pool, to thinking I was at the wrong address in a completely empty council flat but the thieves had in fact not only stripped it of every last stick of furniture, they'd also taken the boiler, sinks, radiators and cooker.

I really needed to learn about the people I was dealing with and my way of achieving this was to talk.

"You alright lads?' I asked with smile, once we had the two men up on their feet. "No injuries?"

They shook their heads.

"Anyone you'd like to call once we're down the station?"

"Nah man," the black youth said, "Why you going after us for, anyways? We're not the criminals. We're the victims innit."

Mark scooped up and bagged their drugs paraphernalia as evidence.

"Cos you're taking drugs," I replied, "*But,* if you would care to share with us where you got them, then we could go after the *real* criminals, couldn't we?"

This, naturally, was met with silence.

"See, we need your help. We don't know where you've got your drugs from otherwise we'd go and arrest the dealers."

"So we arrest users," Mark added. "It's a pain for you and frustrating for us,"

"It is what it is," the white lad chipped in.

"Exactly," I said.

"Well, we ain't grasses," the white lad confirmed, before adding, "Why do you talk so funny?"

"What do you mean?"

"I think he's referring to your accent, Mike," Mark said. "He's a Yorkie."

"A what?"

"From Yorkshire. Up north."

"So what you doing down here then?"

"Well, we solved all the crime up there so we've come down here to sort you lot out."

"Yeah, right."

By the time we were back at the station we were chatting quite pleasantly; we'd never be best mates, but I kept it up and kept it friendly and they weren't too bothered about being arrested. They would be charged then bailed and would end up with a slap on the wrist; they certainly wouldn't receive a custodial sentence. It was more of a bureaucratic pain than anything else as far as all of us were concerned, but I was learning and I hoped that these kids were learning that the cops weren't all bad.

We were just doing a job and we wanted to make life better. And it worked both ways. I was being educated. I was discovering that not all drug users are monsters or nasty types, for example, and they could even be helpful. I already knew way more than most people who hadn't met a drug user and, despite our social differences, I almost felt like I had two new allies by the time we parted.

When I asked these lads, and many others, about why they used I got replies along the lines of:

"Try living in that estate, man."

"I'm the wrong colour for this world, man."

"Try getting a job. Burger flipper, if you're lucky."

I felt sorry for them. I was just a few years older, the same age in a few cases. I'd been a bit wild back home in Yorkshire but I had a family, a safe home and a rock solid community, so I was never going to overstep the mark and I never felt the need to turn to drugs to escape my life or to feed the need for love caused by a broken home.

They'd been in that estate, watching it fall apart for too long. The lack of community had made them more insular and they couldn't see a life beyond the borders, they didn't even leave those borders. They were walking distance from some of the greatest museums, galleries and buildings in the world but they had never crossed the Thames. The only people they knew who did, I was told, were those who went robbing tourists.

I always said they could talk to me if they ever needed to, completely anonymously, if they wanted help or they were in trouble.

"I know you're not used to thinking of us this way but don't forget we want to make things better, not worse. And drugs are making things a lot worse."

I could see the words going in but I don't think they stayed conscious of them for long. They wanted better lives, just like anyone else, but until they had another option that they could understand was better and had the potential for reward, they just fed their brain's desires with an artificial satisfaction that would, over time, and one way or another, through overdose or through the steady disintegration of their internal organs, send them to an early grave, perhaps burdening society with various state benefits and expensive medical treatments.

I talked and talked, and talked my way around my beat until everyone knew me. The law-abiding local residents eventually became pleased to see me and a few members of the local gangs had reached a point where they thought I was 'Alright for a cop,' (which was still the social equivalent of a piece of dog poop) but some of the younger ones did start to engage with me when the older ones weren't around and vice versa. But while I seemed harmless by day, the Clark Kent of beat policing, by night, I donned my cape and put everything I'd learned during my beat into action to identifying and catching street robbers, users and dealers; not that I had made much headway in terms of getting to the dealers.

I loved the work but I was frustrated by just how fast the estates of Battersea were sinking under the weight of drug associated crime, the most worrying aspect of which was the fighting between rival gangs, which was getting out of control. It felt to me like it was something tribal, like the stories of blood feuds in hillbilly America or in Albania, which can go on for generations, or until all of the young men of one family are dead. In Battersea the feuding families were gangs. It all seemed so pointless. Instead of trying to make their lives better, they spent their youth fighting over a patch of land that they hated.

I was out one drizzly night early in the week when I was called to a stabbing, 999'd by a local shopkeeper. I was just a street away so, after a quick sprint, I found a young black male at the reported location. He didn't look that bad to me; he was standing, albeit a little disoriented in appearance, drunk or stoned perhaps, swaying gently in the rain.

"You alright mate?" I asked as I came to a halt beside him.

The rain had developed from a drizzle into a steady and unpleasantly cold downpour but the man made no sign of noticing, nor made any move to get under shelter of nearby shop canopies or a covered bus stop. He was tall, could have been in his late teens and had wispy hair on his chin and upper lip. He was wearing a loose-fitting blue tracksuit and a black baseball cap. I hadn't seen him before and my cop gut was telling me that he wasn't local.

He suddenly realised that I was addressing him.

"I'm fine, I don't need no fucking ambulance," he said.

At first, I had to agree. I couldn't actually see an injury. I got a bit closer, looked him up and down and caught a glimpse of a hole in his loose white T-shirt. It was at chest height and there was a small bloodstain.

"Fair enough," I said, as I spotted the approaching ambulance, lights on, sirens off. "Why don't you just let the paramedic take a quick look, ok?"

"Back the fuck off man, I'm fine and I'm going home."

"Better safe than sorry."

"Nah man."

But he didn't move, made no effort to start walking away.

The paramedic, an unshaven man in his thirties with dark shadows under his eyes and very much of the been-there-done-that school of medicine, took one look from a safe distance and said: "If the mop (member of the public) is right in that he's been stabbed and that's a puncture wound, it looks like it's close to his heart. He could be bleeding internally."

"I need to take a piss," the young man said, finally starting to amble down the street.

"Mate, let me take a look," the paramedic said, "If it's nothing you can go on your way but you could be in trouble."

The boy turned back around and opened his mouth but the words never came. He fell, hitting the pavement with a horrible wet slap.

We both ran over and, despite the rain, a crowd started to gather while the paramedic, by now joined by his partner, set to working on reviving or at least stabilising him. Finally, the been-there-done-that paramedic looked up at me.

"He's gone."

"Gone?"

"Life extinct. My guess would be the knife sliced the heart and he bled out, pumping his blood into his body cavities. That's why he wanted the loo, he was full of his own blood."

I looked at the young man's body. I'd seen plenty of dead people by now in my duties as a police officer, people dead of old age in their home, people dead of overdoses and heart attacks, but I'd never seen someone die right before my eyes.

And then it hit me.

This was murder.

The paramedic continued to look at me.

"This is a crime scene," he said helpfully, kick-starting my professionalism, which gradually overcame the shock that had gripped me.

"Let's get him covered," I said, before shooing the small crowd to back up.

I called it in and a minute later Patters skidded up in the area car with Stevie, another old-sweat in his mid-forties. Married with two kids, he only ever moaned about family life and referred to his wife as 'her indoors'. He called WPC's 'plonks' (person with little or no knowledge) and never smiled.

"You alright Mike?" Patters asked. I nodded.

"First murder, is it?"

"Yeah. He just dropped. Barely a mark on him."

I explained what had happened while Stevie called the CID and we then sought out the shopkeeper who'd called it in. Gradually the wheels of justice started to turn, starting with cordons, the arrival of the forensic officer, which in those days consisted of a lone civilian in a small van, and then the Murder Squad, staffed by the crème de la crème of the Met's detectives.

'I'd love to work with those guys,' I thought, although at the same time, I knew in my heart I was a community police officer. These guys dipped in and out of communities as they cracked some of the biggest crimes in the capital. I preferred to be part of the community I worked in.

'Still, I wouldn't mind the experience,' I thought, to work one or two murders with those guys would be quite the education.

The Murder Squad would never find this young man's killer however. As far as I know, if he wasn't killed in some revenge attack, then the murderer is still out there, walking the streets today.

London had changed for the Murder Squad. Just a few years earlier, murder cases were dominated by white working-class gangsters who robbed banks and security vans and killed grasses and rival gang members. After bank security was improved in the late eighties and early nineties, career criminals had turned to the low-risk, high-profit world of drug importation. Now it seemed as though the murderers were kids who were involved in low-level drug dealing, who claimed they killed over issues of respect and territory, but whose crimes were in fact rooted in drugs, poverty and social exclusion.

And then came a killing that made no sense at all.

# CHAPTER EIGHT

# SENSELESS

As almost any beat police officer will tell you, we suffer mixed feelings about the job. Policing the community is a privilege but at the same time you never know what you'll be called to deal with next and sometimes, for a single bobby, it can all be too much.

I seemed to be on an unfortunate roll as a few nights after the young man's murder I had barely left the station on my patrol when a member of the public called 999 to say they'd seen a man beaten to the ground. I was close by so ran to the location and sure enough, found a man lying face down on the pavement. I felt his neck, then wrist. No pulse. He was a white male, looked like he was in his early twenties. I jerked my hand away in horror when I felt his head. It was soft and sticky from where his skull had been smashed in. He'd had no chance; dead before he'd even hit the pavement.

I stood up and looked back over my shoulder. Battersea nick was in plain view, less than a hundred metres away. This young man had been murdered right under our nose.

"It's Mike, isn't it?"

I turned to see a middle-aged black lady I'd met and chatted to a few times on the beat. Her name was June and she'd lived in Battersea most of her life.

"I seen them, three white lads, they came from nowhere, the man wasn't doing anything, just walking along. No reason, far as I could see. Is he going to be alright?"

June was shaking, clearly in shock. I didn't want her to see the body. I didn't want to have to tell her she had witnessed a murder, but that was exactly what I was going to have to do.

I stood up and gently guided her back inside her house. "I'll be along in a minute, maybe pop the kettle on and we'll have a chat about it, ok?"

Within minutes the estate was covered in flashing blue lights. The forensic officer arrived in his little van and recognised me.

"You again?" he asked as he pulled out two small padded briefcases that contained his paraphernalia.

I nodded. "Just call me lucky."

He put down one of the cases and offered his hand.

"Bruce, I'm new to the area. Was working Westminster before I was sent here. Not your week, is it? Or is it always like this south of the river?"

"It's been getting steadily worse, mate," I said, "And I don't think it's going to get better anytime soon."

The constables of Battersea paired up and did door-to-door enquiries. Timbo and Trist found our victim's girlfriend, a lovely girl called Mary who was studying to be a nurse, and had to break the most awful news she would ever hear in her life. The victims' name was Jon, he was 22-years-old and had been about to embark on his final year of study for a degree in business studies. Jon had just dropped Mary off and was walking home when he was attacked.

It was a senseless crime as far as anyone could tell. No motive and no leads. So, a few days later, we launched a major publicity campaign asking for witnesses, or for anyone who knew one of the attackers to come forward (something along the lines of: Did someone you know come home in bloodstained clothing? Has anyone been talking about the killing? Been acting strangely?).

A week later, Darren (Doctor Death) was in Battersea nick's reception when a middle-aged, middle-class white woman walked in and said her daughter's boyfriend was responsible for the murder.

Twenty minutes later the Murder Squad arrived at a semi-detached house in a nice part of Battersea.

"Can this be right?" I asked. Having seen the woman after Darren had brought her through to make a statement, I just didn't quite buy it.

"Takes all kinds," Darren said, looking suitably grim.

The boy who was arrested, and he was a boy, a puny-looking eighteen-year-old dressed in white tracksuit and white baseball cap, came from a well-educated, well-to-do middle class family. He had told his sixteen-year-old girlfriend about the attack, although he didn't reveal that their victim was dead, but once she saw the appeal she put two and two together and told her mum.

Minutes after the boy was arrested, Bruce emerged from the shed with the murder weapon, a baseball bat made from maple. It had been wiped clean but not thoroughly enough, not to microscopic level.

There was no way this lad could have done this on his own, we thought, and sure enough, as soon as we applied some pressure, he quickly confessed to having two accomplices. We picked them up from their place of work. All three of them had good jobs: mechanic, office worker and trainee chef, and came from decent, hard-working families.

"I weren't the one who hit him though," white tracksuit boy said through his tears.

"Why did you do this, what was the reason?"

"We would just go out louting you know, something to do. We'd pick fights with random people and that. I never meant for anyone to get killed though."

A few nights later we were gathered around the wobbler in a fairly sombre mood, discussing this case when Trist said: "Sometimes, there's just a meanness in this world."

He wasn't wrong, mores' the pity. This was an utter waste of life that broke the hearts of many good people: the family of the victim, his girlfriend and June, the witness who would never really recover. The police are much better at witness support these days, but back then, people who witnessed terrible crimes or were unfortunate enough to find a dead body (even if it was from natural causes) would suffer severe mental trauma and often found themselves psychologically wounded by the experience.

Finding dead bodies certainly affected me but I was fortunate enough to have a family of police officers who knew and understood what I'd been through. This in itself acted as a short cut through conversation and we could talk about the terrible things we had to endure with a sympathy that was as unconditional as it was comforting.

I would always talk to June whenever I ran into her on my beat and stopped by a few times after the crime, to offer her that sympathy that came from the experience we shared, but I don't think this was enough. After all, she had to walk past that same spot every time she left her home.

Then there were the families of the boys who committed the crime. A trial for them to endure and then prison visits, parole and the burden of living life with a criminal record that was never going to go away. As for the boys, they were each sentenced to eight years for manslaughter. With time off for 'good behaviour', they would be out in four. For many, that didn't feel like justice.

# CHAPTER NINE

# MIKE THE MERCILESS

Crack and gang warfare arrived long before the days of CCTV cameras. At the same time cheap mobile phones were still a few years off, so it wasn't as easy as it is now for dealers to operate behind closed doors, or for those at the top to run their empires without coming into contact with the drugs or the criminal minions.

We saw the terrified victims of robberies, businessmen and women who'd been targeted after leaving Clapham Junction railway station after dark by gangs of up to six knife-carrying men. When you see the victims, and the awful psychological, confidence-knocking effect it has on many of them, it makes you want to tackle the bastards that terrorised them head on.

The problem was, how? We couldn't find the street robbers and catch them in the act, even though I knew who they were; Clapham Junction covered a huge area and the robbers struck with incredible speed in different areas at different times.

I started work on creating a file of known street robbers, the bad boys of Winstanley and the surrounding area and with the help of Pete's database I eventually created an album of 140 faces, which I then memorised. We'd show this to the victims in the hope they would ID their attacker but, what with it being night-time and because the criminals often covered their faces with scarves or hid in hoods, shouting at their victims not to look at them, it had limited success.

My early morning arrest of the pharmacy thief had become something of a trademark of mine, in that I liked, if possible, to give the robbers the rudest possible awakening. A strike back for the victim, time to give their cowardly attacker the fright of their life. They were always in bed and rarely had woken by the time I got to their bedroom, even when we used the battering ram.

In one case a robber had threatened a young lady before ripping her bag from her shoulder. But she'd seen his face, picked him out for us and so it was a case of door in, down the hall, into the bedroom and there he was. I threw back the sheets: "GOOD MORNING! IT'S YOUR WORST NIGHTMARE!" He not only hit the roof but peed himself. The room was full of stolen credit cards, jewellery, under the bed, drugs, hunting knives.

"Get up, get up, you lazy sod, time for your ID parade!"

The robbers had become so confident that no area was off limits (a famous QC was just one notable victim) and the phrase "shots fired" came over the radio every day.

I was moved to the robbery squad where I was given a long list of suspects to track down. Many were Yardies on the run from the US and Jamaica, who were arriving in the UK in droves, ready to make some serious drug money on the UK's virgin crack shores.

The term Yardie is used to describe Jamaican-born gangsters who set up drug dealing operations in the UK. The name comes from the young, bored men who hung about in the back yards in the slums of Kingston, Jamaica, slums that had grown in the wake of British decolonisation. When the occupiers left for good in 1962, they took the infrastructure with them – teachers, doctors, administrators, police officers, court officials, etc. Subsequent years of social and fiscal mismanagement, along with political violence, caused the rich-poor divide to widen and the slums to grow. Many young Jamaicans left their homes to find work in the UK and sent their wages home to their families, with the hope of escaping the slums. Many young parents left their children in the care of grandparents. Many stayed for far longer than they intended and soon, the aging grandparents found themselves unable to cope with teenage grandchildren who were tempted to join in with the growing get-rich-quick drugs trade and/or into the violent struggle for power between the main two political parties. These children never really grew up and many, having never learned respect from their parents, adopted a live-fast-die-young attitude that became the Yardie hallmark.

They were unorganised; 'leaders' didn't last long before they were killed or launched operations in other territories. There was little loyalty between Yardies and they often fell out with one other, settling squabbles with the gun.

Jamaica was a stopping off point for South American cocaine being smuggled to the North and into Europe and, with the emergence of crack, which is easy to make, addictive and affordable (at least at first, before a user becomes addicted) the Yardies, with plenty of family connections to the UK quickly saw a way to get rich quick.

The Yardies, who at this time were not officially acknowledged as a gang by the Met (the leadership didn't want to admit there was a problem or create panic), but they were starting to make their presence felt in London and they inspired copycat behaviour in some similarly-minded British-born black youths who were drawn to the "glamorous" gun-toting image. One such youth was 21-year-old Gary Nelson aka 'Tyson' (he looked just like the famous boxer, in build, expression with the same killer instincts and fighting skills). Gary was known to be part of the street robbery scene but also had a reputation for being shrewd, way smarter than your average street criminal who was determined to reach the top of South London's underworld or die trying. I learned later that a well-known criminal had taken Nelson under his wing, after he copped a short spell in prison. This older criminal had given the young wannabe gangster a master class on everything you need to survive as a professional criminal, from how to evade conviction to how to set up and run your own gang. It was this, combined with Nelson's home-grown Yardie mindset (Nelson was ruthless but child-like, as if he'd never really developed into a full-grown adult) that helped propel him up the criminal ladder.

The first time I saw Nelson, swaggering up the road towards me, I was walking the beat with Mark on a bright sunny evening.

"Alright Gary?" I said, adding firmly, "We're going to have to search you."

He said nothing and stared me out, putting his head back and looking down his nose, but he let us carry out the stop and search. This was always done respectfully and followed the GOWISE mnemonic. Grounds (Nelson was on our list of robbery suspects), Object (I explained what we were about to do and why), Warrant Card and Identification (made sure he saw it and knew who I was), Station (where I was from), and his Entitlement (he had seven days to get a copy of the record of the search). As I performed the search I carried on chatting, in the Yorkshire way I was known for, friendly but firm and clear about what I was doing. There was no misunderstanding in terms of knowing who would win a fight if he decided to kick off (and there was no way I would have tried to have stopped Gary without Mark by my side). Gary did not fear the police. He knew the law and believed he could brazen his way out of any situation (and often did). In my experience professional criminals always made it their business to know and understand the law as well as we did and they were plenty of characters who were able to avoid convictions that would have been, for a less well-educated criminal, a dead cert.

Gary was clean and we sent him on his way. Other prime candidates for the stop and search were Gary's henchmen: Richard Watts, aka 'Chen', a giant who looked liked like an Inuit, and Tony Francis, aka 'Lips' a big-mouthed drug dealer. Then there was Jason Miller, another one of London's chief shit-bags. He was wanted for three knifepoint robberies and the armed robbery of a bookies, but we'd been unable to find him as he'd been lying lower than a snake for weeks. It got to the point where there was practically a competition among us to be the one who nicked him.

As usual, when I searched Titch, a prolific mugger and wannabe gangster dressed in top-of-the-range trainers and designer clothes, I got chatting and mentioned the problems with battles between rival gangs. Titch talked of the "disrespect" of the gangs that had "invaded" their territory.

"It's hardly worth dying over though, is it?" I said.

"You die for your crew, you die with respect."

This was part of the strange world of gang philosophy. Kids and more junior members would talk about 'respect' and how their fellow gang members were like family but those at the top were only in it for the power and the money and if that meant screwing over fellow gang members, no problem. However mistaken they might have been about their reasons for being in gangs, it was clear that junior members felt (however mistaken they might have been) just the same as police did in terms of family. Their fellow gang members were brothers in arms and they would die for them.

Titch was clean and I let him go about his day. I watched him walk away.

'You don't die with respect,' I thought. 'You go in a hole in the ground, your body rots and your crew goes on robbing and dealing and forgets all about you.'

***

If there was one thing about all the gangs from Tooting, Clapham, Brixton, Battersea and Peckham that crossed into our patch, they were all united in their hatred against cops. Street robbers smoked crack before going out to 'work' and fought harder when we jumped them, so when we arrested them, we had to go in hard.

I was parked up in the Astra with Mark when a 999 call came: four youths had just robbed an elderly lady at knifepoint and had fled the scene in a stolen red VW Golf. A moment later we saw them fly out of the estate.

"Gogogo!" Mark yelled and I floored it. Our bodies filled with adrenaline as we took off, hearts pounding, racing after the robbers, crossing the river via Battersea Bridge, along the Embankment and through Chelsea on into Fulham. And then the old adage, normally applied to foot-chases, suddenly gave me an opportunity. The VW had to slow for an obstacle, in this case a busy roundabout, around which an articulated lorry was slowly turning, taking up two lanes as it prepared to take the next exit. I saw the VW's brake lights, saw them skidding and Mark voiced my thoughts: "Now we've got them mate!" I gave it everything the Astra had, all I had to do was slide to a halt in front of them, and be out of the car and on them before their driver could even think about finding reverse. The little Astra's engine screamed as I floored it and, seeing we had them, I hit the brakes, prepared to skid and – nothing!

"BRAKE!" Mark screamed.

"I fucking am!"

I'd been so focussed on the chase that I hadn't noticed the smell coming from the Astra's engine, nor the smoke that signalled the car's overheating.

Any police officer who drives a vehicle on the job needs to have passed a standard training course and I had duly taken the relevant course with much enthusiasm and had passed without too much trouble. The words of one of the instructors, a former police driver, suddenly came back to me: "Spare the brakes in a chase if you can, pump them rather than apply them flat out, because they *will* overheat, then you'll be out of time and your target will get away."

I cried "Shiiiiit!" pulled the handbrake swinging the wheel at the same time. This was our only chance, we were going to crash, of that there was no doubt, but there was still a chance for us to emerge unscathed. We skidded side-on into the VW and shoved it into the side of the lorry that was still trying to squeeze past, bringing everyone to a halt.

Mark and I looked at each other and spoke simultaneously: "You alright?"

And then, remembering that our job wasn't yet done, we leapt out – well Mark did – I tried but found I was pressed up against the robbers' car, the guy in the front passenger seat was looking at me, wild-eyed with fear. I followed Mark out of his side and drew my truncheon. These were street robbers, armed with knives. Their adrenaline would be pumping at least as much as ours was.

We proceeded to show no mercy.

We jumped on the VW's bonnet raised our truncheons and brought them down like Thor's hammer on the windshield, smashing the glass, until we were able to reach in and pull two of robbers out onto the bonnet. All the fight had left them and we dragged them to the ground as the other two, still trapped in the back seat, raised their hands in surrender.

"Blimey, you guys don't mess around, do you?"

It was the lorry driver. He had climbed out of his cab only to see two deranged cops destroy a small car and manhandle its occupants out onto the street. Mark and I looked back at him panting, red-faced and still wielding our truncheons, hands bloody, our car steaming away behind us and past that, a traffic jam of epic proportions was developing.

"Apologies for the inconvenience," I said, nodding at his truck.

"No worries mate," he replied in a strong Australian accent. "Truck's not mine, is it? And I'll be telling this story for years to come."

It was a great result, caught in the act with the goods on them, a witness and victim prepared to testify and a whole load of driving offences to throw at them to boot. Mark and I were delighted. What other job is there that would let you hurtle around London at high speed and crash your car into a gang of robbers, all in the name of justice?

We arrived at Battersea nick about an hour later and as we walked in, we bumped into Patters in the hall.

Our clothes were a mess; bloodstains covered our shirts from where we'd cut ourselves on the windshield.

Patters took one look and said: "Lads, I don't think those are regulation."

"Eh?" was all I managed.

"Your truncheon, Pannett."

Both of our truncheons, now back in our holders, were studded with broken glass from the VW's windshield. They looked like some of the adapted weapons I'd seen at the Yard's Crime Museum.

Although we were castigated for the damage caused to the Astra (there was an unofficial points system for damaging police cars and if you ended up with twelve, the traffic department would petition to have you banned), we celebrated our success long and hard that night. All of our crew was just as determined to being justice to Battersea and we (almost) played as hard as we worked. I was lucky enough to be of an age when hangovers didn't really happen, where one could smoke ten fags a day and still run a mile in full uniform without breaking into too much of a sweat.

It felt as though I had two families, one in Yorkshire and a band of brothers and sisters in Battersea, to whom I would give my life to protect. We would spend just about all our free time socialising, celebrating and commiserating, depending what had happened to whom that week.

Although we had some successes, they were still small compared to the number of crimes and the numbers of people committing them. We were reactive, in that we came running when called, but it was only by sheer luck we'd been in the right place at the right time with these four lads. More often than not, all we could do was pick up the pieces. The vital thing we were missing was intelligence. And with no informers to speak of, we needed a spy in the midst. One way or another, I was determined to be that spy.

# PART THREE

**1** am. A man is screaming in the street. He is drunk. His car has hit a bridge. I try to calm him.

"You alright mate?"

He can't speak, the shock has him. Blood is on his clothes but I can't see any obvious injury. I steer him onto the pavement. Alcohol is strong on his breath and I imagine what his blood alcohol content might be; I think of the breathalyzer, but first the car.

Trist is behind me, blocking the road with our panda, going for the yellow cordon tape for safety and to preserve the scene.

The car is twenty metres ahead; it's red, a four-door; the engine is still turning over, somehow, although it's wheezing like an old man halfway up a long flight of stairs. The left side of the vehicle, from the passenger door to the boot is pressed at an angle into the bridge wall, crumpled like a screwed up piece of paper; the right side is near perfect. Bricks are cracked and have fallen into the road.

I call control so they'll alert the railway; they'll need to close the line while engineers check it's safe.

Oil is on the road. I walk quickly to the driver's side; the door is open and I reach in to switch off the engine. And then I see her. I look, breathing in the strong smell of petrol, knowing she's dead and there's nothing I can do but I check anyway. The top of her skull is missing. I play the scene in my mind. She was leaning out of the car window, in party mood, loving life. He, drunk, possibly doing 50mph (it's downhill, a long road with no turns until a gentle right-hander one hundred metres past the bridge) probably turned to look, turned the wheel to the left as he did so, wobbled then lost control. A second and one life ends, while others change forever.

I wouldn't be a traffic cop. They see this all the time but worse even, on our motorways and A-roads where we forget how fast we're going. We don't see this sort of thing often in the congested and speed-bumped roads of Battersea

Trist has cordoned off the road behind us and is with the bloke. I become aware of an audience. People are emerging from a row of terraces that line this section of the road; others stare through the windows. We need to cordon the other side of the bridge and I jog to get the tape. A car goes past on the opposite side of the road at a crawl, taking it all in.

Trist has the breathalyzer and has explained about the need for a roadside test. The man can refuse but it's an arrestable offence and we'll force a specimen out of him back at the station. The man is in shock but complies. As he blows, I am behind, Trist looks at me and I shake my head and mouth the word. Spare him the sight at least. I wait and watch and Trist tells the man he has failed the test; he is almost double the legal limit and he is going to arrest him.

*** 

A decade, that's the maximum sentence. But it's rare for anyone to get the maximum. If you kill someone with a car, whether passenger or pedestrian, it's not seen as serious as killing someone by punching them. You could argue that by hitting someone, you intended them harm and their death was a consequence of that and when someone kills a person through driving, it is totally accidental.

But if you are drunk, taking risks, speeding, texting, then you are engaged in activities likely to cause other people harm. It signifies you don't care about the lives of other road users. Death by dangerous driving is not less of a death than death by knife.

How many people have driven after two pints of lager, a large glass of wine, a double scotch? All are enough to put you over the limit. How many have texted and sped while driving? Raced to beat a red light?

Perhaps there is among us a feeling that we all engage in risky behaviour when driving, and we could easily find ourselves in this sort of situation – as defendants. We drive at speed in our half-tonne metal boxes and we all know it only takes a second. Perhaps we feel for the speeding driver, or the over-the-limit borderline driver, or the texting driver. We identify with the driver and forget the victims too easily.

But, at the age of twenty, I saw a young woman not much older than me, whose whole life had been ahead of her, missing the top of her skull.

I drive like a Sunday School teacher.

\*\*\*

Soon the tape is across the road and multiple lights are turning. The road is closed properly now. Barriers hide the gruesome scene as the fire crew cut the lady's body free. Now we will find out who she is and find the person we will have to break the news to in the small hours of Sunday morning, and watch as their world is snapped in two and a future of waking up from dreams where their loved one was still alive.

We will ask them if they want to see the body. They do not have to identify her. We can do that scientifically, through dental records and matching latent fingerprints left at her home or workplace.

I suspect the officer who visits them will say something like 'You don't want to see her luv, don't put yourself through it,' but if the Coroner or the undertaker can make the body viewable, then perhaps it is better to see, to have the truth of the situation in front of your own eyes.

The driver will be out in a couple of years and will have a shot at some sort of future (if he manages to reconcile his mind with what he's done).

For the girl's family, there is nothing for them to do but live with the facts.

# CHAPTER TEN

# THE ALL-SEEING EYE

Sitting on top of Sporle Court, a 22-storey tower block on the Winstanley Estate, looking across Battersea with a pair of oversized binoculars (after Inspector Barry had authorized their use) for weeks on end, I was happy as a pig in the proverbial. Ok, so it was cold, lonely (I hated having no one to talk to; if I wanted company I had to share my sandwiches with the pigeons) and some days nothing happened at all but my bright idea was leading to some fantastic results. I watched, recorded and broadcast the activities of known street robbers over the police radio – and more besides.

It was quite surreal, being so high up above the city. The view was spectacular, with views across the Thames to the luxury multi-million pound residences of Chelsea Wharf to the northeast and the old riverside houses of Putney and Fulham to the west, the open space of Clapham Common to the south and rows and rows of houses beyond that to Wimbledon. As tempted as I was to turn my binoculars to the view, I kept them firmly focussed on the comings and goings of our persons of interest.

I'd once made the mistake of commenting on the nice views from Sporle Court (named after Sidney Sporle, Battersea's youngest ever mayor who pushed forward the building of the estate, completed in 1966) to a resident who told me: "You can keep the bloody views, I want to know what they're going to do about the damp, cracked walls and crap heating!" Bathrooms had no ventilation and bacteria-carrying mould spread like wildfire in bathrooms and kitchens.

Children, forced to live so high up, have nowhere to go and play. If they lived on a street the kids could step outside and the parents were just a yell and a few seconds' stride away. Here, they were prisoners with no outdoor space save for the small balcony. There used to be a playdeck on the tenth floor but that ended up so vandalised it wasn't safe to use. It was closed in 1969 and replaced with six more flats. And if the lifts were broken it took about half an hour to get up the stairs with small children (I walked those stairs often enough myself; it's an ordeal that no one who lives there should have to go through). If you're a single mum with kids and a pram, you won't make it. And those kids who did go downstairs only had a small play area with some crap swings and a roundabout next to the car park. Families with children were "high priority" in terms of finding them somewhere lower down to live but even urgent cases were a couple of hundred families down on the eight-hundred long list.

It was incredible to me that almost 4,000 families lived above the fourth floor in the London Borough of Wandsworth (in which Battersea is situated) and 950 families lived above the tenth. Although I enjoyed the views, I was able to see how living all the way up here could lead to feelings of isolation, loneliness and frustration – and withdrawn and miserable children. I could see how that view would be depressing if you had little, because everywhere you looked you could see wealth and growth, the living, breathing city and somehow you'd been overlooked, packed away above it all, out of the way. Even families who'd been told they could transfer on medical and/or psychological grounds had to wait for months, if not years for a chance to move.[1]

It was easy to see how this place had only added to the conditions that bred crime among the estate's young. But we had to do something to try and turn it around and I was starting at the top, so to speak. All the CCTV cameras in the world (that's if they're working or switched on and of good enough quality) can't beat a knowledgeable police officer with a big pair of binoculars and a radio.[2]

I knew all about the people who would be up to no good and I began to build up an idea of where stash houses might be, where most activity seemed to be taking place and who was coming and going from the estate at any one time. This would prove to be extremely useful in the case of street robberies.

There was one character we'd nicknamed Jonny Rotten because his nicotine brown teeth were arranged like gravestones in an old graveyard, twisted and turned by the roots of ancient trees. I spotted Jonny Rotten walking across the estate one night and I watched him leave and turn towards Clapham Junction. Minutes later I got a call from Trist.

"Hullo old boy, we've got a mugging just happened round the corner from the Junction, any word on who's in the area this evening?"

Jonny Rotten came into view just at that moment, heading back to wherever he'd come from and, while I kept reporting his position, Timbo and Trist, in the Astra, quietly pulled up

---

1    Not much has changed today, although repairs have been made to the flats (the lifts and the heating still fail on a regular basis, however) and plans for gardens, day nurseries, entry phones, and a community centre have been shelved. Austerity rules.

2    CCTV cameras, which are today run by the council, can of course be incredibly useful but the people operating them just don't have the specialist knowledge that makes all the difference.

with all the lights off and nabbed him as he turned a corner. Unable to run or ditch the goods, Jonny was nicked, fair and square.

One day I was up by the water tanks when I heard one of the lifts approaching. I was positioned directly above and would sometimes hear the shouts of cursing residents travelling up the shaft when the lifts were out of order. When they were working, I'd always hear them clunk into action and would automatically glance down as they whirred upwards. On this occasion, the lift came to a halt just below me and I noticed that something had been left on its roof, out of sight of everyone but me.

It was a large holdall.

I waited for the lift's passengers to disembark before climbing down from my hiding place and, after I'd arranged for the council engineer to hold the lift, I made my way onto its roof.

I opened the bag.

Two sawn-off shot guns.

I wondered whether to leave them where they were and wait for the person to come and claim them but we didn't have the numbers to be eyes-on 24–7, so the best course of action was to remove them. A lad from SO19 (the Met's specialist firearms unit) checked they were unloaded, put them back in the holdall and walked back to the nick.

As part of my new role as the 'eye-in-the-sky', I had been designated the Sector Intelligence Officer and this meant I worked closely with Pete the collator, feeding him information about who was doing what and where. When I got back to the station I showed Pete the guns. He raised his eyebrows, which was a major reaction for Pete, and he sat back open-mouthed.

"Where'd you find those then?"

"On top of the lifts."

"You check the other lifts, by any chance?"

Once the guns were turned in, Bruce the forensics guy was able to link them to a robbery of a post office, where shots had been fired into the ceiling.

Meanwhile, I ran back to the estate and, as discreetly as possible, searched the roofs of all the other lifts on the estate. They were clean but I did go on to find six more guns, a crossbow and dozens of rounds of ammunition in and around the lifts and water tanks of the estate before the criminals cottoned on and changed their hiding place.

***

I was in position one warm, sunny lunchtime and was finishing my sandwiches, throwing crumbs to the pigeons, when I saw a familiar-looking shape crossing the estate. I grabbed my binocs and zoomed in.

"Holy shit, it's Jason Miller!"

What was he doing out and about in broad daylight? I took another look just to be certain and then after some excited fumbling, during which I nearly managed to drop my radio down the lift shaft, I called for backup. Miller was violent, was more than likely armed and would most definitely resist arrest. To my delight, it turned out that the nearest response team was the dog squad, who were just a minute away. I guided them into the north side of the estate, twisting and turning as I watched both Miller and the dog van. I was pleased to see that the two dog handlers were burly-looking guys; they'd need to be with Jason. I guided them in over the radio.

"He's just on the opposite side of the block you're in front of now. Once you turn that corner he'll see you, give it five more seconds so he's good and close. Be careful lads, he's a real bad one."

The handlers crouched down, ready to release what were in effect two extremely fast and precise homing missiles, a pair of

German shepherds called Bert and Ernie. Miller was warned to stop and surrender the moment he turned the corner, but took to his heels, so Bert was released and got to work, legs ablur, teeth bared. It's amazing how fast humans can run when you give them enough motivation and for a few moments, Miller managed to maintain his distance but, realising his time was fast running out, he leapt onto a parked car. Bert jumped right up after him but Miller kicked and his heavy boot connected with the dog's head sending him tumbling back to the ground with a yelp. With Bert out of action, the handlers released Ernie before chasing after him. Bert meanwhile, was up on his paws again, as if nothing had happened. With my binocs I could see the fear on Miller's face as the dogs closed in, wary of his feet and, sure enough, the thug raised his foot to kick out only to collapse when the two handlers pounced from behind and felled him like a tree with a pair of calculated truncheon blows to the legs. Unfortunately for Miller, he rolled off the side of the car opposite to the handlers, and Bert and Ernie, their blood well and truly up, 'restrained' him for a second or two before the handlers could give them the 'release' command.

This was an amazing arrest; Miller had terrorised local people and I'm sure he would have killed or seriously injured an innocent bystander during one of his robberies. A jury found Miller guilty and the judge sent him down for twelve years.

I also watched the estate at nights and one morning, as dawn's fingers were about to curl over the horizon, I decided to set off on my way home after what had been a long and uneventful night when a call came in that a woman had been robbed at the entrance to a neighbouring block.

I raced over and found her sitting on the floor just inside the entrance to the lobby. She was covered in blood, blood was all around her on the floor, on the door and was dripping from her hands at quite a rate.

"It's alright love," I said, crouching down beside her. "Help's on the way. Where are you hurt?"

The woman, who was white and in her early twenties held up her trembling hands to reveal two bone-deep knife slices all the way across her palms. A man had attacked her as she arrived home from work (she was a night cleaner in a large central London office block) and dragged her to a stairwell, where he had pressed a hunting knife to her throat and started to rape her. In instinctive self-defence, the woman had grabbed at the blade with both hands. Her attacker had fled when he saw the blood.

I called for an ambulance and put pressure on the wounds to try and slow the bleeding.

"What's your name, love?"

"Janice." Her voice was weak, faint.

"You live here do you, Janice?"

"On the first floor. Right above us."

"Anyone there Janice?"

"My husband, he's sleeping."

Good god, it was just so awful, to be attacked so close to home, so close to her husband. Janice's physical wounds might heal but psychologically, I wondered whether she would ever recover.

"And the man who did this?"

"He ran away when he saw the blood."

"Did you get a look at him?"

Janice shook her head and looked down.

"It's alright sweetheart," I said, "We'll get him don't worry."

But I wondered.

"That's the fifth rape/attempted rape by a man armed with a knife in the south London area in three months, but the first in Battersea," Sergeant Phil told me. "It's likely to be the same man. All of them were brutal. He dragged one girl through a hedge and practically cut her ear off in the process. We've got his DNA, so all we have to do is find the bastard and he'll be done."

DNA technology still had some way to go at this time; it was very slow due to the complexity and the number of people involved and this made it extremely expensive, but for crimes like this, it was a case of expenses be damned.

I sat with Pete and we went through the index cards, looking for likely suspects we could pass onto the special squad that had been formed to find the rapist. We gathered a small pile, but no one looked familiar, or they were in prison, or completely different from the descriptions we had from some of the other victims.

Just as I was about to chuck it in for the day, Pete passed a card to me.

"How about this one?" He asked. "David Corkhall. He's local, got a record for sexual assault, looks about the right age, colour and height. You ever seen that face?"

"Bloody hell Pete, I have! I stopped and searched him on the Winstanley less than a week ago!" Although Corkhall was a white male, average height, in his thirties and completely unremarkable, he'd stuck in my mind because his attitude screamed 'guilty as hell,' but he had nothing on him, and a Police National Computer (PNC) check revealed nothing outstanding. I'd taken his address, but a quick check revealed it to be a false one.

"At least we have a lead," Sergeant Phil said. My recent sighting pushed Corkhall to the top of the suspect list. It was an extremely tense time; having a serial rapist on your patch is no joke and so I spent even more time in my watchtower, scanning the estate, until finding him became an all-consuming obsession.

## CHAPTER ELEVEN

# HOLDING THE LINE

I had been forced to abandon my rooftop perch for a little while, as it was my turn to stand guard near to the world famous black door of 10 Downing Street (Met officers are simply selected for this role by availability, so it wasn't something I did regularly). Nothing too unusual about that you might think, but this was November 28 1990. The world's press, wrapped up against the cold, were arranged, firing-squad-style, to the front of me and, to my left was a microphone stand, awaiting Prime Minister Margaret Thatcher, who was about to leave Downing Street for the last time.

Suddenly, the call came: "The Head Girl is on her way out."

I watched as the press leapt into action, flashbulbs firing, questions shouted; I looked to my right and Mrs T was right there; her husband Denis just behind her shoulder.

As a rule, police officers (who tend towards conservatism) liked Mrs. Thatcher (some far more than others, it must be said) and this feeling was reciprocated. Although some moaned about budget shortfalls along with equipment and staff shortages, she always made sure we knew we had her full support and let us get on with our job with minimal interference (some might say she kept us on-side to do her dirty work).

On the downside, just a few months earlier, Mrs. T had helped to create a situation in which no police service on Earth, no matter how well equipped, could have coped.

\*\*\*

Saturday, 31 March 1990 was a fine and warm Spring day and news started to spread around the Met that a far, far larger than expected crowd had descended on London to protest the Poll Tax (60,000 people had been expected but over 200,000 turned up), so much so that there was only one police officer for every hundred people – and word was spreading that although the majority of protestors were doing so peacefully, there were signs that a few thousand were out to cause trouble.

This was the week before the new Community Charge was due to come into force in England and Wales. The protestors had renamed it the 'Poll Tax' because everyone listed on the electoral roll, also known as the poll books, would pay the charge, which was supposed to be an improvement on the old domestic rates, which were levied on houses instead of people, so someone who lived in a house alone had to pay the same as a family of six living next door, even though the latter might have a large income and were using more council services. The Community Charge was instead a flat-rate per capita, in that every adult would pay the same amount without taking into account their income.

The Community Charge was seen by the majority of the British public to be unfair but Mrs T wouldn't listen and insisted it was here to stay. Hence the protest. Some left-wing extremists, realising just how many people hated the Poll Tax, saw this as their chance to strike back at their bitter enemy, the woman who'd kept the Conservatives in power for over a decade.

Three days before the protest, the organisers contacted the police and said that Trafalgar Square, with a capacity of 60,000, was going to be too small and asked if the main venue could be changed to Hyde Park. The Met turned them down, stating that this was too short notice to re-organise and, to be fair to the police, the Home Office had just reduced the police budget and so money had to be saved by cutting back on overtime, meaning only two thousand officers were available on the day.

The stage was set.

*\*\*\**

I was due to go off duty at 2pm but by this time the Met command had decided to order every available officer to stand by. Inspector Barry made sure no one left the station, so the canteen was unusually full for a Saturday afternoon. We monitored the protest over the police radio, as well as via live BBC radio reports from the scene.

A group of about 150 anarchists, marching under a banner 'Freemasons against poll tax' had joined the rear of the march. According to undercover officers from Special Branch's Special Demonstration Squad, they were drinking and taking drugs, and had picked up supporters from pubs along the route, which had started south of the river, in Kennington Park.

The demonstrators' mood was still thought to be "reasonably good" as they approached the river and crossed the Thames. Perhaps it was the sight of Parliament that inspired violence. At 2.16pm, the arrest of a violent protestor led to bottles and other missiles being thrown, followed by a couple of smoke bombs.

By 2:30pm, Trafalgar Square was chock-full of protestors and the march, which was still making its way up Whitehall started to grind to a halt. The police radio reported that the "Socialist Workers Party hardcore [had] stopped outside Downing Street."

Not the best situation. Two of the police commanders had a debate about how to get the crowds moving, with the Gold

Commander, the officer in overall charge recommending that they give the crowds "a little more time." But no one moved and by 3pm, the protest had come to a complete halt with thousands of people in Whitehall, in sight of to 10 Downing Street (Mrs T was away, attending a conference of the Conservative Party Council in Cheltenham).

Some of the protestors, with nowhere else to go, began a sit-down protest. The Silver Commander (in charge of implementing tactics, as directed by the Gold Commander) reported that he wanted to "divert [the] crowd – Bridge Street towards Embankment and onto Trafalgar Square if sufficient serials and stewards. Crowds in Whitehall very slow."

The police blocked each end of Whitehall to stop any more people backing up the already huge crowd. More units were sent to join those few officers standing in front of the gates to Downing Street who were by now faced by hardcore anarchist groups and a group called 'Bikers Against The Poll Tax'.

But it wasn't enough. At 3.06PM, officers radioed in: "Area opposite Downing street – barriers now pulled down."

Inspector Barry, who had joined us, was by now practically hopping with excitement. "They should have made the call already! If that's not urgent bloody assistance, I don't know what is!"

It kicked off about five minutes later when a drunken section of the crowd reacted violently to what was later reported to be heavy-handed attempts by the police to move the enormous crowd, including a charge by mounted police.

It wasn't until 4pm that the call finally came on the main set: "All units more vans required!"

The wheels had come off the bus, the police, hopelessly outnumbered, had lost control.

Barry slapped his hands together and said: "At last! Come on lads."

We followed him to a lock-up at the back of the station. Barry opened the steel shutters to reveal rows of riot helmets, shields, fire extinguishers and staves – clubs the size of pick-axe handles.

"I'm not trained in public order!" I said, panicking ever so slightly. I'd had two days of public order training at Hounslow, which amounted to marching backwards and forwards with shields and occasionally holding a line against some 'rioters', our fellow police officers in mufti.

"Just follow my lead," Barry told me with a wry smile, handing me a stave.

The equipment had dust on it. And there weren't enough helmets and shields to go around. Nevertheless, armed with our sticks, we climbed in the vans and flew with the blues and twos blazing towards Trafalgar Square.

"We're going to pick up prisoners," Barry said as we rocked to and fro in the back, "Throw them in the van and go hell for leather to any nick that's got room, then straight back for the next lot. No mucking about, right?"

I had no idea what I was going to find in the square. I was both scared and excited at the prospect of what would be my first public order 'situation'. Mark and Timbo were sat either side of me; Darren was opposite. No one said anything and the mood was "apprehensive".

Radio messages were coming in from officers under attack. One such report said: "We are unable to hold at Northumberland Avenue and will withdraw to reinforce the cordon across Whitehall."

It felt as though they weren't getting through to anyone, nothing seemed to be coming back, no commands, not even a suggestion or a question; all we heard were the gradually worsening reports from the officers on the front line.

I didn't know central London that well, but knew enough to recognise Whitehall as we approached from Parliament Square.

The streets were fairly clear of people, banners, boards and papers were everywhere. I was just wondering where the police cordon might be when Barry, who was driving, skidded to a halt.

"Fucking hell!"

Two hundred people armed with bricks, petrol bombs and sticks were running towards us.

"Where did they get all those weapons from?" Darren asked.

"You can fucking ask them yourself if we don't get out of here!"

The bricks and poles had come from a building site right next to Trafalgar Square – just opposite the police's centre of operations.

Bricks started to hit the bonnet as Barry ground into reverse; one bounced up and cracked the windscreen. I never saw anyone drive backwards so fast. Barry swung the van around once he had enough distance from the crowd, causing us to tumble over each other in the back.

There was so much mayhem we didn't know where to go but then Mark spotted a PC out cold on the ground, missiles landing all around him.

He yelled at Barry to stop and we leapt out, forgetting about our riot gear, and grabbed the officers as bricks landed around us. The officer was dead weight and we struggled to get him; at some point Sergeant Phil came to help and as he hefted the unconscious officer's feat, and a half-brick whistled past my head and hit Phil full in the face. The rioters cheered as Phil buckled but didn't go down, and despite spitting teeth, he held onto the officers' legs and we got him into the van.

Once we were in Phil, his mouth a shock of bright red blood said: "I'th done thirfy fuffing years and now thif!"

He wanted to go back and retrieve his teeth but there was no way we were going back out to face that lot without serious back up. By now 30,000 people were rioting and instead of picking up prisoners, we became a rescue unit, picking up injured cops, many of whom were half-conscious with head injuries.

More reinforcements arrived, including trained riot officers but it wasn't enough. The rioters' blood was up. At 4.52pm an officer reported: "shield serials are not making any headway into the crowd," and this was followed at 5.04pm by an officer stating: "mounted charge has had no effect. We have lost the ground we had gained."

The trouble quickly spread and looting started north of Trafalgar Square, with the police helpless to stop them and then we heard: "Holding line outside South Africa House. I do not presume to push further." South Africa House was home to the South African Embassy, and as the release of Nelson Mandela and the end of Apartheid was still three years away, some rioters saws this as a legitimate target and many windows had been smashed. Along with Met officers from the Diplomatic Protection Group (DPG), armed officers from the South African police were inside the building, and they had the right to defend their sovereign territory from the rioters according to South African law, so it was crucial that this line was held.

It turned out that there was a problem with the police radios; many communications from those in charge weren't getting through, or were suffering from a five-minute lag thanks to a computer malfunction.

We eventually drove up to a small group of core trouble-makers, who were being contained by an equally small group of police officers and we helped bundle them into the van. They carried on rioting and fighting us in the back, trying to kick the doors off and the mesh windows out as we raced through central London, trying to find cells to put them in.

We pulled up outside Charing Cross Nick and a sergeant, in torn shirtsleeves came running towards us. "You can't come here!" he yelled, "There's no more room!"

"What the fuck am I supposed to do with this lot then?" Barry shouted back, the van rocking from side to side thanks to our prisoners who continued to kick off in the back.

At some point, during one particularly confusing melee, we lost Barry (who had seemed to be the only officer who was in his element). Sergeant Phil, who refused to go to hospital, took over. It was chaos, with hundreds of people already nicked, we were struggled to find a place for our prisoners, eventually dropping them at Kentish Town Nick before racing back to the centre of town. The riot was still in full swing. Part of the reason for this perhaps, was the fact that the main underground stations had been shut (to prevent rioting on the tube) and Trafalgar Square had, more or less, eventually been sealed by lines of police officers, making it difficult for people to leave.

By now the Square was full of smoke. The builder's cabins next to the building site had been set on fire and people were standing on the scaffolding, throwing bricks and scaffolding poles at police officers below. Someone had managed to lob a Molotov cocktail through a broken window of the South African embassy and a room was ablaze. Hopelessly outnumbered, we were forced to watch crowds rampage, destroying anything they could get their hands on.

The smoke eventually got so bad that no one could see to fight, in Trafalgar Square at least, and for about twenty minutes, until the fire was under control, there was a lull which then developed into a stand-off between cops and rioters, which quickly broke down when we opened the southern sections of Trafalgar Square in an effort to get the rioters to move on. Some law abiding protestors had been trapped in the Square and they quickly made their way back across the Thames to where their coaches were waiting but the main bulk, who were hardcore rioters, actually pushed north and broke through the police line, taking the riot to the West End.

From the Trocadero Centre and Stringfellows' nightclub to the shops and bars of the West End and Soho, windows were broken and buildings were looted; cars were overturned from Piccadilly to Covent Garden. Shops and cafes were set on fire. One officer reported at 6.56pm that a "very large crowd [were] now making their way back to Oxford Circus from Portland Place, smashing everything in sight. Unable to do anything on my own."

And on it went:

7.19pm: "Windows being smashed, Hanover Street."

7.51pm: "A thousand demonstrators towards Oxford Street. This is now another march. No police at head of march. Serials trying to police from the rear."

8.02pm: "Tottenham Court Road police station under attack. PC on his own."

8.21pm: "Charlotte Street, W1. Large number of youths rampaging in streets smashing windows."

9.37pm: "Looters have entered a sports shop in Leicester Square and taken crossbows and knives."

The rioting eased from 11pm but it wasn't until 3am that the fighting finally finished for good.

When we finally rolled up at Battersea, Constable Sophie was just coming out of the station. Our van was 'limping' in that one side of the suspension had gone, the bonnet was dented from the impact of dozens of bricks and the windscreen was white with cracked glass; one side was black from where we'd caught a molotov cocktail; the blue lights were all askew and had been half smashed off (although one light was on and couldn't be switched off) and the exhaust rattled along the concrete below. Sergeant Phil was a bloody mess, like he'd just stepped out of *Night of the Living Dead*; every one of us had at least one black eye and/or a bloody nose and our uniforms were ripped and stained.

Sophie stopped and stared, open-mouthed.

Sergeant Phil, lisping through his broken teeth, didn't bat an eyelid: "Tried to nick a granny for thoplifting and it got out of hand."

I think it was perhaps down to the adrenaline, but we all fell about laughing.

It was only once Phil had been packed off the hospital and we were a little bit cleaned up and gathered around the wobbler that Pete the collator asked us what had happened to Barry.

"Not sure," Mark replied, "The last time I saw him he was taking command of the other Battersea van. But he looked like he was actually enjoying himself."

A few minutes later we were still in the canteen and watching the late-night news reports on the rioting when the camera closed in the footage of a van, right in the thick of the action in Trafalgar Square.

"There he is!" Mark cried. "Right by the van, in the thick of it!"

"Bloody hell," Pete said, "Looks horrendous."

It most certainly did. I was amazed to think that I'd spent the day amongst that and was still in once piece.

Barry was pulling a badly-hurt colleague into the van and simultaneously holding back the mob by waving his stave at them; they charged as he dragged the injured officer inside and he just managed to bolt the rear doors as a scaffolding pole was thrust through the passenger window. To add insult to injury, someone had set the van's tyres on fire and as the van accelerated way, it left a trail of smoke as it vanished down the Mall, towards Buckingham Palace.

Barry, as it turned out, was just fine. He arrived the next morning, fresh as you like (apart from two black eyes and a swollen nose), invigorated even, a spring in his step.

Over 5,000 police officers and civilians were injured that day (I don't think a single police officer escaped injury). We had lost control. We hadn't had enough officers and the British public had seen for the first time just how narrow the thin blue line really was.

This was also the first time that Mrs T's leadership was questioned openly and after a couple of Tory heavyweights (Geoffrey Howard and Michael Heseltine) criticised the PM, Mrs T called for a vote of confidence via a leadership contest. After the first round didn't quite go her way, the Iron Lady realised, after eleven years as PM and fifteen as leader of the Conservative Party, that her time was up.

*** 

And, after having been at the riots just a few months earlier, I was there to see her go. She said something about how she'd left Britain in a better state than when she'd found it but I couldn't hear much. What I do remember is seeing tears in the former PM's eyes as she waited for the car to drive her out of the iron gates that had, just a few weeks earlier, almost been torn down by people who couldn't have disagreed more (I also happened to be on duty in Downing Street the day Mrs T's successor, John Major, arrived and one of the first things he did was to abolish the poll tax and replace it with the property-value based council tax we have today).

Like most police officers, I'd appreciated Maggie's admiration of the police but she had failed to see (or had ignored) the effect of some of her policies on the young and the poor. Young people from working class backgrounds had seen a few people get rich under Thatcher; it was more a case of the rich getting richer. The poll tax was more than just a protest against an unfair tax; it was a protest against Mrs T's government. The vast majority of the 200,000 strong crowd had wanted to protest peacefully but the 30,000 who decided to riot gave the world a very visual demonstration that all was not well in the UK.

# CHAPTER TWELVE

# LOOK A DEVIL IN THE EYE

The relationship between the cops and robbers of Battersea was an unusual one. The street robbers, dealers, shoplifters and burglars could be roughly split into two groups: Those who wanted to do the police harm and were set on the path to a career in criminality, and those you could talk to when they were on their own. These were under the influence of the hardened types yet – I felt – still had a chance to save themselves from a life of crime. A great deal of my intel came from these guys. I'd pretend to know a bit more than I did about an incident or person and it was amazing how much they'd presume you already knew but didn't.

I'd never, ever betray those people to their friends but would not hesitate to pick on those abhorrent scumbags that made it impossible for us to walk, let alone park under any of the windows of the estate, whether on or off duty. Take the example of Hot-Head Jonny, who needed little excuse to drive to call-outs at break-neck speeds, who one day had skidded to a halt on the Winstanley, hoping to interrupt a burglary in process. Timbo was with him, and they rushed to the flat in question to find that not only were there no burglars, but no one there had called the police. Then came the bang. They rushed to the balcony to see that someone had dropped an old car battery from one of the flats onto the car's roof. It had to be towed away.

My chance for revenge came whenever I saw a group of these scumbags hanging about on the street. I'd great them with a cheery wave and say something like: "Nice one Del, thanks for that tip, it worked out a treat!" That would ensure he got plenty of grief from his mates. They accused one another of being grasses all the time and this was a simple way to create discord.

A day didn't go by when I didn't question someone and among those who did talk to me, one name always got a reaction: Gary Nelson, aka Tyson. Whenever I mentioned his name, the response was usually something like: 'Don't go there,' or 'You don't want to mess with that guy,' and 'He's bad news and that's all I'm saying.'

A few weeks after this, I was rooting around in lock-ups in the Vauxhall area, in the arches under the railway, acting on a tip off which I was hoping would lead me to a load of stolen electronic gear (TVs, fridges, washing machines, all lifted from a warehouse). I emerged from one arch after finding nothing when I bumped into a glum-looking market trader wheeling a stall barrow into his lock-up.

"Alright mate?" I asked, helping him lift the garage-style door and holding it open while he wheeled the barrow inside.

"Nah mate, it's not," he replied. "It's hard enough trying to put food on the table without these bleedin' protection rackets but what can yer do? You lot ain't gonna do nothing about it are yuz?"

"What? What protection rackets? Who's been paid off?"

"Come on, everyone knows, that black lad and his gang."

"I don't."

He looked me over. "You're young, must be new, right?"

"Fairly."

"We pay protection money so our stalls don't spontaneously combust, or so we don't have any accidents while crossing the street. You guys take a piece, so he can carry on what he's doing."

The allegation was ludicrous but first things first: "You said a young black lad. Does he by any chance look like Mike Tyson?"

"Yeah, he does, as it goes."

The trader started to arrange empty boxes into a stack.

"I can assure you, no cop is taking a cut from Nelson. We're doing everything we can to stop him."

"Oh yeah? Well he's been working these markets for a long time now, and the money's going up and up and I don't see no sign of any cops carting him off to the nick."

Our new Chief Inspector was Hugh Orde. Hugh, whose career would reach spectacular heights,[3] already had a great reputation for getting stuck in. Just a few weeks earlier, he'd been driving the van on night relief when he'd arrested an extremely large drunk and disorderly rugby player. Hugh's prisoner had stayed docile until he realized he was being charged, whereupon he decided to fight his way out of the police station and Hugh, on his own at this point, had yelled for help. By the time the relief piled into the charge room however, they were too late; they found their Inspector sitting on the prisoner sprawled below, now promising to remain on his best behaviour. When I told Hugh about the extortion racket he ordered me to check it out. I went with Dr Death, dressed in plain clothes, in the unmarked Astra. Our timing was remarkable. Just as we reached the top of the New Covent Garden Fruit and Vegetable Market and started to drive down the long straight road to the trading area, I spotted Nelson with his best mate, Chen. While Nelson was a compact muscle

---

3   Hugh (OBE, QPM) was the President of the Association of Chief Police Officers, and therefore one of the most senior police officers in the country before he left in July 2015

powerhouse, much like Mike Tyson, Chen was a heavyweight giant, the size of an All Black No.8 with long arms that looked as though they could bend iron bars like they were rubber.

They were walking towards a top-of-the-range Audi, each carrying a large holdall. They put the bags in the boot and climbed in.

My heart started to race. All my instincts screamed that we'd just caught them in the middle of something really big and if we tried to stop them, they would try to get away by any means.

"Darren, we need to be onto this," I said, genuinely scared, tearing my eyes away from the Audi and sinking low in my seat. They hadn't driven off; they were just sitting there and we were about to drive right past them.

I'd stopped Nelson a few times by now and he knew my face. Each time I'd stopped him he'd been clean and although he hadn't said a word to me, he'd done what I asked and then went on his way. If they were in the middle of something dodgy now they would kill to get away, I just knew it. There was no way Darren and I were going to go up against Chen and Nelson without some serious back up.

We drove past and pulled in about sixty yards ahead of them. Darren got on the radio, called Control, asking for backup, explaining we thought they were armed, to send officers from the Tactical Firearms Unit (SO19).

"Mike, they're moving!"

Sure enough, they were driving in our direction and they slowed as they drew near, practically coming to a stop as they pulled up alongside. Unable to stop myself, my heart pounding, knowing we'd been spotted, I turned to face Nelson, who looked me in the eye. He was handsome, shaven-headed and chisel-jawed, but his expression was cold, cruel and murderous. He sneered at me as he kept one hand on the steering wheel, the other, closest to the door, was out of sight.

I had no doubt that he was holding a gun at that moment, and was wondering what we were up to. Was it coincidence that we were here? Had we been following him? Were we part of a larger operation? Was he about to be hit?

After a three-second stare, Nelson revved the engine and span the wheels, burning rubber, giving me a last look before he released the brakes and absolutely floored it, taking off down the long straight road, through the market, heading south; the engine screamed as he picked up speed, 30, 40, 50.

"What the hell is he doing?" Darren asked. "He's going to kill someone!"

"And himself," I replied, watching, horrified, my eyes pinned to the Audi, suddenly remembering to take the number plate, an instinctive cop reaction, as it approached the first of two crossroads at over 60mph and he was through the first, just missing a white van by a second and then through the second between two saloons, both of which slammed to a halt as he continued to accelerate away, vanishing out of our view.

An Armed Response Vehicle arrived three minutes later.

***

Nelson seemed to be everywhere, and yet we rarely saw him. On my own time, I started a file on Nelson and tried to compile what little information we had about him into some kind of record. The file was thin. I added my own thoughts and deductions to file, personalising it somewhat, to try and understand something of the man.

Things Nelson could not tolerate, in no particular order:

Disrespect.

Rivals.

People who didn't pay their debt.

Police officers.

Anyone in a position of power, no matter how small. Anyone, in fact, who felt they were in a position to try and tell him what to do.

All of these groups would face the uncontrolled wrath of Nelson, supported by his henchmen, cowardly bullies who were too scared to even think for themselves, let alone challenge him, and who would let Nelson take the blame for everything, if and when the time came.

Nelson knew how to be charming, friendly and loyal and lots of people called him their friend. But get on his wrong side and you would immediately know about it (alternatively, if you were really unlucky, you wouldn't know about it until it was too late). He also possessed the mental self-discipline of a professional sportsman. He practised the art of pugilism and used weights to create an impressive physique that required focus and organisation. When it came to personal interactions however, discipline went out of the window.

Nelson divided the world into two groups: the haves and have-nots. He wanted the cars, the clothes, the luxury pad and the women. He needed power to get these things. In some ways he was intelligent. He studied the law, got to know the crimes, what you could do to mitigate any offence should the cops bring you in, and he believed he would never do serious time.

Nelson's rise was fuelled by the emergence of crack that arrived in the UK via Jamaica. Before, weed had dominated the drug scene. It could be argued that smoking weed was at least social and pacifying, in that helped deal with feelings of hopelessness and malcontent. Selling it was profitable but not wildly so for the smaller dealers, many of whom sold it to maintain their own supply.

Crack use, on the other hand, is a lonesome activity; a short, minutes-long high that leaves all the wrong feelings burning more intensely in its wake. Once crack has you, you can't be employed, not for long anyway, and that means, to raise a stake, crimes have to be committed.

Nelson would become a role-model (of sorts) who appealed to younger, weaker men and boys, alienated by society, who were looking for something to which they could belong, and which they could use to escape from the sense of hopelessness that filled their lives. As we were learning, dealing crack, even small amounts, could be insanely profitable and therefore there was no shortage of people wanting to sell it, to get rich quick. Men like Nelson fed the myth that all dealers got rich, wore labels, bought guns which got you girls ('No gun, no girl,' was a popular saying of the time) and won respect.

Nelson wanted to be King and like his nickname namesake Tyson, he wanted to be heavyweight champion – but of the Underworld, an untouchable, who fed lesser dealers their supply, taking the lion's share of the cash and never even touching the drugs (he could pay people to do that). Nothing was going to stop him. Nelson wasn't at war with any particular gang – he was at war with anyone who was stupid enough to get in his way. Violence is cyclical; kings can only stay kings as long as they provide their people the spoils of war, and that means always being at war, a state of being that suited Nelson to a tee.

Something that helped reinforce much of the above was the information we had about Nelson's one and only conviction, which was for kidnapping.

Saltdean, a seaside suburb is famous (locally) for two things: its Art Deco, Grade II* listed lido, built in 1938, and its cliff-side walk that runs towards Brighton's Black Rock.

The chalk cliffs, about a hundred feet above the stone beaches and concrete promenade, are subject to the occasional rock fall.

Apart from cliff-walkers, they occasionally attract those who wish to commit suicide, although the most 'popular' place for the terminally depressed (or, at the other extreme, base-jumping adrenaline junkies) has always been Beachy Head, a few miles further east, near Eastbourne; a 500 feet drop into rocks, littered with the remains of smashed cars from those who have chosen to drive to their doom.

But 100feet and the peace and quiet of Saltdean by night was enough for Nelson, barely out of his teens, to take an even younger man.

The whole thing had been spontaneous.

Nelson had driven this young man to these cliffs from London in the boot of a hire car (Nelson usually used hire cars so he couldn't be linked to one particular car, making it that much harder for us to spot him when he was going about his business, although the Audi I'd seen him in near the market would turn out to be his car).

They arrived at the beauty spot as dusk was falling.

By removing this boy and himself from London, Nelson knew the boy's friends would notice. They would gossip, as teenage wannabe bad boys do, about what had happened. The fear would spread, Nelson's reputation as a hard man who would go to extremes the moment – the very moment – he was disrespected, would be reinforced, regardless of what the law said. In fact, Nelson wanted, needed to disrespect the law, to show his world who was boss.

Nelson gripped the boy with one hand and pushed him until he was teetering at the cliff's edge. He placed a gun to the boy's head. He could have so easily pulled the trigger and let the body fall and, maybe, if the tide was high, or there was a storm, no one would ever know, no one would ever find him. No one would even miss him. He was nothing. Who was he to defy Nelson?

I'm sure he considered killing the boy. Nelson was yet to shoot someone dead; an act which for psychopaths like Nelson, done once, is surprisingly easy to repeat, a simple and effective punishment that everyone notices and respects.

Maybe he actually needed the money.

Instead, Nelson told the boy to open his eyes and admire the view. If he wasn't paid within 24hours, Nelson said, he would find the boy and bring him back here to this exact same spot, and throw him onto the rocks below.

Nelson let the boy find his own way back to London, which proved to be a mistake. The boy was so scared and had so little hope of repaying his debt that he called the local cops and Nelson was arrested.

A local walker had seen the two men from a distance and backed up the boy. But he didn't see the gun, just confirmed they had been there. Nelson went to prison, but was only off the streets for a few months.

This remained Nelson's only conviction of interest (his 20-odd minor offences dating back to when he was fifteen-years-old didn't count for much) and was a key moment on his path to the top. This experience had taught him that showing mercy was not a Kingly act, mercy was for the weak and from now on, Nelson would show the world just how strong he was.

# Chapter Thirteen

# GOBBLERS' GULCH

Cops have a sense of humour that's drier than Death Valley and blacker than deep space.

It comes from the experience of dealing with all the world has to throw at us, the folks who have to learn to run towards danger instead of away from it. We have to laugh; it's either that or cry and cops don't cry (rarely anyway, and it's not encouraged). We have to sort out chaos, relieve misery and physical pain (at least until the ambulance comes), quell anger, negotiate with lunatics and, if all else fails, fight (and/or get beaten up). It's a tough career but we hold the line together like a family would, we look out for one another, understand one another because 'normal' people can't; until you've been the first on scene to a murder, a road traffic accident or an accidental death, you can't understand what it's like. Part of that understanding comes from sharing a laugh, sometimes when we're at work.

It was shortly after midnight and Darren and I were on Clapham Common, sitting in an unmarked car, lights off, on surveillance, of a sort. Clapham Common was then developing its international reputation as a site for gay men to cruise for sex.

We weren't so much bothered about that, although some efforts had been made to curtail the activity at the start of the summer as it seemed every gay man and his dog was out trying to get some; so much so that even some liberal-minded locals were starting to complain – we even rather distastefully – and privately – 'codenamed' the area 'Gobbler's Gulch'.

One woman walking her dog arrived at the station to report three men sunbathing in Speedos, which, while possibly offensive to some tastes, wasn't illegal. Mark didn't help matters by suggesting, just out of the lady's earshot, that they were, ahem, 'undercover' officers engaged on a 'sting' operation, and I developed a sudden coughing fit.

"Is something funny officer?"

"No. Not at all. Tell you what, I'll cruise by the Common now and see if I can find these young men and give them a stiff talking to about public decency."

The Common is popular because it's big and dark with lots of places to hide but at the same time it's not *too* dark, so people go there thinking it's safe compared to other famous cruising spots. It appeals to men – if a similar area operated for heterosexual men with the promise of erotic encounters with like-minded women, they'd flock there, I'm sure. It's unemotional, deals with nature's most powerful urge and the people you meet are like-minded, don't want to talk and won't ask questions.

A famous story, told by Patters, described how a solicitor was caught having oral sex in the bushes by torch-wielding police officers. They wanted to charge him under the Sexual Offences Act, outraging public decency, and the Public Order Act.

"On what grounds?" the solicitor asked.

"You were having sex in public."

"I was not. I was having a very private encounter, hidden by a bush. No one could see us and you only found us because you were carrying torches and looking for people having sex."

He had a point, common to all these laws was the fact that someone had to have witnessed the act (and be offended) and most people would not think of going for a stroll through the Common after midnight. And, as the solicitor argued, police officers tramping through bushes looking for sex didn't count. He was released without charge.

The real problem, in terms of crime, was that the sheer number of cruisers meant there were plenty of vulnerable victims for muggers with violent tendencies, who also flocked to the Common after dark in search of easy prey.

Then, one morning, a dog walker found a dead body. We thought it was murder until a post mortem revealed the 30-something man (who was married and had two children) had had a heart attack after inhaling Amyl Nitrite (i.e., poppers) while engaged in an erotic encounter. His wife knew nothing about his late night activity and breaking the news was difficult to say the least, as she was adamant the officers had the wrong address, until she was taken to view her husband's body.

Nevertheless, we needed to do something so, to bolster the number of observers, I'd been dragged down from my midnight perch in the tower blocks and posted to the Common. After a few walk-throughs of the Common, warning the cruisers and letting them know that we were on the case, we had staked out the park.

We were bored. It's no excuse for what followed I know, but we were *so bored*. Both Darren and I liked action. When Darren wasn't chasing criminals, he was chasing ladies and if he wasn't doing that, he would drive off in his VW camper van to some secret surf spots in the southwest.

So, we smoked fags until we could barely breathe and ate so many crisps and sweets and drank litres of pop that we were high on sugar and e-numbers. We racked our brains for something to do. And then I had an idea.

"Fifteen," I suggested.

"No way. More like twenty."

"Serious? How much then?"

"Tenner."

"Pfff."

"Alright then, twenty. And the loser cleans out this car, it's in a right state."

"So closest wins?"

Darren nodded. "Naturally."

"Right then."

I reached under the dash and brought out the blue light and clipped it onto the roof.

"On the count of three."

"One, two, THREE!"

I turned the headlights on full beam and flicked on the blue light. A dozen men appeared as if from nowhere, emerging from behind bushes and trees, and ran frantically in all directions in various states of undress, trouser legs flapping; one gentleman was completely naked and ran hell for leather with his clothes in his arms.

"I make that thirteen," I said a few moments later as Darren switched off the lights and started the engine.

"Best of three?" he said.

"Fair enough," I said as he started the engine and we drove off to another part of the Common to continue the waiting game.

# Chapter Fourteen

# DRUGS ON THE BRAIN

Despite the demands of Gobblers' Gulch, our main priority remained street robbers and burglars. They continued apace and, with at least six or seven reports each day, it was decided that we needed to strike not at the robbers but at the reason that drove the robbers to strike: the crack houses.

We were still in our infancy in terms of dealing with the meteoric rise of crack in London. As I've already said, crack is the most addictive substance known to man. Users will do anything for it. Teenage girls sell their bodies in filthy crack houses, teenage boys rob and beat women on the street and above it all, the dealers rule with the gun. Within a year of us first seeing it, crack had spread like the common cold across the estates and beyond.

Something that helped crack spread in the poorest areas of London was the fact that it was cheap, at least to start with (as little as £5 for a few good hits on the crack pipe) and it fulfilled a need among the young and disaffected. Those that had grown up without loving families, or those who had been physically, sexually or mentally abused, found salvation in crack, which lights up the most powerful parts of the human brain, the sections that regulate feelings of love and affection, blowing their minds and setting them on the road to addiction.

Crack is a magnet for the psychologically weakest in our society. Addicts do not choose to become addicts. Addiction is the result of many complex processes involving biological, chemical, neurological, psychological and – vitally – social and emotional factors (this is supported by decades of scientific research). The key thing to remember is that addiction is extremely complex – and we shouldn't judge drug addicts (even though this is sometimes impossible).

Drug addiction involves:

1. Compulsion and preoccupation with the drug/s of choice.
2. A lack of behavioural control.
3. Persistence, even when serious physical, emotional and social harm might result.
4. An extreme craving for the drug when it is not immediately available, which grows in intensity.
5. Promises to quit but quick relapses.

Drugs don't cause addiction. Addiction is already in the person who takes drugs, otherwise doctors wouldn't be able to prescribe anti-depressants and certain painkillers. Some people do become addicted to certain drugs after taking them just a few times but they are in the minority. Exposure to a mind-altering chemical does not make a person an addict. The person is already at risk. And once this person takes a certain drug, their descent into addiction is incredibly hard to stop as their tolerance quickly increases, and thereby their dependence.

What puts a person at risk? A lack of control (powerlessness), lack of emotional interaction (love) and stress are the key factors that create the neurobiology required to kick-start addiction. Three factors that were top of the list among the complaints of many young people in the estates of Battersea and beyond. They felt that they had no control over their destiny, no way out of poverty, and living this way is extremely stressful, exacerbated by the nature of life on the estates. Many of them came from broken or breaking homes, with high numbers of absent fathers having left single mums struggling to raise their children on benefits in a testing environment.

Many suffered for a lack of love and this weakened their brains' neurobiology, allowing crack to take over. Cocaine, the substance from which crack is made, along with other similar stimulants leads to huge and sudden increases in dopamine – a chemical that makes the brain feel really, really good. It's this that leads the user's brain to produce wondrous feelings of untold possibility accompanied by superhuman exhilaration.

People who have suffered from stress, powerlessness and lack of love have fewer dopamine receptors than average, so they will really feel the high of crack. It literally fills a gap – a synaptic gap – that has never been filled before. Crack blocks the re-uptake of dopamine back into the cells from which they were originally released. They hover in the synaptic gap and it is this that creates the sense of joy and exhilaration. Natural activities that lead to an increased number of dopamine molecules in the synaptic gap include sex and eating. Having sex doubles the amount of dopamine molecules but this is nothing compared to drugs like cocaine, which increases dopamine activity in the synaptic gap by 1200 per cent. After each use, the number of dopamine receptors will be reduced, so each time the user takes a mind-altering substance the brain has to work harder to get to the same high. Most drugs like cocaine provide a short high, only sticking around the receptor sites for a few minutes and, as the buzz fades, the urge to take more is redoubled.

One of the many downsides of crack use is that it kills off dopamine receptors, leading to tolerance and therefore a need to take more of the crack to recapture that initial wonderful high. Once a certain amount of crack has been taken, removal of the drug leads to the pain of withdrawal, which involves fatigue, depression, feelings of paranoia and alienation, and it is this that leads to addiction. All common drugs can create addiction: heroin, morphine, amphetamine, crack, alcohol, caffeine and nicotine.

This change in the brain's state leads to drastic changes in the user's emotions and their everyday existence. Just to demonstrate how powerful the centres at which narcotics make their way into the brain are, consider the ventral tegmental apparatus, (VTA), which sits in the midbrain. When activated, it creates feelings of elation or desire. The VTA also triggers the release of dopamine in the nucleus accumbens (NA), at the front of the brain. These two brain components make up a system known as the incentive-motivation apparatus. It responds to reinforcement. All it takes for the NA to start firing off dopamine is a cue, something associated with a pleasurable experience one has had in the past. For drug users, those cues are people (fellow drug users), paraphernalia (the sight of a fresh needle or a crack pipe) and places (the dealer's house, street corner or pub). These triggers are so powerful that they often cause addicts who are trying to quit to relapse. Addicts often say how much they miss the process of getting high, from scoring the drugs to preparing the hit and, as hard as it is to believe, find these processes almost as hard to give up as the drugs themselves.

The brain processes described so far are all key parts of our limbic system, the emotional centre of our brain. They process emotions like anger, fear, happiness and love. Emotions are supposed to be able to help our survival. They tell us when to flee or fight and when to love or help a loved one. We are drawn to positives (love, food and water) and repelled by negatives (physical attack and poisons). For most people the limbic system runs perfectly, allowing beneficial social interaction, helping us to fall in love and protecting us from those who would do us harm. If the limbic system is damaged in some way then our emotions will do us more harm than good. Addiction is one of the most common and disastrous results of a damaged limbic system.

Scientific studies have tied addiction to the orbitofrontal cortex (OFC), near the eye socket, which is closely and powerfully connected to the limbic system. The OFC decides moment-to-moment how we should respond, based on the emotional intelligence sent from the limbic system, to people and situations. It tells us whether to respond with love and is constantly assessing our relationships with other people – whether we should show them love or anger, for example. The OFC helps us inhibit harmful impulses (verbal or physical violence) and helps us balance short-term needs against long-term consequences. Many neuroimaging studies (which record blood flow, activation and energy consumption) have shown that the OFC fails to do its job in the brains of drug addicts. Drug addicts are well known to accept short-term gains (getting high, fighting to evade arrest, robbing to get money for their fix) over the risk of long-term pain (illness, damage to relationships, prison, their own career and financial stability). Addicts who say they cannot stop taking a drug, even though it has been a long time since it held any pleasure for them, are subject to the commands of the OFC, based on experiences the user can no longer consciously remember. The OFC has by this time been conditioned to create an irresistible urge to use, thanks to the creation of extremely robust neural networks, and it releases dopamine, increasing the addict's desire to use, displacing thoughts of unpleasant consequences.

Imagine a child that no one ever smiled at, that never heard love in their parents' voices, was never cuddled or played with. Imagine the kind of adult that child would grow into. They would grow up at an extremely high risk of becoming dependent on drugs to make up what their own brain is lacking. This is what we were seeing in Battersea.

Countless studies have revealed that most drug addicts have suffered from childhood traumas, such as sexual, physical and emotional abuse, domestic violence, the death of a parent, divorce, or drug/alcohol abuse. For each one of these experiences a person goes through, the chances of their becoming an addictive drug user are increased two to four times. For addictive alcohol use the rate is two to three times.

Physical and sexual abuse are perhaps the strongest predictors of addiction. Some people who have suffered childhood abuse and who are predisposed to addiction never find out. But for those who do finally try heroin or cocaine or alcohol, they are hit with overwhelming sensations of euphoria, comfort and security. Their experience is far more intense than for a 'normal' person. As well as the euphoria, they experience sudden and sheer relief from the anxiety and stress that has accompanied them throughout their life.

Addicts take drugs for respite from the emotional pain caused by the agonies they suffered in their pasts and the hopelessness with which they view their future. Those who have lived a relatively happy life with a loving and supporting family have a much weaker reaction to drugs and are able to 'manage' their use.

We didn't know any of this at the time and, as a young police officer, I didn't understand drug use or the addicts (even today, most people don't understand addiction, even the addicts themselves). Some seemed quite nice; others were like monsters. Besides, it was difficult to show much sympathy with a crazed addict when they were trying to kick you in the head in order to escape your clutches. We were seeing more violence from both addicts and dealers, who were turning more and more to gun use as a way to hold onto territories and to deal with rivals.

This section barely skims the surface of what we now understand about drug addiction. We simply didn't know anything at the time. We were, as police, reacting to a situation that was threatening to run away from us. All we could do was fight back the only way we knew how, through raids and arrests and marvel at the speed with which this drug had gripped the capital.

***

Thanks to my incessant friendly chatter, several users ended up becoming low-level informants who sometimes, albeit with reluctance, gave me a snippet about someone who might have carried out a particularly nasty robbery which was, apparently, a violation of some street robbers' unofficial code of conduct.

Our greatest sources tended to be local residents who understandably wanted to remain confidential. Once they knew they could trust their local beat officer, they would often make the approach, volunteering crucial intelligence.

One breakthrough came via George, who had moved to London from Ghana when he was a young man, with his wife June, who had worked for thirty years as a nurse in UK hospitals. George, who was in his late seventies, had been an electrician for London Underground.

I was in their neighbourhood one morning when I bumped into George, armed with his copy of the *Daily Mail*.

"Mike, you're a good man. I can see you're trying to make a real difference."

"Trying's the operative word, George."

"Things have always been a little bit 'interesting' around here," George answered, emphasising the word 'interesting', "And to be honest Mike, my wife and me, well, we turned a blind eye to a lot of it but now ..."

"You mean the muggings?"

"I'm talking about the crack. My granddaughter, you see. She and her mother, they don't get along so well, since her father left, you know? She's a teenager now and she … She's, well, she's been hanging out with the wrong crowd."

"She's started using?"

"Yeah, yeah she has. And she's changed. She was such a sweet girl, bright, she used to sit on my knee and giggle when I told her silly stories, you know? But now the things she says and does; the things she says she has to do to get her drugs…"

"I'm so sorry, George."

"Don't be sorry Mike, I just want you to do something about those crack dealers. I been asking around. And my granddaughter told me some things. She doesn't know how to be careful. If I tell you where and when…"

"Give us the information and we'll act, I promise you that."

"There are some nasty people coming here. Senior nasty people, if you see what I mean, bringing in big amounts of drugs. People who run south London. I know who and I know where."

## Chapter Fifteen

# RUMBLED IN THE JUNGLE

A few days later I was in the back of an obs van, essentially a hired Luton. We were staking out what was, according to George, the mother of all crack houses. It was a supposedly empty flat in the Winstanley estate but we soon saw a lot of activity, even in the daytime.

Sitting in an obs van from dawn until after sunset (or the other way around) is hard and boring work, particularly in summer when, despite the temperature, one can't risk opening the windows, when your only toilet is a bottle in the corner and when one has to watch your suspects go about having a good time, getting high, drunk and making money. All one could do was look forward to the day we would bring righteous retribution down upon them.

Mark and I had to spend up to fourteen hours a day in that van, taking it in turns watching and writing the log. We couldn't just come and go as we pleased. It was down to another officer in plain clothes to park the van, leave and then return to drive us off for a debriefing and we'd offload all our intelligence into reports and summaries onto index cards for Pete the collator.

It was only our second day but it was clear to us that this was a place of interest, and we wanted to move things on, keep up the momentum George's information had started. I also felt huge pressure to act soon, for George's sake. I had to show him that I hadn't made empty promises. I also wanted to show everyone in the estate. If we failed, then people would be less likely to come forward with information for us.

We were thinking of having a couple of punters pulled by uniform officers a bit further on and seeing what they'd bought, as well as trying to get intel from them as to what was happening inside, when Mark said: "Hang, on something's happening mate."

I threw aside my newspaper and joined Mark at our little peep-hole, which was disguised as an air flow fan. A black guy in his twenties was on the balcony looking down at us. He was pointing at the van and talking with someone we couldn't see who was behind the crack house's door.

"What's he up to?" Mark said.

"He's looking at us!" I replied.

He came downstairs a minute later, and stood in front of the van, his arms folded, as if he were trying to out-stare the vehicle. One hand seemed to be clutching a bulge in his jacket.

"You think he's carrying?" Mark asked.

Then he banged on the side of the van. "Anyone there?" He shouted. "Because I can smell the stink of bacon!"

I was by now radioing the station. "Come and pick us up mate, we've been rumbled. Better bring back-up. Suspect's possibly armed. Keep them close but out of sight of the bad guys, ok?"

Two minutes later, our plainclothesman, Darren (always considered a safe bet in this role because you'd never think that this spectral, stick-thin figure was a police officer), strolled up in plain clothes.

The black guy asked him outright.

"Are you police?"

Darren, who was smoking a roll-up for a bit of extra authenticity, snorted at the questioner. "Nah mate," he answered in his finest cockney accent. "Why? You in trouble?"

\*\*\*

Back at the station, after a short debate about whether this guy was the doorman for the crack house (as Darren put it: "Does the Pope wear a hat?") we realised our cover was probably well and truly blown. Chief Inspector Hugh wanted us to stay eyes-on on the crack house and get something more definitive about the operation before he authorised a raid.

"We need to know when the gear arrives, Mike," he told me, "We have to be able to catch them in the act. The more drugs in there, the more people in there when we come crashing through the door, the better."

Although I agreed, I was of the mind that we should strike before this doorman was sufficiently spooked to demand the gang move operations elsewhere. At least if we raided them we'd show them that we weren't about to take this sort of thing lying down. If we stayed on top of them, going after them at every opportunity then maybe they'd stop, go elsewhere or we would get lucky and manage to arrest, charge and send them away for a good few years of thinking time.

Still, I was up for finding another observation point and, after strolling through the estate in plain clothes at 6am, I found that there was only one place in the whole estate where we would have a decent view of the flat in question, a place where no one would ever think to look.

Unfortunately, it happened to be in the huge metal box in which this block's water tank was situated and the view, through slats in a ventilation grill, was extremely narrow and therefore extremely uncomfortable. And even though it was summer, being right next to the water tank inside this little box that never saw the sun, it was freezing cold. We could only come or go in the small hours, so we wouldn't be spotted, and Mark and I spent fourteen-hours a day in there, sharing the eyes-on position in hourly rotation over a ten-day period. It's amazing how much one is prepared to endure if one wants something badly enough. And we wanted to take these guys down so badly it hurt. If ever we grew tired or fed up (which was often), we just had to remind ourselves why we were there. It helped, no doubt, that we were young, unmarried and childless and had bags of energy and enthusiasm.

We took down the registration numbers of cars that came to the flat to score; they arrived from all over London and beyond, and when we PNC'd them, they came back as being owned by some real nasties, including a number of armed robbers who were suspects in pending Flying Squad operations. It seemed, thanks to improving bank and money van security, bank robbers were looking to move into the lucrative drug trade, where the risks were lower and the rewards far higher. Most bank robbers escaped with just a few hundred pounds. Pros could manage a few thousand every now and again but it was high-risk stuff. The Flying Squad even reported that some robbers hit banks and money couriers to raise a stake that they could use to invest in the drugs trade. One thing was certain, whatever was being sold in that flat, everyone who was anyone in the underworld wanted a piece.

It was still possible for us to see people coming and going after dark, thanks to the balcony lighting and when the flat got busy, after about 8pm, we'd often count upwards of fifteen people inside.

On about the fifth day, Mark noticed something interesting.

"There's that girl again."

"What girl?"

"That one." He passed me the binoculars. "I've seen her go in there every day, she's in and out in a minute. That's quick, even if you just want to score and run."

Most users, desperate for their fix, stayed to smoke at least some of their crack in the house before leaving. Some stayed there all night, depending on how much money they had to burn.

"Hey, yeah, I've seen her too. Maybe twice a day."

"Well look where she goes."

I watched as the young lady entered the stairwell, crossed to the other side of the block and then walked up to the fourth floor. We were completely new to this game and had no idea about the gang's tactics, but it was then we finally realised that this girl was bringing a fresh supply of drugs from another address, so that only small amounts of drugs were in the dealing house at any one time (this way, the police or robbers who were crazy enough to target drug dealers would only yield a small return). The second flat was for storing large quantities.

"Perhaps they even make it there?" Mark wondered.

"You know what that means, don't you?"

"Yeah. Two raids for the price of one."

The next night I saw Nelson and his henchman, Lips. They turned out to be regular visitors.

"Are they involved, do you reckon?" Mark asked.

"Blokes like that? Bound to be. From a gangster's perspective they'd be stupid not to."

After ten days we went to Chief Inspector Hugh with everything we had. We laid it on a bit thick and by the time I'd finished saying my piece I don't think I'd taken a breath in five minutes of talking.

We needn't have worried. Hugh was a pro-active copper; he liked to get up and close and personal with the criminals. He would soon go on to become a Superintendent in the Territorial Support Group (TSG). If the raid went ahead, everything would depend on the TSG, the Met's muscle (they're sometimes unfairly known as the Thick and Stupid Group). Incredibly fit, TSG officers are expertly trained in public order and remain on standby throughout the capital, ready to rush to the scene of any violent incident or to the rescue of any officer/s in need of urgent assistance. They also take part in most of the Met's most dangerous operations, such as raids on crack houses or on the homes of particularly dangerous criminals.

Hugh rubbed his hands as he declared: "Well done lads. Looks like it's time for us to start striking back at long last."

# CHAPTER SIXTEEN

# THE RAID

The briefing at the station was intense. Mark and I were already buzzing from getting the warrant from the Magistrate's Court, where we had to swear (in-camera, i.e., just us and the magistrate, to prevent leaks) on the Holy Bible that what we knew was true, which it was but there were still a few unknowns. We thought it likely that there were guns inside but had no evidence and without evidence we couldn't call on the help of the Met's specialist armed unit SO19, so the plan was to hit them hard and fast with the TSG.

Success depended totally on the element of surprise, which would be hard to achieve, considering we were planning to flood the estate with riot cops in full armour, when the crack house (and criminality in the estate) would be at its busiest. Everything depended on intelligence, planning and a large slice of the cake of good fortune.

The set-up of crack houses was still a bit of an unknown quantity. I'd heard rumours about steel doors and locking iron bars that secured front doors to concrete floors, making normal TSG entry via battering ram totally impossible. In this case we were 99% certain that the door hadn't been customised with extra security. The criminals had grown complacent and had started to feel as though they could operate with impunity. The flat was so busy with people coming and going and the door was always opened immediately that it seemed unlikely. Finally, we were going to show them that this was not the case.

I hardly slept the night before, even though our sixteen-hour days continued. I was buzzing with adrenaline. Fifty TSG officers, along with two Method of Entry Teams (specialised in smashing down doors, which is sometimes more technical than you might think) would hit the two flats simultaneously, at about 8pm (because the operation depended on the element of surprise we needed to make sure no one could see the teams and shout a warning before they reached the door).

There were too many officers for a briefing at Battersea, so we packed out Wandsworth Nick, which was a bit further away. This suited me just fine as this reduced the chances of any local criminals spotting increased activity at Battersea and reporting back to their mates. Chief Inspector Hugh had placed us under strict instruction not to mention the raid to anyone not directly involved in the operation to minimise the chance of any inadvertent leakage.

Mark and I left the briefing room first and installed ourselves in the usual spot, eyes fixed on the flats as we watched the comings and goings. At 6pm Mark was barely able to contain himself.

"Mike! It's Nelson and Lips!"

We watched the two men swagger through the estate, climb the stairs and enter the flat.

"It'd be worth hitting it now!" I said.

"Let's just hope they stay there until zero hour," Mark replied.

Unfortunately, just after 7pm, they left. The other teams weren't on the estate yet so we couldn't even have them pulled for a stop and search.

"I can't effing believe it!" I said in exasperation as we watched them stride away to safety. "The bastards don't know how lucky they are."

An hour later we watched from our eagle's nest as the TSG slowly rolled up into the estate in two large unmarked vans, also with the dogs inside. It was quiet on the estate, no punters in sight. I crossed my fingers.

"Anyone spots them now and it's all over!"

I was completely on edge. I felt like this was all on me. As the final countdown began, I prayed we wouldn't be hearing gunshots.

The Method of Entry teams, who were in fact civilians, were affectionately known as the Ghostbusters because they sometimes carried oxy-acetylene tanks on their backs if they were planning to cut their way through a steel door. In this instance, they were going to use the 'enforcer' an extremely heavy metal battering ram. They edged their way quickly and quietly along the narrow balcony while the TSG formed a silent single-file black queue behind them.

As soon as they managed to get the door open, the Ghostbusters would stand aside and the biggest TSG officer would go in first, removing any obstacles (including people) as he charged into the unknown.

I'm certain that every single police heart was pounding as one at that moment, all filled with a mixture of fear and excitement. I thought how tremendous it must be to be leading the charge. I desperately wanted to be there with them, to take the responsibility for our intelligence, the information that had brought them here, and this made me wonder whether I should consider a spell in the TSG.

Everyone was in place. The police channel crackled as the Guv'nor gave the command.

"GOGOGO!"

The Ghostbusters swung and the sound of exploding doors shattered the mid-evening's peace and quiet. The TSG piled in, screaming "POLICE!" as loud as they could in an effort not to be mistaken for a rival gang and shot before the criminals had time to think.

My heart was in my mouth. I'd never understood the expression until that moment. I couldn't speak, breathe, move or think; I'd lost all physical sensation and my body, shook with adrenaline; I hoped against hope that I wouldn't hear a gunshot, that we'd get the result we so desperately needed.

People started coming out of their flats and houses to see what was going on. And then the TSG started emerging with prisoners, one after the other, hands tied with plastic: ten from the flat with all the activity and two from the flat where the gear had been stashed.

Soon, they were all secured and Mark and I were given clearance to descend. We waited until we could be confident no one would see us emerge from our hiding place – we reasoned that any criminals on the estate would have vanished faster than rats into a hole at the sound of all this police activity- and joined our TSG colleagues as they bundled prisoner after prisoner into the vans. One of the TSG officers gave me a cheery thumbs-up.

"Beautiful job, mate, great result."

Mark and I had been buzzing before but at that moment we felt as though we could have floated up to the flat. It was a mess, and not just because the TSG had charged in and caused chaos. It also stank, a horrible rancid smell that stuck in the throat. This was the stench of crack, suitably evil to match the drug from which it came. Furniture was torn, cracked, smashed and burned, the toilet was an unspeakable horror that would have challenged any search team, had the suspects had time to flush their drugs away, which they had not – in both flats. The element of surprise had worked. This, it would turn out, was the largest seizure of crack so far in London.

"Mike, can I have a word?" It was Foxy, who'd been liaising with the search teams. She was holding a small file of paperwork in clear plastic evidence bags.

"What have you got?" I asked.

"The registered tenant of this flat has two council properties. The searchers found this tenancy agreement for a property on the other side of Battersea, along with some bank statements."

"Looks like he was trying to expand his business," Mark said.

"So what do we do?" Foxy asked.

"Follow me," I said. We found Chief Inspector Hugh on the stairwell, talking to a sergeant from the TSG unit.

"Sorry to interrupt Guv," I said, "But I thought you'd want to know about this," and told him what Foxy had told me.

Hugh looked at the TSG sergeant who said: "What are we waiting for? We should hit it right now!"

Hugh nodded. "Alright Mike, go find Sergeant Phil, take this evidence, explain the situation and tell him we need a warrant for this address. He'll know what to do."

Yes! Two raids for the price of one!

Foxy joined us as we headed downstairs to find Sergeant Phil. We were all in plain clothes and, as we turned the corner of the last stairwell, we met what looked like two local lads coming up.

"Woah, lads!" Mark said, "You can't be in here."

They stopped halfway up the stairs.

"Who says?" the taller one of the two said.

"Yeah, who says?" his mate echoed.

The lights in this stairwell weren't working and as we were standing on the landing, we were silhouetted by the lights above. I took a couple of steps down and held out my warrant card.

"Oh shit!" they both said and turned to run, but only got as far as the arms of two burly TSG officers, who were only too glad to add another two prisoners to their tally.

These two idiots had somehow managed to miss all the excitement and emerged from their flat in the same block to score from the crack house. They had a small amount of cannabis on them and the taller lad was carrying a knife.

"Those idiots need to be locked up for their own safety," Mark said as they were loaded into the van.

***

Prince of Wales Drive, on the southern perimeter of Battersea Park, was home to the great and the good – and many victims of car thieves.

I had come with Sergeant Phil to see 'His Majesty,' who lived in a penthouse in York Mansions, which had a fine view of the park and the River Thames. It was after 10pm and I was slightly nervous about troubling someone so important so late but "Crime waits for no man," as Sergeant Phil said, flashing his new teeth, before adding, "His Majesty is sound as a golden guinea, Mike, you'll see." Preparations for the second raid, which Foxy and Mark had stayed behind to help organise, were already well underway, so the sooner we had this warrant the better.

It was extremely quiet in the thickly carpeted corridor outside the flat and one got the impression that the soundproofing was excellent, a fact confirmed when the door flew open before the chimes had finished resonating, to be swallowed by live piano music and the chatter of a lively smattering of guests. The man standing before us looked to be about fifty years old and was just below average height, fairly round in girth, with curly, unruly hair that curled around his crown like "a perfectly-twirled '99," as Sergeant Phil later put it. He was wearing glasses that sat halfway down his nose, over which he peered at us intensely. It was only then that I noticed he was swaying slightly and holding a near empty glass of red wine in his right hand.

He digested the fact that two uniformed police officers were on his doorstep on a Friday evening and turned to look back into the flat.

"I'm so sorry to disturb you sir," Phil said. "But-"

"Yes, yes, come in, come in boys, delighted to see you. Wait just a moment here and I'll let my guests know duty calls."

He guided us into a large study lined with books ranged upon dark bookshelves, a broad desk, a globe, a drinks cabinet where we waited for a few seconds before His Maj returned, with wine in hand, by now topped up. He beamed at us both in turn.

"You found my car then?"

"Um. Your car?" Sergeant Phil said.

"The thief then?"

"Ah, no, sir, we have, alas not found your car, as far as I am aware. We are here about another matter."

"Oh," said His Majesty in surprise and then followed this with a more serious "Oh," followed by "I see." He then looked at the glass of wine he was holding as if just noticing it for the first time and quickly put it down on a nearby bookshelf.

"Well, er just had a couple, it being Friday you know?"

"A couple of redcurrant juices do you mean sir?"

His Maj beamed, "Yes, yes, fully compos mentis boys, what can I do for you?" He walked to his desk and pushed his glasses back up his nose and reached for a pen, only stumbling slightly as he found his chair.

His Maj was a friendly Magistrate, one of the really good ones, who could be relied upon to issue warrants day or night.

Magistrates are (mostly) unpaid volunteers who hear cases in courts in their community (in groups of three), with a legal advisor on hand. More serious crimes are passed onto judges for the Crown Courts to deal with but Magistrates issue search warrants, as long as we provide enough evidence to support the warrant application. They're public-spirited folk, of that there's no question, but some were better than others. After all, they were civilians and were often naive about criminals and the tricks they and their solicitors pulled in court that stand out like sore thumbs to police officers but seemed to fool magistrates with worrying frequency. From the old 'he's been clean/done nothing wrong for six months,' without adding the proviso 'that we know about,' to 'he's now back home living with his mother,' without mentioning the fact that the mother has a record longer than her son's, Magistrates, it seems to police officers, tend to go far too easy on some of the criminals brought before them.

His Maj was perhaps more motivated than some since his pride and joy, an antique 1950s MK 2 Jaguar had been swiped one winters' night a few months earlier. He always gave us the puppy dog eyes of hope for a walk when he saw us out of office hours; he lived for the day when we would reunite him with his beloved and drag the thief before him during business hours. Despite the fact it was a pretty unique vehicle, it was long gone and probably in someone's private collection by now; possibly even abroad as there was a bit of a craze for antique British cars among foreign collectors.

HIs Maj was the owner of several business in and around Battersea: cleaning, minicabs, 7-11s and a couple of butchers. He was a real community man, born and bred in the area as his parents were before him, and he always acted like a proper gent.

"So what have we got gentlemen?" he asked.

We explained about the raid, the paperwork we'd recovered and the fact we expected to recover more drugs from this second address.

His Maj frowned for a moment. "Yes, well. I see. What kind of drugs are we talking about?"

"Crack," I said.

"Well, we can't allow this new scourge to get a grip can we?"

His Maj turned and looked among the bookshelves behind him. "Now, where's my Bible?" he asked.

Sergeant Phil stepped forward and picked a book up off the desk. "Here you are sir."

"Ah! Lovely thanks." His Maj picked it up and passed it to me. I then held up my right and swore on the Holy Bible that all we had said was true.

His Maj then sat down at his desk to sign the warrant and then paused, his pen poised above the document.

"What's this?" he asked, pointing at something on his page.

Sergeant Phil leaned over and squinted. "Rawson Court, Rawson Street," he said, reading. "That's the address."

"But that's just behind me, over there!" His Maj exclaimed, pointing towards the back of his Penthouse.

"Yes sir."

"I'm shocked gentleman, truly. I mean, I know the situation is bad but literally so close to home, well, I'm flabbergasted. I want you to promise me you won't hurt any innocent people. My children walk down that street every day."

"We'll take every precaution," Phil said. "We'll only be raiding the flat, nothing will take place outside of the front door."

"Good," his Maj, signing the warrant. "Lock them up and make sure they never come back."

"We fully intend to, sir," I said eagerly.

Just as we were about to leave His Maj's office, a beautiful young lady appeared in the hallway. She was tall and wearing a full-length, bright red evening dress. She started to say something but stopped short upon seeing us and glanced down at the signed warrant Sergeant Phil was clutching tightly in his hand.

"I'll be with you in a minute darling," His Maj said, "Just finishing up here."

The young lady smiled, wished us a good evening and walked back down the hallway.

"It's my daughter's birthday," His Maj said by way of explanation, "So sorry to rush you out but I suspect you'll want to crack on."

He beamed at us, at his little joke. I was looking over his shoulder down the hallway, my eyes following the girl as she walked back to her friends and family; champagne cocktails, a buffet, grand piano (how the hell did they get that up here?), a huge apartment exquisitely furnished, with actual paintings (not prints) adorning the walls.

'In less than an hour,' I thought, 'I'll probably be standing in a freshly-raided crack house, a stinking hole without internal doors, let alone any usable furniture, where the only things on the walls would be unidentifiable stains (Blood? Vomit?); with young men splayed on the floor, TSG officers holding them down, with search teams bagging large quantities of drugs, cash and guns. And it's less than two hundred metres from here.'

# Chapter Seventeen

# DEADLY TARGETS

Sure enough, forty-five minutes later, we pulled up in our police vans in Alfreda Street. We'd left a line of trees between us and the target address, a three-storey block of flats that ran the length of Rawson Street, so the TSG officers would emerge from behind the trees, cross the road and run straight into the flat, which was on the first floor. The lights were on, so it looked as if someone was home.

What would happen once that door went in? We had no intelligence on this address; except for the bare facts, in that we knew (thanks to a police officer who'd been inside a flat in the same block) the flat's interior layout, but nothing about what we might find once we were inside.

The TSG were completely up for it; they were looking forward to this 'bonus' raid and I was full of admiration for them. Never one to miss an opportunity, I took the chance on the drive over to chat with some of the TSG guys. They all said it was the most satisfying kind of policing. As one officer told me, "You see the results straight away. You go in, get the bad guys, go out again and on to the next one. It's a great feeling."

I craved that satisfaction, as well as the excitement. I loved community policing but it was slow work and the few successes

I'd had were easily overwhelmed by frustration at how little had changed. Maybe joining the TSG would be the way to go.

First things first: the raid. The TSG had a plan of action. The biggest officer, a giant black-haired lad known as Desperate Dan would go in first and clear the hallway. He would be followed by five officers who'd each been allocated a room, and they would be followed by a K-9 unit which, in this case, consisted of Joe the handler and Jet, a three-year-old black German Shepherd. Another five TSG officers would form up in a line on the landing/balcony and stand by in case reinforcements were needed. I would keep out of the way, along with Chief Inspector Hugh, Mark and Foxy and the SOCO (Bruce, the Scenes of Crime Officer), who would go in as soon as the property was made safe to search for exhibits and secure them forensically.

We were all set. It was 11pm, three hours since we'd struck at the last property. Might the occupants have been warned? Suppose they were armed? Suppose someone got hurt? I panicked at the thought that maybe we weren't at the right address. Suppose we were about to terrify an innocent person?

The TSG were in formation outside the door. The Method of Entry team readied their 'Enforcer' a bright red bazooka-sized, solid metal battering ram and Chief Inspector Hugh gave them the command.

"GOGOGO!"

The door was blasted right off its hinges and Dan charged over it, bellowing "POLICE!" followed by the rest of team, fast and fearless. I was eyes-on; my heart once again in my throat, not daring to breathe and then a huge BANG! accompanied by a flash which led to an immediate increase in both pitch and volume of the shouts coming from the TSG officers and Jet the dog, as the remaining TSG officers piled in. Unable to stop ourselves, Mark, Foxy and I ran left our posts at a sprint, bounding towards the flat; that was a fucking gunshot!

By the time we got to the front door, the fighting was over. The front door was lying flat on the hallway floor and we stepped over it, shouting, alerting the TSG to who we were and the fact we were coming in. The TSG sergeant appeared at the end of the hallway.

"All clear," he said, pointing to the lounge. "Feel free to take a look but better not go in. The SOCO will want as little contamination as possible."

From the doorway we could see four men on the floor, hands behind their backs, fastened by plasti-cuffs. Jet was pulling on his leash, snarling, barking, tail a-wagging at one man who looked utterly terrified, as I think I would have if I were in his position.

Also on the floor, glinting in the bulblight was a silver .357 Magnum. Dan was sitting on its owner.

"Bastard tried to shoot me," he said. "Had the thing in his lap, just lifted it and pointed."

Luckily, Dan had stuck to the old police adage, 'action beats reaction,' and came in so fast and hard that he was able to knock his would-be assassin's arm towards the ceiling. If armed officers had been with us, then they would have very likely shot the man dead. As it was, he would be charged with attempted murder.

The sergeant had by now radioed the all-clear and, as Joe distracted Jet with the promise of some play with his favourite toy, Bruce the SOCO appeared behind us.

"Excuse me lads, lady," he said with a dry smile. "If you wouldn't mind moving aside, I'd very much like to get my gloved fingers on that bullet."

In all that night twenty people were arrested. Ten were punters of varying ages and nationalities while the other ten, all Jamaican (six at the first property, four at the second), were related in some way to the crack dealing enterprise and, it seemed, were also in the business of supplying guns. None of them spoke to us except to deny any wrongdoing, anything to do with the drugs trade, although one did say: "I'm a Yardie. You don't want to mess with us Yardies, man."

My reply was instinctive. "Yeah? Well, I'm a Yorkie and it's my job to mess with you!"

Identifying some of the people we'd arrested wasn't easy but once we were back at the station and got Pete the collator on the case, we gradually pieced together a terrifying picture.

"Good grief Mike," Pete said as we looked at the faxes that continued to roll in, "I've never seen anything like it."

A number of the men were wanted by the FBI in the USA for countless gun crimes – and murder. They'd been convicted in New York *in absentia* for kidnapping, rape, robbery and torture, as well as a whole host of gun and drug-related offences.

They were members of the Shower Posse (they 'showered' people with bullets fired from Uzi sub-machineguns). We marvelled at the length of their sentences: 49 years, 54 years and 63 years.

The record holder of the longest prison sentence in the UK is Nezar Hindawi, who was sentenced to 45 years in 1986 when he gave his unknowing pregnant girlfriend a bomb hidden in a bag just before she attempted to board a commercial flight. She was intercepted before she could board and the bomb was diffused.

Still, these sentences were well-deserved. These young men had between them been responsible for more than two dozen murders, not to mention the fact that they'd fed the crack and heroin boom in the US, literally selling tons of the stuff, and fuelled drug wars through the sale of guns.

They'd fled to the UK after their indictment and had tried to set up shop over here; we soon found out that this method worked the other way as well, with Yardies wanted for crimes over here using fake identities to flee to New York.

We'd been saved by the fact that they'd quickly become complacent – it had taken us a while for us to notice so hadn't bothered about being careful, let alone security – and by the fact that they hadn't really managed to get a grip on a reliable supplier of high-quality firearms.

While the powers that be got in touch with our opposite numbers in the USA and built up a charge list, I was amazed to be asked to appear in court in another case as a 'crack expert' because I'd been among the first police officers to recover some of the drug. (I was also amazed and delighted to receive my first commendation for this raid). I gave evidence about so-called 'crack factories', which in the case of our first raid was simply a microwave in a dingy flat that was used to 'cook' cocaine into crack.

The only problem was, by removing theses Yardies, we'd left the way clear for Nelson. And if we thought the Yardies were ruthless, then we hadn't seen anything yet.

# PART FOUR

You're in the dark, scared, alone and breathing in a suffocating stink, but this is largely overruled by the pain, definitely the worst of your life. But above all that hovers fear, fear of what will happen if you're found.

You might ask yourself how you got to this point. Aged 14, you were arrested along with some other kids, on suspicion of dealing Class A drugs, namely crack cocaine. But by the time I caught up with you, you'd ditched the gear and we couldn't link it to you.

You're part of a gang, a group you call your family, who plague the streets of the Winstanley.

You're a scared teenage boy who doesn't know better. You're angry with your mother who loves you and has taken care of you all your life and wants you to do the right thing.

You're angry with your father, who left when you were two; you always hoped he would return one day, rich and successful but you don't know where he is, don't know how to find him and your mum describes him as a liar, a thief and a cheat.

You live three streets away from the great and the good. You watch from your window people going to and from work.

'For losers,' you say to your friends but deep down you lie. You want purpose. You're not so stupid to think that the way of the criminal is the fast track to success and wealth.

People you know, just like yourself, have been beaten, stabbed and shot – murdered.

You've thrown drugs out the window when the cops came calling.

You've run for your life from rival gangs.

You've carried weapons for the older boys that have harmed, maybe killed people like you.

You're not a fighter. You run from the fight, which is the smart thing to do and you ran today.

No one you know believes in school much. Occasional attendance led to home visits, which angered your mum, which drove you further apart.

You've been in stolen cars driven by men high on drugs and who drove like they wanted to die, who did not care about you.

Your 'family' does not care about you. They do not love you. They will not come to visit you when you go to jail. You can see the place where you work from your window and it fills you with dread. It is boring. A gangster's life isn't exciting, there are long stretches of nothing to do, no purpose.

So many others are doing what you do.

The rustle of money and cellophane. Those little rocks you hold, convert to cash, cash converters.

The smell is always in your clothes and on your tastebuds

The faces, the buyers, people you don't know; the desperate ones, the ones on the hunt for a buzz; the lonely ones with nothing to love but the drug; the dangerous ones who prefer to self-medicate instead of relying on the drugs they've been prescribed. And it's never enough. They always want more, always. Even if they can't pay. One day someone will rob you, meaning you have to go back to your boss who, like some crackpot dictator, will decide if you're telling the truth or whether, even if you are, that it might be worth making an example of you.

Hundreds of people like you spread out over dozens of estates, all over London.

The trains come and go, thousands of people going to and from work.

Every day you wake and see the faces. Same big talk but nothing really changes.

Life is happening all around but nothing feels real. Like it will last.

You're in the system. You're a low-paid service worker. You're in the worst part of it. You're high-risk low reward no hope go straight to jail – then you're as good as processed meat.

You're a slave. Disposable, like the rubbish you're lying among.

***

It's almost dawn by the time we finish searching the area below the flat we've just raided.

"Anyone checked in here?" I ask, pointing at the large communal wheelie bins.

Shrugs tell me I can fill my boots, so not really expecting much I open the lid.

For a second, I think I've found a dead body. Then I see it move, see the white shinbone sticking out of the leg and I call for help, already wondering whether the wound is infected and the leg will be lost.

"Ricky? Is that you?"

He groans. "Oh no, not you again."

"You should be happy to see me, mate. I'm the bloody cavalry as far as you're concerned."

It's as if I'm looking down into hell; that's where he is alright; in the gutter and he's not, like Oscar Wilde once said, looking at the stars.

"What the hell happened?"

"Jumped when you lot came crashing in."

"From the second floor? No trainers, no matter how fancy, are going save you from that height my friend."

He groans again, from his pain, the situation. Busted in mind, spirit and body.

"Cheer up mate," I say as help comes running, "The only way is up."

# CHAPTER EIGHTEEN

# TO CATCH A THIEF

As usual, there were plenty of other crimes, apart from drug dealing, for us to worry about. Car thieves remained a major blight on all owners of four-wheeled vehicles, rich and poor, the length and breadth of Battersea. We woke up to at least ten new thefts every day. A great deal of police time was spent visiting owners and completing crime reports, and it was hard for both victims and cops to keep feelings of hopelessness and frustration at bay.

The cars we tended to recover were the few that were dumped by joyriders. The majority were stolen and sold within hours. Pros had targeted Battersea because of its rich pickings. Thanks to the demand for space, few people had a garage or underground parking and the wide streets around Battersea park were therefore prime parking spots for some top class motors, but this also meant that the cars were just that bit further away from their owners, giving professional thieves space (and therefore confidence) in which to work. One thing was absolutely clear: we had reached a point where we had to think of *something*; not only were we top of the UK crime tables for cars stolen per head of population, we were top in of the European tables too.

Some thieves had become so brazen that they targeted drivers as they parked or picked up their cars, holding them up at knifepoint or, in one case, gunpoint (in which a shot was fired into the air). These scumbag robbers had left their prey psychologically traumatised, sometimes afraid to leave their home, let alone walk to their cars once they'd replaced them. Then there was the reckless driving when the thieves sped away with their prize, or raced one another in the small hours. It was only a matter of time before someone was seriously injured or killed.

I arrived for one morning shift to hear reports from the neighbouring borough of Lambeth that a young mother had, while getting in her Audi, been attacked by a knife-wielding robber who attempted to drive away with her baby still strapped in on the backseat. She had had to beg the robber to wait as she frantically fought to undo the straps.

Apart from the human side, the amounts of money involved were incredible. Half-a-million quid's worth of top-of-the-range cars could disappear from the streets of Battersea in just a few days.

Chief Inspector Hugh called me in to discuss the problem.

"It's out of hand, Mike. I'm prepared to authorise whatever it takes; we've got to start making an impact. What can you tell me about the car thieves?"

As Sector Intelligence Officer, it was my job to get proactive in terms of finding out who exactly was nicking all these cars. I'd spent a great deal of time with Pete, going through his index cards (and breathing in Pete's non-stop pipe smoke), gathering all the information about car thefts from reports made by all the uniformed patrol officers, searching for patterns, connections and possible leads. Looking at the data, stored in a half dozen overfilled A4 ring-binders, it seemed to me as if the car thieves of London had joined forces and decided to descend on Battersea. We'd put posters up and the local press had been great in terms of writing plenty of articles to alert the public, but there were only so many things people could do; the thieves were able to bypass any lock and people tended to ignore car alarms, especially if they went off late at night and the thief, once inside the car was usually able to disable it in seconds.

"I want you to spend all your time on this Mike," Chief Inspector Hugh told me once I'd related all of the above.

We really needed a lucky break if we were going to turn the tide.

I decided to hit the streets and made my way to the area where most thefts had taken place. This was Prince of Wales Drive, a long, broad and straight road that ran along the south side of Battersea Park, alongside rows of mansion blocks. Built in late Victorian times and inspired by the Arts and Crafts movement, these blocks attract professionals, celebrities and families – and now car thieves.

I talked to local shopkeepers, residents, rubbish collectors, postal workers, builders, etc., in an effort to get any information at all that would help but, after several days, I was no closer.

Our break finally came when Foxy called me back to the station. I'd just left to patrol the Winstanley but when I heard the urgent tone in Foxy's voice I hotfooted it back to find a middle-aged man called Lincoln waiting for me. Lincoln worked as a locksmith and we'd crossed each other's paths a few times, usually at follow-up visits to homes and businesses that had been burgled, where he was installing new locks and security systems.

"Hi Lincoln, good to see you," I said, meaning it. Lincoln was a good guy and liked to talk as much as I did. He was from the West Indies where he'd played guitar in various bands before moving to the UK about twenty years earlier.

Also, there's nothing I like more than to see an upstanding member of the public walk into the nick. That meant one thing: some A-star intelligence was about to be delivered.

"Heard about that car theft today," Lincoln said. He had three kids and his first grandchild was on the way. "It's got to stop."

"The young mother with the baby in the back of the car?"

Lincoln nodded.

"Tell me about it," I said. "So you have something for us that might help?"

"Well," he said uncertainly. "You got to promise what I say stays between us right?"

"I'll promise you that as long as you're not protecting yourself or someone else from possible criminal charges."

"No, it's nothing like that. It's my boy; he heard something. He won't come to the police; he's sixteen and if he's seen coming here, well, you know what I mean?"

Sadly, I did.

"For me, it's less of a problem, you see, I run into you guys all the time. My business intersects with the police but I'm separate from you guys, if you understand."

"Sure, fire away Lincoln."

"Well, my boy heard these kids talking at school. There's this one boy, I think he's fifteen. He's got problems, he's not in school much, but he was there the other day. He's hanging out with some bad lads and they were talking and this lad, the troubled one, he was showing off, talking big, listing makes of cars: a Porsche 911s, Cosworths, Mercedes, Land Rovers, BMWs, Range Rovers, Audis and so on. He said that was he was looking for all of these makes because there was some south London gang willing to pay handsomely, no questions asked, to anyone who could deliver them. He said that the gang are making the cars clean by using real parts and paperwork from models that'd been written off in Europe. This kid said he could steal ten cars a week and make a grand."

I glanced at Foxy who was standing behind Lincoln. She couldn't help but grin and give me the thumbs-up. Finally!

The suspect's name was Sam, he was indeed fifteen-years-old and he lived on one of the low-rise estates behind the mansion blocks on Prince of Wales Drive. Hugh authorised us to watch it all night, every night, in an effort to catch what we believed was one of the most prolific car thieves in London.

The address was overlooked by a modest block of new-build flats filled with private tenants. This was one of the many times we would rely upon the good old British public for assistance, and once I'd decided which flat had the best view, I went up and rang the bell.

"Hello officer, what can I do you for you?"

For a moment I was speechless (a unique condition for me) and could only manage an 'Um,' as my brain tried to digest the fact that the door had been opened by one of the most beautiful women I'd ever seen in my life. And then I noticed an equally beautiful woman in the hallway behind her. Both of them smiled pleasantly.

"Um, yes, well, right. May I come in?"

A few moments later I was on the sofa explaining (albeit like a blushing teenage boy unused to being left alone with girls) that I would very much like to use their flat as part of an operation to catch a thief in the act.

"We just want it for observation," I said, "For intelligence, you understand."

These ladies, both in their early twenties and both brunettes, could have been sisters except for the fact that the one who had opened the door was a Russian called Marta, while the other lady, Anna, was from Oxford and spoke like she'd just stepped out of a public-school. They were both intrigued at the prospect.

"When would you want to watch for your suspect?" Anna asked.

"Just after dark, really, that's when he operates."

"So all night then? Until dawn?"

"Pretty much."

Anna and Marta said that they worked nights and that would be fine; I would have the place to myself most of the time.

Mark decided to join me so we could share observation duties. His eyes bulged when he saw the two ladies and was about ready to walk them to the station when they left for work at 8am, I cleared my throat and he let them be.

After they'd gone he joined me on the balcony, pulled up a chair and said: "Trust you to end up with two hot hookers!"

"What?" I said. "They're not prostitutes!"

"Oh really? So what did they say they did then?"

Mark soon persuaded me that we were engaged in a stakeout from a flat inhabited by two young ladies of the night.

"I'd genuinely no idea," I said.

"Well, the less said about it the better, I suppose," Mark replied.

And so, we settled down on the girls' balcony to watch. Luckily summer had at last arrived and with jumper, coat and tea, it was not the most unpleasant of stakeouts.

At about 1am the front door opened.

"Here we go!" I said, tapping Mark on the shoulder, waking him up from a doze. I could see the hallway light but then, the door just closed again. No one came out. Mark returned to his doze.

"Well, what the hell was that for then?" I asked

"Maybe he just wanted some fresh air," Mark muttered.

It happened again a bit later. And again on the next night.

It was peculiar but, as long as no one left the house, then there was nothing for us to do. And cars were still being stolen at the same rate every night. Lincoln was certain that this was our guy but by the third night I was starting to doubt him and I wondered how long the two ladies would be prepared to let us intrude.

Then I finally realised what the cheeky bastard was up to. He was doing his own counter-surveillance and crawling out of the front door, which was out of our sight behind the low balcony wall. I was amazed that a fifteen-year-old would think of such a thing.

He sabotaged his own counter-surveillance, however, when he came home in a Sierra Cosworth. We continued to watch the flat until dawn, when we whizzed around in the car, search warrant at the ready, and knocked him up.

The door was opened by a man, presumably the boy's father. Sometimes you don't need to be a cop for your sixth sense to kick in to tell you that you're dealing with a bad person.

"Sam in, is he?"

"It's six in the morning, I have no idea."

"He usually out at 6am is he?"

The man, who was completely bald, in his late thirties, tattooed (badly) and about six feet tall glared at us with unconcealed hatred and practically spat when he spoke.

"No, he's got a paper round."

Clearly a lie but not our problem. No need to muck about any more, I held out the search warrant and said we were coming in.

The man frowned at the paper as we stepped into the flat. It was desperately untidy. The kitchen was a mess of takeaway paraphernalia and plastic cups, strewn liberally over the countertops and piled up and around an overflowing bin. The smell was enough to make us want to wrap this up quickly. Cops are used to encountering bad smells (the odour of the long dead is quite unforgettable) but this was just as bad as far as I was concerned.

I finally got to Sam's room and threw open the door, ready to do my "GOOD MORNING IT"S YOUR WORST NIGHTMARE!" routine but the words stuck in my throat, thanks in part to the smell, to the mess (even greater in here), the smell (equally bad but different) and the envelopes stuffed full of cash that were sitting on piles of clothes which were covering, I presumed, a table or chest of some sort.

A small teenager, eyes half open, light brown hair springing out in all directions, emerged from beneath a thick and mountainous duvet.

"I'm nicked aren't I?" Sam said.

"Yes, son, you bloody well are."

We 'searched' the room – it would have taken a four-person team a week to do it properly – and recovered cash just shy of £4,000 in four envelopes and the keys to the Sierra Cosworth which turned out to be a spare set the owner had left in the glove compartment; some people can't help helping the criminals. When the Dad stuck his head in the room to see what was going on, Mark held up one of the envelopes with the cash, now in a clear plastic evidence bag and deadpan, said: "Must be the mother of all paper rounds."

It was clear to us that there was more to this story than what we were seeing. Sam came with us and sat in the back, good as gold and soon we were in the interview room with a solicitor and a social worker.

"So, how many cars was it last night then?" I asked when we got the preliminaries out of the way.

"Hands up, you got me," Sam said. "To be honest I'm not a hundred per cent sure, ten maybe? I'll confess to more, the ones I remember anyway, if you want to go through them with me."

When Sam talked about cars he became a different person, animated and confident. Anything else and he was withdrawn.

"Who have you been selling them to?"

"Some travelling types from down Croydon way. They pick them up from me at an archway garage in Wimbledon, round the corner from the stadium. They've been selling them on but every now and again, when one of the cars takes their fancy, they'll race them around the M25, baiting the traffic cops."

Sam was the exception to the rule, a real once- or twice-in-a-career arrest. He gave us all the details, everything he knew – he would go on to confess to over a hundred thefts of high-performance cars – and even showed us how he did it. It never took him more than a few seconds to get the door open and not much longer to start the engine.

"If you want, I can give you some names," he said. "Of other car thieves, and the people I delivered to. But I need a favour in return."

"Oh yeah, what's that then?" thinking he was going to ask for the judge to go easy on him.

"I want to talk to her," he said, pointing at the social worker. Alone."

# Chapter Nineteen

# THE STING

I t was a car thief's dream target: an almost brand new, white Ford RS Sierra Cosworth 4X4 parked on the broad thoroughfare of Prince of Wales Drive. These powerful cars were highly prized by both rally drivers and car thieves and a member of the latter group was soon drawn to the Cosworth like a bee to a Chelsea Flower Show rose.

The car was secured with its own automatic locking system and alarm but this did nothing to dissuade the late-night thief who popped the lock, slid into the driver's seat and disabled the alarm in under ten seconds.

He started the engine, revved it, admired the sound, nodded and grinned, mouthing 'Oh yes!' He turned the wheel, not bothering to signal, and pulled out of the parking space, at which point the engine died. His WTF? expression turned into a frown as he tried to restart the car, looking at the ignition and then under the steering column; perhaps when disabling the alarm he'd disabled some vital electronics. With no solution in sight he turned to open the door and, to his surprise, found he couldn't.

"Having a spot of bother are we?"

Timbo had appeared beside the driver's door and was holding it closed. The thief looked the other way to see Mark, who was waiting at the other door, and who gave the thief a little wave. The thief sat back, looked skywards, closed his eyes and let out a loud expletive.

Timbo opened the door and took the young man down to the station, while Mark and I moved the bait to a different parking slot.

Sam the car thief hadn't stopped talking once he'd spent some time with the social worker. He gave us names of thieves and their operating methods, including their favoured patches in which they sought their prey, their preferred vehicles and, in a couple of cases, their home addresses.

Sam had said it was a relief to be caught. Once he was able to talk to the social worker alone, he'd opened up about how his father had sexually abused him. We passed his case over to the Child Protection Team who nicked the father; it also emerged he had previous for the sexual assault of a former girlfriend. But what he was really into was little boys.

The search teams sifted through the entire house (it must have taken them forever) and found a stack of child porn hidden behind a neatly-made hidey-hole behind a fake wall that covered a chimney-breast.

That already meant prison but, on top of that, Sam – who was going to end up with a slap on the wrist for the countless cars he'd stolen – was prepared to give evidence that he was raped. His story would make compelling testimony. The social worker said his car thievery was actually an addiction. He didn't care about the money, he did it for the rush, the feelings of pleasure it gave him, much like those people who became addicted to crack.

As a result of Sam's fantastic intelligence we set up the sting operation, which we ran every night over a two-week period. We caught some of South London's most prolific thieves, one-by-one, until word had spread and, for the first time since I'd arrived in Battersea, car thefts took a sudden dip, so much so that the people who compiled the stats called to check we hadn't missed a zero.

Also caught were the little terrors who went for car radios and CD players which were stolen by the dozen each night. They'd smash the window to gain access and grab the stereo and anything else they could find in seconds – it always amazed me how many people left valuable items in their cars overnight, from jewellery, designer sunglasses and cash to power-tools and fully loaded shopping bags, when they knew this was a car-crime hotspot. We set up a bait car with tempting knick-knacks in view such as sunglasses and an empty box for a DVD player.

We didn't have to wait long.

We had only just got into the back of the van, which was parked right in front of the bait car and had got settled when we heard the sound of smashing glass. We leapt out only to find there were four of them and three of us.

Timbo somehow managed to grab two of the lads with his shovel-like hands while Mark, a keen rugby man, threw himself after number three who'd turned to leg it and brought him crashing down on the pavement, leaving me with no.4 who seemed to be the fastest of the bunch.

I took to my toes and ran full pelt after no.4, a white lad of about eighteen in T-shirt, loose tracksuit bottoms and trainers. He was quite the gymnast and jumped onto a car bonnet only needing, thanks to his momentum, to let one foot touch the car as he bounded off and onwards into estate land.

I was in plainclothes and had fortunately worn trainers but I didn't feel able to leap a car bonnet in a single bound so I jumped through the gap between the two cars without losing too much speed. I applied the usual match-his-pace-until-he hits-an-obstacle approach, but the little bastard had no problems dealing with obstacles and I was rather surprised to see him perform a one-handed vault over a hip-high wall that divided the walkway from a row of back gardens.

'Ok,' I thought, 'You can do this Mike,' and so I half hurdled, half vaulted the wall only to hear a rrrrip sound coming between my thighs. My jeans were not built for stretching and now had a rather large hole in them but I wasn't about to stop for a clothing malfunction and so carried on the pursuit over a back garden wall and into a narrow alleyway.

I actually gained some ground on the lad as we raced down the alleyway which was barely three feet wide; the lad dived left at the end, so left I went only to run into a wheelie bin he'd pulled in front of him. I pushed it over; he'd had to slow to do this so it hadn't bought him much time and I saw him take a right down a path between two rows of houses that would bring him out onto a short street. I knew this estate well and knew there was a parallel path in front of me, so dived down it and came out to find the lad was actually running towards me.

"Shit!" he exclaimed, dodging my outstretched hands and off we went again, down the street and across a road, through a line of trees and suddenly we were on Battersea Park Road not far from the famous Battersea Dog's Home. It was late at night but both pedestrians and cars were about but I was too breathless to shout "POLICE!" as my lungs were burning and I knew I wouldn't be able to keep this pace for much longer. We passed under a railway bridge, trains rumbling above and the lad darted into Battersea Park Station and up the steps three at a time to the platform. He was hoping to make it onto a train. I gave it everything I had, leaping up the steps three at a time until I was on the platform, along which the lad was already running but I'd made up some ground. A train had just finished pulling in before he could attempt to dart in, I leapt after him in a flying rugby tackle and caught his legs – I got him! Or rather, I got his tracksuit trousers, they had come down to his ankles and he struggled and kicked to free himself until the tracksuit was hopelessly tangled around his trainers.

"Come on now lad," I said, gasping as the train started to pull away, "I've got you now, don't be silly."

We were both lying on the northbound platform, struggling to get our breath, chests heaving, he with his tracksuit bottoms around his ankles, me with my jeans split down both thighs.

Suddenly, a camp voice came from above.

"Darling, if he wants you to stay that badly, then I think you've no choice."

A man, primly dressed in a light suit, was sitting on a bench, waiting for the last train home.

"I'm a police officer," I managed to say between pants before giving up trying to explain anything else.

"Well good for you," the man said, with a friendly smile. "I'm sure you'll be very happy together."

Once we were reassembled and I had a firm grip of the lad, I asked the man to use the station phone to call the police and we were soon in the back of a panda car, on our way back to the station to join his and my partners in crime/crime fighting.

I received plenty of strange looks and was the butt (ahem) of many jokes thanks to my split trousers but I didn't care. We'd achieved what we'd set out to do – which had once seemed impossible – and reduced car crime to a comparative trickle. For my work on the car crimes the team received a commendation (which was my first) but I would like to dedicate my share to Lincoln, the man who came to the police with the tip-off about Sam. He trusted us to do something and without him, Sam might not have been rescued and we might never have been able to get the car thefts under control, certainly not as quickly as we did.

This case taught me two things. First, maintaining public trust was one of the most crucial aspects of policing. The second thing I learned was that whatever the challenge, there was always a way.

# CHAPTER TWENTY

# TITCH

Dawn on the Doddington Estate. One flight of concrete stairs stained with blood, a congealed pool at its base. A body on the stairwell landing. Young, black and dead.

I was with Patters. We had just finished winding police tape around some railings and a stairway pillar, creating an inner cordon. Now, we were waiting for the murder squad.

"You know- sorry, knew him?" Patters asked.

"Yeah. His street name was Titch. Twenty years old. A small-time dealer."

We lapsed into silence. Dead bodies have that effect, if you're given the chance to stare at them for too long.

Titch had the extremely unfortunate distinction of being a 'first'. He was the first Battersea gang member to have been shot dead since I arrived in Battersea. There'd been plenty of stabbings, bludgeonings and beatings, some of which had led to murders in the heat of the moment, but Titch's murder was a cold-blooded execution. Three bullets in the chest, all grouped around the heart.

***

There's no procedure for breaking unbelievably bad news but one has to prepare. Make sure you have all the information. Make sure you have the right address (sometimes it's a good idea to check with neighbours but in no circumstances should you give them the bad news first). Then it's deep breaths on the doorstep to calm yourself and ring the doorbell.

"Mrs Holden?"

The woman standing in front of me was in her forties, she was small, delicate and I felt like I was towering over her.

"Yes."

Trying to keep my expression neutral, I said: "Police Constable Mike Pannett, May I come in?"

"Yes, of course, what seems to be the trouble?"

"Is your husband here Mrs Holden?"

"Please, call me Paula," she said before shouting "Gerald! Police are here!"

"Is anyone else in the house?" I asked.

"No, it's just us. Is it about Michael?"

Titch's real name.

"Yes, yes it is."

Mr and Mrs Holden were going to remember my visit for the rest of their lives because this was the moment their lives were forever changed. I knew that my behaviour, how I handled this, would have a lasting impact. I wondered how they would react – anger, shock, disbelief, violence, silence – and the sorts of questions they would ask. I knew not to say anything trite, like 'Time heals,' or 'You'll get over it.' Police officers vary wildly in their effectiveness at giving bad news and that's to be expected, as we're only human. The key is to try and let the professional police mode take over, but at the same time, to allow your natural compassion to come through.

I was however 'relieved' that the father was there so I wouldn't have to do this twice. Some officers prefer to tell the father first, to try and protect the mother from the details but this is preposterous as it only adds to the distress of both parents. The mother will become angry with the father. Much better they are both united in their grief so that any anger is aimed at you, the messenger.

Gerald came downstairs. He smelled of shaving cream. Must have been getting ready for work. He was six feet tall, in his early forties, completely bald and had long arms made muscular through years of house painting.

"Could we sit down? In the lounge perhaps?"

"Yes, of course."

Paula led the way into the lounge and there they were, the family photos, Michael as a schoolboy, on holiday, pressed up against his mum when he was ten years old, in his football kit.

It was (still at this time) a tradition in the police to send the new recruits to deliver the death message. It was the job no one wanted to do, or do again once they had. It was a terrible thing to send a young and inexperienced police officer on such a mission, and sometimes had terrible consequences for the families. I heard several stories of constables who had got the victims' name wrong and even of a case where an officer had informed a family (they were out when he called upon them) by putting a note through the letterbox.

I wanted to go. I was the community beat officer. I had found Michael's body. I knew the boy. I would be able to answer questions about where it happened and how. I would be able to connect Paula and Gerald to their son's last moments. At the same time however, we would forever remind one another of the worst moment in their lives and one of the worst in mine.

It was time to speak.

Be measured and soothing, leave nothing out. Only the truth, no matter how terrible, will do. A slow delivery with long pauses. Do not under any circumstances invoke religion. Do not hug. Do not fill silences by over-talking, something I was wont to do. Do not use euphemisms (like 'passed on' or 'lost'). Do not criticise their child. Michael might have been a pain in the arse as far us police officers were concerned but he was, for all his flaws, their son and they had loved him, cared for him and would go on loving his memory for the rest of their lives.

"I'm afraid its bad news. I'm very sorry to have to tell you that Michael was found dead this morning."

A pause; breathe.

Unthinkably awful news like this can lead to a number of responses, generated by the associated intense physiological changes – a leap in stress hormones, short gasps and then, an attempt to make an unreal event seem real and logical, the father usually will ask the first question/s. The mother (usually) will wait for more information to come from the messenger.

People rarely remember the answers, however, as the shock some comes rolling in over everything that is rational and real.

The father spoke first. "How do you know it was Michael?"

It's a good question. Just because someone has a wallet on them when they're killed, it doesn't mean that it's theirs. But I knew Michael and, if it came to it, fingerprints do not lie and thanks to Michael's criminal record, we had those on file. I wouldn't have been there unless we were certain. We also had the option of dental records but we wouldn't contact the family dentist unless we felt it was absolutely essential at this stage, before telling the parents.

I explained. I knew not to use expressions like 'the deceased' or 'the body'. Michael had died and he had to be named.

As for the circumstances of the death, it's a good idea to lead up to it, to perhaps let the parents ask the questions that take you there. I explained that Michael had been murdered.

"How?" Paula asked.

"He was shot."

"Was he in pain?"

"I don't know," I said "But I think it was very quick."

A few minutes later, I asked them if there was anyone they'd like to call, to be with them at this time.

Paula and Gerald looked at one another. They had other people they needed to tell. They would perform the role I had for them. Over and over again. The grandparents, his sister, uncles and aunts. A single death affects so many, it's easy to forget this when you're looking at news reports and statistics.

"Our daughter. She's at school."

"I can arrange to have her brought home. We won't tell her what's happened. Is that ok?"

Gerald nodded.

News of the sudden death of a loved one can lead to a whole raft of responses, from grief to anger, guilt to pure, silent shock. As strange as it seems, some people start doing things, are over-come by a need to fill the time with errands. No one is normal at this time, shock unbalances mental and physical processes and the strangest reactions can take place.

"We'd like to see him," Paula said, looking at Gerald, who nodded.

"Yes," he agreed, "We'd like to be with him."

"Of course," I said. "I'll speak to the Coroner and arrange it so that you can see Michael as soon as possible."

It was best they didn't drive themselves, so CID detectives would take them and perhaps bring them home again, unless a relative was on hand to do this. Unfortunately, as this was a murder enquiry, Paula and Gerald would not be able to touch

Michael's body. The Coroner was in charge of Michael's body and would not release it until he was satisfied that all the necessary evidence had been collected. The same applied to Michael's clothing and belongings. I would hand those back when the time was right (as long as they didn't have to be used as evidence), and would make sure they were presented nicely; it's not a good idea to return personal belongings in a plastic rubbish bag.

"We also want to see where Michael died," Gerald said.

Paula nodded. "To pay our last respects."

"Of course, I'll arrange this for you too."

It was a full day before we could visit the scene. The area had been cordoned off for a fingertip search. Although bullet fragments had been recovered from the body, no other evidence had been found that was going to help us identify the murderer, not even shell casings. We had a host of suspects but it didn't feel as though this was going to be a quick investigation. The shooter had been careful enough to strike in the small hours and had collected the shell cases.

Michael's sister, Amelia, was with her parents. She was just fourteen years old. She laid some flowers on the concrete, on the spot where her brother had died – the blood had been spray-cleaned away. She had barely spoken. Amelia left her parents for a moment and came over to where I was standing, a short distance away, beside a path.

"I wanted to say thank you for doing this with my parents."

"Goodness, you don't have to thank me-"

"I do. We appreciate what you're doing."

"Thank you for saying that."

"We knew Michael was with some bad people but to me he was still Michael, my big brother, you know?"

I nodded. "Of course," I replied. "Family's family."

There was a pause. I resisted the urge to fill it; I could sense Amelia wanted to tell me something else.

"Do you know what the last thing Michael said to me was?" Amelia said, looking down and then back at her parents.

"Mum and Dad wanted to do something for his twenty-first birthday, a dinner in a nice restaurant, just the four of us. Michael said he wasn't going to be able to make it. He said 'Tell Mum I'm sorry.'"

Amelia paused again, tears running down her face. "Tell Mum I'm sorry," she repeated.

\*\*\*

I didn't need much in the way of encouragement in terms of doing my duty but Amelia loomed large in my mind as I performed stop and searches, and I can't remember many days when I didn't arrest someone; mostly for carrying drugs or knives.

We all used the stop and searches to target the people we knew to be criminals. Unless we were given reason (i.e., we stumbled across a likely drug deal, or someone using drugs), we didn't trouble people who were simply going about their business.

One break came when Mark and I turned the corner and ran into Lips. He had a warrant out on him and we were able to grab him before he could turn and run. Once we'd finished nicking him I took a look at his phone to see who he'd been calling and hanging out with and, together with officers from Serious Crimes, I went through the list, explaining who was who.

'Mole,' for example, was an ex-Battersea boy whose specialty was robbing brothels at gun-point. These were easy targets and the owners didn't often report the robbery for obvious reasons. Nonetheless, Mole was on the Flying Squad's radar. Mole's number was also in the phone but Lips wouldn't say a word to us, except for 'solicitor' and although the warrant had proven useful, it was for the minor offence of possession of a Class C substance, so we weren't able to keep him off the streets for long.

Number one on my list of targets was, of course, Gary Nelson. He was the most dangerous man in London and he had taken on the mantle left by the Yardies. Nelson was king and to be king, you had to terrorise so that no one would doubt the lengths to which you were prepared to go. He had established himself as being crazy or even crazier than the Yardies, and these days, whenever I mentioned Nelson's name, people clammed up and walked away or ushered me out.

As far as I was concerned, Titch's death was just the beginning of a new drug-fuelled crime wave featuring guns. Alongside the rise of crack, the structure of London's underworld was changing, making life in the city – where poor lived alongside rich – a more dangerous place for everyone. It was only a matter of time before innocent people started paying the price.

# CHAPTER TWENTY-ONE

# BABY MOTHERS

It was about 9pm on a June evening, I was with Stevie in the Panda car with the windows down and had been admiring the twilight and the 4,000 lightbulbs (LEDs today) on the Albert Bridge while Stevie moaned about 'her indoors' and his horrible kids who always seemed to be in lots of trouble at school, or were ill, or needed braces, or some other sort of expensive dental work. I'd learned to zone out once Stevie got going and could meditate on all manner of things while he rambled, until my brain picked up on a keyword – my name, or something to do with the job usually. In this case the keywords that brought me back to reality were: "What the fuck?"

A black VW Golf with black windows was weaving across the narrow bridge and, despite being a small hatchback, only just made it through the traffic calmers – and this was after the driver stopped, fiddled to get into reverse, grinding the gears in the process, before straightening up and suddenly leaping through the gap.

Driving along what was the very straight Albert Bridge Road, it cruised at a steady 20mph in an unsteady S-shape, attracting the attention of some late evening dog walkers, joggers and us. Without another word, Stevie flicked on the lights – leaving the sirens off- and pulled out onto Albert Bridge Road, and we cruised behind the car for about a hundred metres but the driver, apparently, still didn't notice us. Stevie then hit the siren and the car jerked to a sudden halt.

I got out, leaving Stevie in the driver's seat, just in case the VW decided to take off and give us a run around town. The VW's engine was still running as I came up beside it, as was the sound of a stereo, which emitted a deep bass hum. It was impossible to see through the windows, which remained firmly wound up. I also noticed that the car was hot, so hot in fact that it was like standing next to an oven. I tapped on the window.

"Switch off your engine and lower your window!" I shouted.

The engine's hum suddenly died and, a moment later, the driver started to wind down the window. I felt tremendous heat coming out of the car, quickly followed by a smell so overpowering that I took a step back into the road.

A young black man was at the wheel. His clothes were soaked in sweat and perspiration covered his face. It was a hot June evening and still about 20 degrees outside; it must have been more than double that inside the car.

"Get out of the vehicle sir," I said.

"Ociffer, I can explain," the man slurred quietly.

"Out!"

"Shiiiit," the man said.

I beckoned Stevie over as the man climbed out.

"Hands on the roof," Stevie said, "Legs apart," and he started to search the man.

I, meanwhile, had a good look inside the car. I'd never seen anything like it before and I never have since. It was like a mobile cannabis factory. There were sixty plants of varying sizes (I eventually counted them) that filled every available space in the car. The back seats had been removed and heat lamps had somehow been wired up to the car's battery. Criminal entrepreneurs never ceased to amaze me but this really took the biscuit.

"He's clean," Stevie said and we arrested the man, whose name, like the bridge, happened to be Albert, for a variety of drug-related offences and had the car lifted onto a low-loader and taken to the station yard, where it attracted the attention of the entire nick.

***

That same June night, in Victoria's SW1 Club, just behind the train station, an altercation was taking place between two men: Gary Nelson, who was running the club's security, and Mohammed Massaquoi, a south London criminal. Witnesses later said that the argument was over a girl. Nelson had previously fired his gun at Massaquoi and this time, after saying: "Remember me? I'm the guy that was buzzing shots at you," Nelson pulled a pistol from his waistband and opened fire. Chen, who was in a balcony on the opposite side of the nightclub, also started shooting. Massaquoi was in fancy dress, in the style of a Wild West outlaw, and his life was saved by the metal bullet-bandoliers that criss-crossed his chest. Nevertheless, Massaquoi ran limping from the nightclub with bullets in his thighs and buttocks. This was the second time in a few weeks that Nelson had opened fire in a nightclub. The first time the victim's life was saved when the bullet ricocheted off the zip on a pouch he was wearing round his neck.

At the time we had no idea about Nelson's involvement in this shooting. Massaquoi claimed not to have seen the shooter's face and the few witnesses that police managed to speak to all claimed hadn't seen anything. While this may have been true, I can understand people being unwilling to give evidence against someone who was prepared to shoot someone dead in one the UK's busiest and most densely populated areas.

***

That night, Stevie and I were celebrating our prize catch. Albert, aka Ice Cream Man, aka ICM, was part of a new-ish phenomenon, as it was back then, of home-built cannabis factories, but had been evicted from his flat for non-payment of rent, so was moving across town, from Earls Court to Brixton. Albert not only grew, he also delivered his produce hence the nickname, reinforced by the fact that, like the ice cream man, his arrival was usually announced by the broadcasting of loud music over his car stereo, except instead of *Here We Go Round the Mulberry Bush* or *Row Row Row Your Boat*, Albert played reggae.

Albert was practically deaf and the interview was carried out at an intense exchange of yells until, between protests – first that the drugs were not his, second that ok they were but they were herbs and therefore harmless and third, he was – thanks to the munchies brought on by excessive cannabis consumption – terribly hungry- he could finally be charged and held for court the following morning, at which point he would, most likely, be remanded.

Once Albert had been locked up, I went to the canteen where I found Pete and Foxy. They beckoned me over to their table. I felt like an old hand by now, and the days when I approached canteen dining with nervous apprehension were long gone. Both Pete and Foxy had been working on Nelson's file and they told me that they now reckoned that he had more than a dozen so-called 'baby mothers' spread out all over south London; some of them were teenagers, at least two of them were carrying his child.

I looked at the names. "Hang on! This one doesn't fit the profile."

"You know her?"

"Just a bit. She was working at that pharmacist that was robbed. You remember, don't you Foxy?"

"I remember the burglary but I didn't meet her."

"She's smart, beautiful. What on earth would she want with Nelson?"

I was genuinely slack-jawed in amazement.

"Honestly, I've never understood this phenomenon," I said. "What makes criminals like Nelson so attractive to women? He's got about as much charm as a rattlesnake in a cage full of mice."

Foxy looked at me despairingly and then exchanged a look with Pete that said something like 'poor naive fool' before she took up the mantle.

"Put it this way. You're young in the no-hope world of this or that estate; maybe from a broken home and maybe school didn't work out as well as you'd hoped, i.e., not at all. You're poorly-qualified in a world of stupid, violent men with one-track minds. Prospects are slim to none. Perhaps you've got a job like your friend in the chemist but what prospects are there? You want to do that for the rest of your days? There are plenty of girls like that around here.

"So these girls see other girls who have managed to make school work and have started to do something with their lives. It feels as though life is slipping you by. Then an older man shows up. He pays you complements, shows interest. He's good looking, has money and has a reach beyond the estate. He even travels to other countries and offers you a chance to go with him, all expenses paid – you who've not even crossed the river. These are girls who have barely finished school, think they know it all but are extremely naive in the ways of the world and buy Nelson's lines, confidently delivered, like they're the Gospel. As far as they're concerned, it's win-win; after a lifetime of struggling for recognition, and in some cases love, they are at last getting it; they're being saved from a life of dull poverty."

"He gets them pregnant," Pete said. "Either sets them up in a rented flat or they queue for a council place. Then he has a multiple bolt-holes, so we'll never know where he is on any given night, and places where he can stash things, or where friends can hide out if they need to. They all take part willingly precisely because his affections are spread far and wide; he's gone a lot of the time so although they might be angry when he first shows up, they don't dare risk pissing him off and pushing him away."

"But not all of them are like that. There's also those with Bonnie-and-Clyde-syndrome."

"The what?"

"Hybristophilia," Pete chipped in.

"Bless you," I replied.

"It's when women get excited by dangerous men," Pete said.

"It can work the other way too," Foxy answered.

Pete raised his eyebrows. "Yet to see it that way around, professionally and personally speaking," he said with a slight smile. "Anyway, the more dangerous the man, the better. And the lousy conditions on the estates of South London are a perfect recipe for this. Poverty, despair, poor housing, a weak social network. Men tend to respond to despair and so on with crime and violence. Women tend to turn to the strongest, most dangerous men for support."

"And there's none more dangerous than this guy," Foxy said.

"There are different versions," Pete said. "For example, some women who feel as though they can change him, turn him into a good man. We've seen that in the crazy people who write to serial killers in jail like Ted Bundy and Jeffrey Dahmer.[4]

"They claim to love these men and some of these letters get pretty sexual; some of them have even married, like serial killer

---

4   Mass murderer Anders Brevik and the Boston Marathon bomber have also received plenty of fan mail.

Richard Ramirez. This is only in the US mind you, where they seem to allow this sort of thing."

"Got to be one of the weirdest experiences possible for the priest," Foxy said. "How's he going to get through the wedding vows? I mean 'til death do us part?' Come on!"

"But that's not the case here. It's more one or a combination of basking in the fame of being the girlfriend of the most dangerous man in South London and she gets respect as a bi-product of that reputation. Also, it feeds a fantasy. He's the perfect man in that she doesn't have to look after him; he's never there, none of the day-to-day boredom of cooking or washing his smalls; she can imagine that he loves her, is thinking of her and will come to her when he can, which isn't often because of his hi-risk life, which he spends increasing his fearsome reputation. It's very easy to maintain the fantasy of a perfect relationship." Pete paused before adding: "And he's so Alpha it's off the scale," Pete said. "If you look at it from an evolutionary angle,"

"Oh, here we go, evolution as an excuse for sexism," Foxy said.

"Not at all, but men are the hunter gatherers and alpha males are effective at protecting women and their children, as well as providing for them. There may be a rational, modern part of their brain that says this guy is bad news but the old brain, the bit that's been with us since before humans learned to stand on two feet says he's providing for me, and life has never been so exciting."

"They're so wrong they're right, you mean," I said.

"Exactly. Just look at literature," Pete said. "Mr Darcy was an Alpha male. Then if you want to get blatantly obvious there's Beauty and the Beast, the Phantom of the Opera, King Kong. The more dangerous the Alpha male the better. This figure is in almost every romantic tale going. They believe he will kill for them and it doesn't get more romantic than that."

# Chapter Twenty-Two

# A NICE CUP OF TEA

Plain clothes in a cafe north of the Thames, waiting, waiting, third cup of tea, fag on, paper read and re-read. I needed the loo but didn't dare leave my position. I ordered another tea. Cops have bladders of iron. It was supposed to be my day off but, hey, when this informant tells me to meet, I obey.

Informants are as rare as gold.

Reliable and trustworthy informants are as rare as unicorns.

Sergeant Phil was eyes-on the cafe, sitting in another cafe across the road, making sure he didn't see any familiar faces. I had a radio in my lap and all it would take was three clicks from Sergeant Phil for me to know that we were in danger of being rumbled, or one click to let me know he'd seen our source.

As always, I was confident that we'd done all we could to protect the source and ourselves but of course, as with so many areas of policing, there are always degrees of uncertainty and random variables that one just can't control.

Normally, the police (the detectives of the Criminal Investigation Department in particular) 'flip' criminals, transforming them into informants. I'd seen this in action myself when, having just finished a smoke around the back of the station and about to board the van with Patters on an equipment run, the CID 'tecs rolled in with a prisoner.

"Alright son?" one of them asked. He was tall, smartly dressed but his face was saggy and blotchy and he smelled of last night. I wouldn't trust him any further than I could throw a blue whale. His partner, an overweight unshaven man had stayed in the car with the prisoner.

"Not bad, ta," I replied uncertainly.

"Need to use your van for a minute."

"Um."

"We're not going to take it anywhere, just need a bit of privacy in the back."

I was completely nonplussed until Patters stuck his head out of the driver's window and yelled at me to get my lazy arse in the van so we could get this over with.

"Alright Patters," the detective said, walking to the driver's window. "The delay's my fault, was just chatting to your mate here."

"Alright Jim, I see. Need us to stand aside for a moment?"

"If you wouldn't mind."

"No problem." Patters climbed out. "Come on Pannett, tea's on you."

"What the hell was that about?" I asked, once we were out of earshot.

"Pannett, you are but a naive young constable and some things are probably best left untold."

"Oh come on, I've been here for over a year now."

Patters thought for a moment. "Ok then. Those are two of our best detectives, right? Put more bodies in the rusty nail than the rest of us put together."

I found that slightly hard to believe but let it go and nodded.

"Well, one of the many secrets of their success is persuading criminals that, in order to possibly save their own skins from a fate worse than death, if they deigned to testify about this or that, or provide information about the other, it would be deemed so useful that they might be allowed to return home and go about their business. Minus any criminal activity, of course."

Nobody tells you about this sort of thing in training school.

Criminals are by their very nature opportunistic and disloyal and often aren't members of one clearly defined gang, so detectives try and identify those they think they can turn, i.e., recruit to assist the police. It's not illegal but it is a specialised subject, with plenty of grey areas. These days we call informers Covert Human Intelligence Sources (CHIS), who are run under the auspices of the Dedicated Source Unit (DSU).

Criminals call them grasses, snitches and squealers.

I called them snouts.

They came to us in a number of ways:

Sometimes they walked in, or approached a police officer directly, which happens more often than you might think. Of course, one has to be careful about their motivations.

Sometimes a person came to us about a loved one or family member that they know to have been up to no good and that for their own sake, they come to us to deal with it because the family is unable to stop them.

Sources can also be witnesses, innocent people caught up in a criminal incident, whether they've walked into a fight or seen a drug deal from their bedroom window and decide to come forward, or volunteer information during house-to-house enquiries (which is why going house-to-house is so important, by visiting everyone in the area, no one can be singled out for talking to the police), or a media appeal. If it was serious enough they would be given witness protection, which is today dealt with by a top secret police unit.

I had started working on finding sources as soon as I started patrolling the Winstanley. I wasn't trying to 'turn' criminals per se but sometimes one of the lads might talk out of carelessness or because he didn't approve of someone else's operation. You have to remember that they cannot be trusted (which makes acting on their information alone a risky business, so corroboration is always important). Talking to the cops is a high-risk strategy for those who associate with, or live close to criminal gangs. They might be motivated by money (we didn't pay at our level, just £10 or £20 for 'incidentals' like travel and refreshments, but it was always possible that they wanted to put a rival out of business); to save their own skin if they'd annoyed someone mad and bad enough who was looking to harm them or pay someone else to harm them; tricking us tying us up in one part of town while they did their business in another, for the sheer thrill of it and therefore probably mentally unstable; to gain intelligence to try and find out what we know about a criminal or criminal operation or out of public spirit.

This last option was the one I liked the most. But it was also the rarest.

A short time later, the detectives let us know our van was good to go.

"Any luck?" Patters asked.

The taller of the two detectives gave him the thumbs-up. "Sweet as a nut."

Once a criminal is 'turned', they're given a story to cover their arrest, for something minor, nothing to do with the actual crime they were nicked for otherwise it would look more than a tad suspect.

You need to make sure your supervisors know about the source, especially if they're a participating informant in that they will 'have' to break the law to maintain their cover.

At that time, if the case was extremely serious, detectives would alert the existence of their source to the Regional Crime Squad, which dealt with organised crime and major drug trafficking (today's equivalent is the National Crime Agency), otherwise they would notify their DCI.

Once that's done, it's time to set up tightly-controlled meetings with cover stories (reasons why the source is there) and back up, with someone staying eyes-on to make sure no one's followed the source, and, ideally a bunch of contingency plans should it all hit the fan.

These meetings are always interesting experiences. The source will tell you what *they* want you to know but you have to find a way to make sure you know everything you need to know but of course, you can never be certain. And then you will want to task them to find out certain things and to do this you need to come up with a plan together that is legal, as safe as possible and that the source is confident that they will succeed. After the meeting, you write up notes and make sure everyone who needs to, knows what's going on but all the while keeping the source's actual identity a secret – the less people who know, the better and the easier it is to know that a police leak didn't blow their cover or jeopardise an operation.

Of course, once you have a source, there's all sorts of other issues that crop up such as health and safety, i.e., physical harm to the source, their families, yourself, fellow officers and anyone else you can think of; not forgetting legal and ethical issues, such as whether we will have to rely on the source in court to secure a conviction, and what are the chances of everyone, especially the source's, of getting through this both physically and mentally unscathed?

And, first things first (certainly from the source's perspective), are we doing enough to protect their identity?

To that end, I was meeting my source on my day off, dressed in plain clothes – I'd even gone unshaven and un-ironed my jeans, always a dead give-away that you're a cop, that, and the short, smart haircut- in a part of town a long way from Battersea, in a cafe that offered cubicle seating a stone's throw from a central train station, so nice and busy.

The intelligence we had from this informant had become so reliable that we were planning to get the Regional Crime Squad involved as we were, bit-by-bit, gradually building up a larger picture of how the drug supply network worked, up to the point of import, in other words, from the moment it entered the country.

The streets outside were busy and I people-watched, wondering about their lives. Everyone has a story. From birth to death, we all share many of life's experiences, rich or poor, privileged or deprived and we all have similar desires; whether it's a good life for our kids, a career, a degree of wealth, a secure home – and fun. We go through so much to achieve our wants and, as life tells us, sacrifices have to be made; we sacrifice time for money; boredom for progression; our own needs for our children's.

Sometimes, we have to make especially unpleasant sacrifices.

Ms Philpott, son of Ricky, the one-time pharmacy thief, took the seat in front of me.

"Sorry I'm late but couldn't just rush out, you know, not until Ricky's gone."

"I understand, of course no problem."

Ms Philpott had appreciated our efforts on the Winstanley but Ricky had emerged from a short spell in a young offender's institution even more determined to embrace criminality than when he went in, and was on his way to becoming an extremely well-connected young man, criminally speaking. He was trusted among his compatriots – a prison record always stands you in good stead in terms of criminal credibility- and was seen as someone to be relied upon should an errand need running, a favour done. Ricky was full of ambition but lacked the brains and/or experience to see it through. He had worked out, however, that undying loyalty to the cause of whomever he was serving at the time was an effective way of advancing up the ladder. He was, in effect, the archetypal 'yes' man.

Ms Philpott, who worked as an administrator for the newly-created Child Support Agency, had had enough of trying to control her son. She blamed his father, in part, rightly, for he had never shown an ounce of responsibility, and Ms Philpott could not oversee Ricky 24-7. Ricky had found father figures on the estate, even though they were only a few years older than he was. They seemed to know what they wanted and how to get it, and were certain about what was right, what was wrong and who you could trust, who you should distrust and that in this world your family were your mates and mates looked after one another.

Ricky saw his mum as a pain in the arse who wanted him to study hard, work hard and carve out a career like she had. But when Ricky was offered more money than his mum earned in a week for a few hours' work each day, running here and there, carrying packages, stashing things, bolstering numbers when certain transactions were due to take place, he couldn't say no.

Ricky didn't know what to do with the money, this thing that everyone was chasing. He had ready cash but what to spend it on? He couldn't wear his brand-new trainers most of the time, brand new designer clothes in the Winstanley labelled you for what you were, made you stand out to people like me. Ricky didn't dare offer any cash to his mum; she was not going to support *this* career, even if there was potential for advancement.

Ms Philpott first overheard Ricky talking to his mates in his room when she'd taken the afternoon off work for a doctor's appointment. It seemed as though Ricky's room had become a clubhouse of sorts during the day. This time, however, no one heard her come in, thanks to the music and, listening at the door, she read through the street talk to pick up plenty of details about what exactly Ricky had become involved with.

"I'm scared of the boy," she told me. "Since he came out of the young offender's place, he's got a lot worse. And he's so tall now. I mean physically he's a man, but with the mind of a boy, you know? I look him in the eye but I see him looking back and he's thinking there's nothing I can do to stop him doing exactly what he wants. The day is coming, believe me, when he will tell me to screw myself and I will have lost him forever. I'll read about him in the paper, for all the wrong reasons. Better for all if I act now, right?"

And then there were the other mothers, who were also neighbours. Some of them actually supported their children; they benefited financially. They were also loose-lipped with each other, unable to contain boasts about the things their sons were up to, the responsibilities they had, and the things they'd been able to buy as a result.

All Mrs Philpott had to do was listen and chip in, pretend to be part of it.

This was a big deal. If her cover was ever blown, I didn't doubt that her life would be in danger, she would have to seek help from the witness protection people and she would say goodbye to her son forever.

"I know some drugs are coming from Canada, and a shipment of cocaine is due in the next few days but I don't know where yet. I can give you names of the people supposed to collect. But the reason I'm here is because I know a load of crack and weapons are being stored at a flat on the Winstanley."

After we'd finished talking, Ms Philpott headed off; she was visiting her mother who lived in a flat in the Peabody buildings off Pimlico Road.

If it was up to me, I would have paid Ms Philpott a reward. Some high-level criminal informants make a very good living. Payments can sometimes run into the thousands, on occasion, or a participating informant might be allowed to profit from criminal enterprise to further their credibility with the criminals and increase their worth to the police. To me, Ms Philpott was worth her weight in gold. After she'd gone, Phil and I made our own ways back to the station for a debrief. When we were in a quiet corner of the canteen, I told Phil everything Ms Philpott had told me.

"So what now?" I asked when I was done.

Phil flashed his new pearly whites at me and said: "I think we need to take a look at this address, don't you?"

# CHAPTER TWENTY-THREE

# MR DRASTIC

It was the start of another hot summer's day on the Winstanley when I arrived at the little row of shops on the edge of the estate. A pair of sunburned and shaky homeless-looking alcoholics were poised in the green space just opposite the off license, anxiously awaiting opening hour so they could take advantage of the six cans of Tennent's Super for £4. This, along with Jamaican-brewed Red Stripe, was always on special offer. The shop owner knew his client base.

I knew of one alcoholic who used to stagger to this shop with the usual morning withdrawal symptoms, shaking so much that he was barely able to open the door. The shopkeepers not only happily sold him a crate of Special Brew, they would also help him down to the post office to cash his giro so he could pay his tab. His alcoholism killed him eventually but there always seemed to be a ready supply of hard-core drinkers, young and old, who couldn't get enough of that high strength lager.

As a cop, the amount of alcohol-related grief we had to deal with was extraordinary, from pub fights to domestics, to drink driving to alcohol-related trips, falls, stabbings and murders committed in what papers always described as "a drunken rage."

Although cops are no strangers to alcohol and it is used as an 'off' button by many stressed and overworked officers, one can't help but wonder whether it's simply crack by another name. A single can of high strength brew contains more alcohol than the government's recommended daily allowance – and I've never met anyone who drinks super-strength lager socially. The only people who drink it are addicts.

It was clearly a tough market for these little shops. The bookie's window was starred with the impact of a sore loser's boot, the bin outside the mini-supermarket was a blackened stump, the result of casual arson, and someone had decided to leave a stained, shiny green three-seater sofa in front of the greasy spoon. Yellow foam stuffing was blowing in the soft summer breeze, which judging from the state of the ripped cushions, arms and back of the sofa had been torn free by one of the estate's many fighting dogs.

I walked into the greasy spoon, bade the three people inside a cheery hello and bought a cup of tea to go ("Do not ever even *think* of buying food from that place," Bry had warned. "The sausages are spiced with botulism"). My plan was to visit each establishment under the pretext of performing door-to-door enquiries about a Ford Cortina that had been set alight in one of the estate car parks but my main reason was to get to Sandra in the chemists.

This was the same chemists that had been subjected to the pre-dawn burglary by Ricky Philpott and his friend Little P. The damage had long since been repaired and no raids had occurred since. I suspected there was a particular reason why.

Sandra was one of the many women dating Gary Nelson.

"Morning Sandra," I said smiling. "How's things?"

I was pleased to see that the shop, never a bustling centre of activity, was completely quiet.

"Not bad, thank you officer. And you?"

"Oh you know, the usual, fighting crime and so on. I'm just checking on the car that was set on fire near here. You heard about it?"

"Yeah, but I can't help you there. No idea who that might've been."

I looked around the chemists. Still empty.

I turned back to say something to Sandra but she beat me to it.

"Can we talk?" she said, looking serious. "But not here."

"Sure, anywhere you like."

"Somewhere we won't be seen. And not in that getup."

***

"Babe, help me out; you're a chemist aren't you?"

The words that changed Sandra's life – and not for the better.

At first, the extra money it brought in was most welcome and the work was easy. But it developed into a full-time job, on top of the job Sandra was already doing. And by then it was too late; she had to do what she was told and keep her mouth shut, otherwise...

Supervising the cooking of crack and breaking it down into different weights was not the kind of job one 'fell into' but Sandra had fallen for Gary when they met at a night club. At first she thought it was love.

She supervised two other girls who did the smashing up of the rocks and wrapped the measured weights in clingfilm. This set up was often repeated. The girls cut the drugs and the boys handled deliveries.

"It was like how I imagine work in a lab to be like," Sandra said. "Quiet, monotonous and you don't talk shit."

The girls worked in near silence under the casual but constant supervision of two men who lived in the flat, who toyed with their handguns and rolled joints in between playing video games and watching TV, one eye on the production line.

"Gary came along at the right moment, well the wrong moment maybe," Sandra told me when we met in a cafe in a park north of the river. "Mum had died, cancer; she and Dad had split up and he'd never been around much in the first place. I was lonely and I just wanted to have some fun, you know, get out of it and all that.

"I fell for him like a bomb," Sandra said. "Good looking, strong, rich and he lived the attitude 'live for the moment for tomorrow we may die'. Who wants to live to get old? All that kind of stuff. I wanted to be with a bad boy and I knew he was into shit but I didn't know just how bad he was and how far he planned to go."

I'd often wondered what motivated ambitious criminals like Nelson. There was money and power to be had and he was good at getting it but what drove him? Sandra didn't know either.

"Some warped masculine psychopathology shit going on there you know? But I liked it. I liked the fact he was a bad boy and I liked the fact that going out with him gave me power. I thought no one can touch me – not that anyone ever did before but, living here, there was a fear that one day something might happen and with Gary that fear was gone. Word soon spreads."

"But then came that favour which became a career. It never even came from Gary. He never talked about what he did. It was associates of his, the crowd we mixed with. I carried bags, hid them in my flat. I never looked inside them but I knew they contained drugs and weapons."

I thought of my encounter with Gary and Chen in the New Covent Garden Market.

"I didn't ever think about the cops. It was like you guys didn't exist, you were so far from Gary and his underworld you just didn't seem real. And if you'd caught me, I would've said nothing and done the time. That's how much I loved the man. And he wouldn't have come to see me in prison but I would have said that was because of course someone like him couldn't come somewhere like here.

"Now I know he can suss out a girl faster than you can tie your shoelaces. I never loved him. I might have thought I did but he was just there at the wrong time in my life, he tapped into my psychology. And then I started to see less and less of him which made me want to see him more and more and made me insist to myself that he loved me, that he was just too busy to be with me, he was doing gangster shit, building the empire and I was a key part of that. I eventually realised that this was as good as it was going to get, there was no palace in which I would live with my prince at the end of the rainbow. But then it was too late. I didn't realise how deep I'd gone until it was too late. The 'job' became hell on earth."

Sandra was absorbed in her task one day when she looked up to see that one of the men had raised his handgun and was pointing it at her. He smiled and pulled the trigger. It wasn't loaded.

"He said something like, 'You ever fuck us over, then we'll blow your brains out.' Those idiots are on some stupid power trip. Girls show up at the door and offer their bodies to them in return for crack all the time. And these guys are just the most disgusting men you'd never want to be around, let alone touch."

"I know too much for them to let me go. I want to leave but it's going to take something drastic. So that's where you come in. You're my Mr Drastic.

"I know everything about everyone in this area. I know who's selling, who's got the guns and I know which addresses you should hit and when. I only know to come to you because of those other raids. I saw them and thought 'I'm either going to end up dead or in jail.'

"You hit all that at the right place and the right time, his empire is gone, the stupid assholes will be too busy worrying about their business and trying to stay out of jail to bother about little old me.

"But you better watch it cause these boys are bad. They're always talking about how they dragged rivals from their cars and beat them up. They're deadly enemies with everyone and they'll stab, shoot, break, burn and bite their way through any enemy, whatever it takes. They've trained pitbulls to bite people and those beasts don't let go once they've got their teeth into you."

"I'm more worried about you than us," I said.

"I got some money saved. I'm going to get on a bus out of town to somewhere a long way away from here and I'm never, ever going to come back. Just being somewhere else is going to be the greatest feeling in the world. I might even go abroad. I'll get another job easily enough. Then I'll start studying. Find a way to get to university. A fresh start. Clean break. And you, Mr Drastic, are going to make that happen for me. Just don't expect me to testify or nothin' like that."

She passed me a piece of paper. "There's two addresses. The first one is the lab. The second one is the where all the action takes place. That's where you'll find the drugs and the dealers, and maybe even Gary."

I looked down and had to stifle a shout of triumph. The second address was the same as the one we had from Ms Philpott. Corroboration, fan-bloody-tastic.

"You don't want to be there when we go in," I said.

"You just tell me when I shouldn't be there and I'll vanish in a puff of magic pixie dust."

***

A few days later, at 4.30am I was in standing in front of Penethorne House on the Winstanley. With me were two representatives from SO19, the Met's firearms team. They'd brought two specialist officers with them. Suffice it to say, they were ex-SBS (the army's world-famous Special Boat Squadron).

We had a problem. The target flat was deep in the Winstanley, on the fifth floor of Penethorne House, at the end of a corridor. This was another unfortunate side-effect of the estate system, in that they had unintentionally created impenetrable fortresses in the sky as far as the police and drug dealers were concerned. With lifts only big enough for four at a time and narrow stairwells and corridors, it was impossible to get to the door without those inside knowing well in advance.

As Chief Inspector Hugh had said: "If our intelligence tells us they have guns, then we need armed officers and the element of surprise. Without both of those factors I won't authorise a raid of any kind."

On top of this, the door was reinforced with steel plates and the so-called New York latch, which made it almost impenetrable. The Ghostbusters, specialists in door demolition were scratching their heads as to how to solve it.

"Even with hydraulic jacks we can only break the frame," they told us. "If the steel door is held in place by a metal bar fixed to a plate drilled into a concrete floor, well, it's going to take forever to get in, and bang goes your element of surprise."

They talked about using explosives but, concerned they would do a Michael Caine in the film the *Italian Job* and blow the whole block up rather than just the 'bloody doors,' we racked our brains trying to think of a smart way in.

And then one of the SO19 guys mentioned the ex-SBS officers: "They could abseil from the top of the block and go through the windows," he said. "It's a standard SAS/SBS move. They've done it a hundred times."

And now we were checking the possibilities an hour before the crack of dawn, so as not to be spotted.

"I think we can do it," the taller of the two former SBS men said. He was extremely broad, with huge chest and shoulders but spoke like Prince Charles. He radiated the kind of confidence that only SBS soldiers can.

"Are you sure?" I asked, "It's a long way up."

The flat was about a hundred feet from the ground and about thirty feet from the roof.

"There's only one way to find out."

He walked up to the side of the block to where there was a gap about four-feet wide between two parallel exterior walls that divided the block into two sections. He jumped and, using only his hands and feet, left and right on opposite walls, he quickly started to climb while I watched, open-mouthed. One slip and he was dead but as his compatriot said: "If we're going to abseil from the roof, we need to know the lay of the land first."

"I could've got the keys from the caretaker and we could have gone up another time," I said. "All he had to do was ask."

"Saves time this way, and he's going to check for any obstacles that will interfere with the overhang and the abseil."

He quickly reached the top and then in a movement that nearly caused me to cry out in surprise, he pushed and jumped from the gap so that he had both hands over the roof's edge and pulled himself up in one smooth, easy movement (at least that's how it looked) and swung himself onto the roof.

He came down the same way about two minutes later. Back on terra firma, I noticed he was barely sweating.

"Let's do it," he said. "It's the kind of operation we live for. I checked the roof and there's air vents up there that will support us no problem. We'll start prepping things our end but it'd be great if you could sort access to the roof with the caretaker's key so we can get our gear up there the night before."

We shook hands and, as we went our separate ways I couldn't help but wonder at the thought that if you'd told me a year earlier that I would soon plan and be part of a raid on a crack house inhabited by the UK's most dangerous man, with both cops, criminals and the SBS all armed to the teeth, and that the SBS would kick things off by abseiling through the windows carrying MP5 Heckler and Koch machine-guns after detonating flash-bangs, then I would – most definitely – not have believed it.

The next thing we needed to do was observe. Mark and I had made this into something of a speciality but now the whole shift got involved. The key thing was to not to let too many people know what we were up to. Some police officers are habitual gossips and tell their families the gory details of operations they're involved in, and this leads to gossip at football grounds, the school playgrounds and coffee mornings and before you know it, the wrong person has overheard. I noticed that there was an empty flat in the block opposite Penethorne House with a view of our target property and wanted to get my hands on the keys so we could use it for observations but wasn't keen on alerting the caretaker, who seemed like she could keep a secret, but you never knew. The only other approach meant going through the council, which I also felt was hazardous so, in the end, we set up an operation where we pretended to be from British Gas. The flat needed a new boiler and pipes, we said and we received the keys and had a cover story to boot. Once night fell we took it turns to sit in the dark, eyes on the primary target, watching the comings and goings, trying to get some sort of insight into what was going on. The water tank of another block gave a view of the front door and Mark and I watched from up there.

It was a huge joint effort, which we ran alongside all our regular policing duties. We spotted Nelson, Chen and Lips, among many others, all of them nasty lads. They parked their cars some distance away and swaggered to the flat, a rather sad attempt at counter-surveillance.

We took down registration numbers of all the cars and when Pete checked with the Flying Squad and the Regional Crime

Squad (RCS), they all came up as belonging to persons of interest for everything from shootings to robbery, from GBH to drug dealing. Everyone wanted a piece of what was going to be a huge operation.

Because of the dangers, I didn't think we'd get the go-ahead but the powers that be were so desperate to take out South London's new kingpins, they gave us the green light after three weeks of observations. We were going in.

# CHAPTER TWENTY-FOUR

# STRIKEBACK

**3**.30am and the entire shift held their collective breath as nine officers from SO19 crept quickly up to the roof via the stairs. The slightest noise would have spelled the operation's doom.

I'd barely slept for the past two nights but felt wide awake, no sign of fatigue at all when I arrived at my hiding place to spend yet another six hours watching the flat. I was eyes on as SO19 ascended. Silence reigned over the Winstanley and although a single light was on inside the target flat, this was normal. No one ever switched it off. We didn't know why. Maybe someone there was scared of the dark.

'Well, if they take a look outside now,' I thought, 'they'll get a bloody fright, right enough.'

A whispered call confirmed that SO19 were completing the last stage of their climb via the fire escape and a minute later they were in position. Now they had a long day's wait ahead of them. Their plan was to spend the night and all of following day up there, until the late evening, when the strike would take place – at a time when the flat would hopefully be at its busiest.

I couldn't wait. At the same time, I was full of dread with all the possible outcomes and thoughts of what might go wrong.

Earlier that day I'd bumped into Bruce, the forensics officer and he'd asked so many questions about the op that by the time we parted company my head was spinning. He was planning to come equipped with two back up officers, including a specialist fingerprint officer and, he added, with a chuckle that he would come 'armed' with as many forensic firearms kits as he could carry, in case it all 'kicked off'.

"With so many guns knocking about, it pays to be ready," he said.

Then, during a briefing at Clapham (briefings for big operations like this never took place at the local nick, to prevent leaks), one of the firearms officers who was going to abseil down the side of the building said to me that he'd "never done this sort of thing before," but that "it should be interesting."

They'd all had experience abseiling down buildings and swinging through windows in training exercises but of course, as I was rapidly realising, this operation included a number of firsts, and not just for me and Mark.

The TSG were planning to create a diversion at the front door once the attack began, to wrong-foot the criminals inside. The Ghostbusters, who were civilians, council workers from Wandsworth, were up for it. In a way, they would be in the safest place as they would never actually get through the door, they would just jack the frame and then one of the abseiling SO19 officers would release the New York latch from the inside, letting in the TSG, who would provide 'overwhelming support', in case any criminals were foolish enough to try and kick off. The TSG would then start removing any prisoners from the property, by which time Bruce would already be trying to connect people to any drugs, cash and/or guns that might have been discarded.

The plan was for three abseilers to drop with crowbars, smash the windows, shout "Police!" and toss the flash-bangs. They would 'stand' aside, being immediately followed by the next three armed abseilers (their MP5's set to single fire) to swing straight through the broken windows first and, all being well, secure the property and let in the TSG. Two of the SO19 officers would stay on the roof in case of any problems with the equipment, and would remove all of their gear once the raid was over.

"Sounds simple enough to me," Pete said upon hearing the plan.

"Easy for you to say," Foxy answered, "Especially from the safety of your broom-cupboard."

***

And suddenly, it was 10pm and the raid was about to happen. I was eyes on the property and felt a huge surge of adrenaline as I received word that the convoy was finally rumbling through the streets of Battersea. I was proud to be part of this unit, to be a small piece of this powerful machine that was about to show – at long last – just what it was capable of. We were the biggest gang in London and that night we were going to show the criminals that we would stop at nothing to take them down.

And best of all, Nelson was inside. Perhaps his luck had at last run out.

The convoy held back as we neared the estate and waited until the three abseilers were in position. It was truly surreal, seeing three dark shadows drop quietly off the balcony and sail past people's windows; my heart was in my mouth, I was worried they might end up outside the wrong flat but soon enough they were outside the right address, five floors up from the ground.

Just before they'd started their descent, the two Ghosties, supported by four TSG officers, had driven into the car park in an unmarked van. A couple of people were about, but they didn't seem to notice the black figures as they climbed out of the van and jogged up the stairs with their equipment.

We were seconds away now. I waited, waited, waited. I couldn't see the stairwell but I could see the balcony and it felt like they were taking forever to arrive.

And then the door to the flat opened, a figure stepped out and ambled along the balcony walkway to the fire door that opened onto the landing where the lifts and stairs were – and where the Ghosties and the TSG had to be by now.

"What's the hold up?" one of the SO19 officers hissed over the radio.

"Someone's come out of the flat, standby," I whispered back.

The figure opened the fire door and stepped out of my sight and onto the landing. Another moment and the Ghosties appeared, followed by three TSG officers. They must have nicked him and the fourth TSG officer was holding on to him. I would have loved to have seen his face when he stepped out onto the landing and walked into two dozen police officers in helmets and body armour.

I wanted to be there with them, on the front line and would have gladly swapped places. It was at this point that I realised I really wanted to join the TSG, it was the most exciting job going, the sharp end of policing.

Then the Ghosties and the three TSG officers quickly moved along the balcony until they reached the target door; the Ghosties knelt down and prepped their equipment.

"In position."

"GOGOGO!"

And the night exploded. The blast at the door was, seconds later, followed by the sound of breaking glass, cries of POLICE! Followed by the flashbangs going through the windows. The three abseilers, legs bracing them against the wall, dropped until they were under the windows and suddenly the next three were there, they slid at breathtaking speed and swung in almost perfect synchronicity through the windows, one hand on the rope, the other on their MP5s, and they were in. Anyone inside who'd reacted to the door would now be completely thrown by the flashbangs and the impossible appearance of armoured armed officers at the fifth floor windows.

More screams followed, male and female; lights were coming on around the estate, dogs were barking; was that the sound of one in the flat? I had binoculars; I pressed my binoculars to my eyes so hard it hurt. The Ghosties had retreated and downstairs, the rest of the police convoy had driven in at speed and the entire shift, led by another troop of TSG officers was piling out, while the TSG team upstairs were waiting, waiting, waiting and then finally, the door flew open and they were in, amid more shouting and screaming. A few minutes later, I decided to release myself from my position as the operation's 'eyeball' and started to run to the scene.

As I jogged up the five flights of stairs, I was fit to burst with excitement. Had it worked? Was everyone safe? What had we found? What about Nelson?

"All clear! Prisoners under control," came over the radio.

I found Nelson calmly sitting in an armchair, hands in plasticuffs, trademark sneer on his face.

I tried to catch my breath so I sounded casual when I spoke.

"Alright Gary?" I said, "Don't wear out that sneer now."

The flat was, as one might expect, a mess. Glass covered the floor; a barefooted prisoner was bleeding from his feet; two of the TSG officers were trying to stop the bleeding and dress the wound.

There were thirteen prisoners in total. Three women, ten men (no dogs). Two of the 'men' looked as though they were under eighteen.

"She was still smoking crack when I grabbed her," one of the TSG officers told me pointing at the young woman. Nothing terribly unusual about that, addicts sometimes try to take everything they can if they're facing imminent arrest, but the shocking thing in this case was the fact that this young woman was several months pregnant.

The flat stank of stale sweat, damp and crack.

"Someone open a window," Bruce quipped, stepping over glass from the broken windows. "It bloody reeks in here!"

One of the women, who was in her late 20s, was kicking off, trying to resist arrest, spitting in the face of the cop who was trying to restrain her, so I stepped over to hold her arms while he got the cuffs secured. The other woman, also in her mid- twenties, was quiet; she'd peed herself from sheer terror. The men, in various stages of intoxication sat in sullen silence, a silence they were determined to maintain.

I went to join Bruce, who was in full forensics mode.

"Anything?"

"Two imitation firearms, a chunk of heroin, not massive, a few rocks of crack, again not a lot. Looks like there's a few more bits lying on the carpet. Needs a proper search now."

While SO19 were delighted with the operation, I had mixed feelings. I was over the moon that we had safely shut down this particular operation but this was only disruption – it wasn't an end to drug dealing on the estate, not by a long shot.

And Nelson knew better than to carry anything that could incriminate him. As all the drugs were on the floor and because the flat wasn't his, ultimately, although we nicked him along with everyone else, Nelson was bailed and then released.

But for now, it was pats on the back all round as the operation had gone smoothly and safely; we had shown the public we were taking action of the most extreme kind and word would spread among the criminals that they had good reason to fear us; there was nowhere we would not go, no one we wouldn't challenge. We were tackling organised crime head on and it felt to me like this would be the raid we would look back upon as the moment we started to turn the tables.

The following weekend, we went out to celebrate, a day at the races in Epsom, Surrey. We ate, drank and got merry as we let off a lot of steam after a long, tense surveillance operation. The job had truly become my life, my obsession. I rarely went home to Yorkshire and on those few occasions I did, I rarely talked about what I was doing in London with my other family.

At the end of our day at the races, I started to wonder if we'd really achieved all that much. Teamwork, ok yes, but we hadn't been able to connect Nelson to any crimes and he was still free, still doing god knows what to maintain the power he so desperately craved. Now his reputation was even greater. Even cops armed with machine guns hadn't managed to nick him. It seemed as though he was truly untouchable.

*** 

A few weeks later, a postcard arrived in my pigeonhole at the station. On the front was a picture of a lavender field and a big, blue sky. The message was short and made me smile:

Safe.

S. x.

# PART FIVE

One of the usual addresses. Domestic violence in the Black Prince Road.

We see him and we know what he's done. He knows what he's done. He is on the hallway floor, his head is in his hands and he is quiet, not sobbing as you might expect, just very still, as if meditating.

There are two sentences for this crime. The first is prison. The second is a lifetime of regret trapped in the kingdom of your skull; drugs and alcohol won't set you free, even for a moment, they'll just take you to places you don't want to go.

But what can we do?

Two women a week are killed by a violent partner. 104 women a year. 2,080 women in my police career.

The woman's body lies in the kitchen, on the floor, her torso pressed into the corner, between two cupboards. She is thirty years old. She is emaciated. Her skull is cracked. Blood is on the countertop and covers her face. Her eyes are closed and her jaw has fallen open. There is alcohol everywhere. The mess of dinner on the walls and on the floor. The smell of food, alcohol and death.

Did he isolate you? Was he jealous? Did he make you feel loved? How did he insult you? He criticized everything you did and yet – you said – you still loved him. You even defended him to us.

He knew your weak points. He knew you thought you needed him but he knew that you did not. He had to hit you to remind you that he was in charge. He shoved you, squeezed your arms; I remember the finger mark bruises you forgot to hide. But then he'd apologise, say he was sorry, that he loved you and would never do it again and then things were ok, until he thought you were getting above yourself and he threatened your family, told you he knew people who would make accidents happen. He controlled everything. His mood switched like lightning, Prince Charming one moment, the Black Prince the next. He took your money, sent you to the shops for beers and chips and timed you to the second. Be late and the Black Prince would be waiting, even if it wasn't your fault, even if there was a queue at the chippy. You tried, you did whatever you could to keep him calm, even things that you once loved that later disgusted you. It got so you couldn't think for yourself anymore. Booze helped; hit the pain where it hurt, when he let you drink, when he wanted you to drink, which was another kind of horror. He destroyed your nice things; your clothes and knick-knacks from your mother (he sold your good jewellery a long time ago), and smashed the furniture. He tried to kill that cat you befriended. He liked to scare you, would push you into the road and pull you back again, so the cars just missed you. He'd lock you out, lock you in; tell you how to dress, how your hair should look, then that you should do something different but not tell you what and every decision would be wrong, wrong, wrong.

I know because it was written in your face, your home, your body.

It was written in his face, his breath and his voice.

And we saw it for ourselves. We would come

And yet there was nothing we could do. You wouldn't press charges. You always stuck by him. Stand by your man, as the song goes.

The boiler clicks into life above you. It's cold.

The lights are spinning and we're here now. We're all here.

# CHAPTER TWENTY-FIVE

## AMATEUR DRAMATICS

Summer had ended with a raft of storms in the middle of August, which I'd spent on leave in Yorkshire, and I returned to work to find Battersea in a much colder climate than when I'd left it.

I started on nights and was wearing jumper and jacket when I left the canteen to join Patters in one of the marked Sierras.

"Hurry up Pannett!" he yelled. "Burglary in progress!"

I ran across the car park. Back to work with a bang.

By the time we were close to the scene, we were told that the burglars, two black youths, had not only escaped the property with cash, jewellery and electronics, they'd also fled in the house owner's BMW after finding the distinctive car key ring lying on a hallway table.

Patters stopped driving and parked up.

"Shouldn't we be driving about?" I asked.

Patters looked at me disdainfully. "Have you learned nothing Pannett? Tell me what street we're on."

"Black Prince Road."

"At the junction of?"

"Kennington Park Road and Kennington Lane."

"They were last seen driving from the scene of the crime in a southerly direction. So if they're going any distance at all, it's very likely they'll come through this junction." Patters paused for a moment before adding: "And here they come."

A silver BMW shot through the junction, turning right into Lambeth Road, losing a hub cap as it clipped the kerb of a traffic island. The hub shot past us as Patters spun the wheels of the Sierra and let loose our clarion call.

Being in a high-speed car chase is a surreal experience. Cars are dangerous enough when one sticks to the rules and obeys the speed limits but when you're hurtling along the Old Kent Road at sixty miles an hour on a Thursday evening, well the stakes are significant to say the least, especially when our prey, obviously fancying himself as an expert driver, pulls a handbrake turn which, I have to admit, was done professionally enough – (turn wheel, pull handbrake a second later with the clutch down, release and into first the moment you're facing the direction you want to go and floor it before the car's stopped moving – and he executed an extremely sharp right turn, catching Patters out, forcing him to pull right and brake so hard that I found myself thrown up against him.

"What the fuck are you doing Pannett?" Patters said through gritted teeth, as I fought a hopeless battle against the forces of gravity.

"Smmmghph!" was all I could manage with my face was pressed into Patters' shoulder.

We came about in the side street but had lost ground to the BMW, so Patters pressed pedal to metal while I called in our position and, by the time we'd reached the end of the street, we were joined by India 99, one of the Met's helicopters. Other units were scrambling to form roadblocks while, for now at least, the tight-lipped Patters remained the solo pursuit car.

Patters had been a bit of a closed book to me. In fact, he was the kind of book that turns up in *Night of the Living Dead* – with a large padlock and chain and an evil face that screams "Do Not Open!" As far as I'd been able to tell, he was all about The Job and nothing else.

Even though he came along to our day at the races, it was as if he had come under duress, as if he were doing his duty rather than joining his friends on a fun day out. He reminded me of Judge Dredd, the justice-obsessed cartoon character, in that dispensing the law was his life (and they had the same square jaw). And although I'd only been at Battersea for a few short years, I knew Patters as well as the next man, for he revealed nothing about himself and only ever talked about the job.

Despite a series of handbrake turns (they were proving to be somewhat of a speciality of our car thief's) and some dangerous driving that made it clear that these lads were desperate to get away, were prepared to do anything in fact, Patters, old stony-face, managed to close the gap until we were in Peckham and our nose was on their rear bumper.

"Standby Pannett, that big roundabout up ahead, I'm going to PIT stop him."

"PIT? What the hell's that?"

"Pannett, you need to start paying more attention. Precision Immobilization Technique, or Pursuit Intervention Technique. Some call it a TVI."

"TVI?"

"Tactical Vehicle Intervention. Personally, I like to call it the Tombstone. It'll earn me nine points but I think it's worth it in this instance."

"The Tomb-?"

At that moment Patters moved left and then accelerated as we approached the roundabout and started to nudge the BMW before the driver had had a chance to think about making a handbrake turn and, for a moment, I felt the resistance of the BMW against our Sierra and thought we were about to lose control but instead Patters held his course straight and true while the BMW skidded, turned 180 degrees and ended up facing us, and we were nose to nose as the driver of the BMW found reverse and started to drive backwards with Patters still on his nose, now pushing him; I locked eyes with the passenger of the other car and I think we looked equally terrified as I heard screaming over the radio, the chopper overhead, the sound of crunching metal, squealing tyres, screaming engines and then an almighty bang as the BMW hit a black cab that had just pulled out of a side street and we came to a stalling halt. All doors flew open at once and I went after the driver while Patters went for the passenger. I had managed to leap out of the car that bit quicker and threw myself after the thief in a rugby tackle, catching one leg and we both came crashing down in the middle of the road. My quarry immediately kicked to get away; I'd lost my grip in the fall and his boot connected with my face, snapping my glasses in two; I tried to grab hold of his legs again but he kicked again and this time my nose crunched under the impact and I let go; we struggled to our feet and the thief started to run but by now furious, I caught one of his shoulders and let him have a couple of solid blows to the kidneys, pushing him into the side of a parked car.

"I give up! I give up!" the lad cried as I twisted one of his arms behind him. "You want the other guy, he's fucking mad; I would have stopped sooner but he made me drive with a knife to my throat!"

A moment later we were joined by another Sierra, crewed by two blokes from Peckham.

"Can you take this one?" I asked. "My mate's gone after the other lad and might need some help. This one says he's got a knife."

"No problem mate," one of the men said, broadcasting this update over the radio as I ran off to find Patters and the car's passenger, not really having any idea where they might be, until I noticed that the helicopter was hovering about a hundred metres to my right, its searchlight pointing straight down. I sprinted towards it, knowing Patters was facing a crazed man on his own.

They were locked in a struggle when I arrived, Patters was trying to hold onto the boy and I could see the shine of the knife blade reflecting the street lights as the boy swung it back and forth, aiming it at Patters who was trying to dodge out of the way.

"OI! POLICE! STOP!" I yelled, hoping this would persuade the lad that reinforcements had arrived and it was now time to cease and desist but, to my horror, this only led to the intensification of the knife movement but still Patters would not let go. I dug in and sprinted for all I was worth and threw myself at the lad, pulling his arms behind him, allowing Patters to get in one, solid knockout blow. The lad was suddenly a dead weight in my arms and I quickly lowered him to the ground. Sirens signalled the sound of reinforcements, called to our location by the chopper. I looked up at Patters who was standing just in front of me, breathing heavily.

"You alright?" I asked. It was only then that I noticed the glint of the knife's hilt poking out of his side, about halfway up his midriff.

"Shit! Patters, you've been stabbed mate!"

Patters looked down. His arms and hands were a bloody mess of small cuts and scratches, inflicted as the knifeman had carved his knife back and forth trying to force Patters to release his stubborn grip.

Patters stayed standing as I left the lad on the floor and ran over to him. Unable to think of anything else to say I asked "Does it hurt?"

Patters shook his head. "I don't know Pannett. No, not really. Can't feel anything in fact." He looked down at the knife. "I've never even been stabbed before," he added, and then reached into his jacket, where the knife had gone in.

"Don't!" I yelled. "You'll make it worse!"

"It's alright Mike," Patters said, sighing with relief as he grabbed the hilt with his right hand, "I'm fine, look."

He removed the knife, then, from the inside of his coat pocket, he removed a thin paperback book and held it out to me. There was a hole where the knife had entered it.

"Bloody hell!" I said. "I thought you were done for then!"

I looked more closely at the book. It was a copy of *A Midsummer Night's Dream*.

Patters took a seat on the curb, while I went to check on our prisoner, who was still dazed but nevertheless trying to coordinate his limbs in order to get away.

"What are you doing with that book anyway?"

"Amateur dramatics," Patters replied with a small embarrassed laugh. "I'm playing Puck in our local production."

***

Just a couple of miles from where I was doing my best to absorb the fact that Patters was a keen amateur actor, an altercation was about to take place.

Builders who drive white vans are not known for their patience in traffic, especially in London. Gary Kewell was no exception and he had grown increasingly exasperated by the midnight-blue BMW in front of him that had slowed to a crawl at every junction. There was no room to overtake and Kewell drew close to the car's rear bumper. He could see a couple in the car; a man was driving and a woman was in the passenger seat; they seemed to be having an animated conversation.

Kewell flashed his lights at the BMW and was met with a series of obscene gestures from both occupants. He then beeped his horn. At this point he could see the couple looking back him, exchanging heated words. And then the driver gave him the finger. Kewell started to feel uneasy; something told him that it might be a good idea to leave them to it. A right turn was coming up, so he decided to take it and switched on his indicator.

Glancing back at the car he saw the woman reach down into the footwell and hand something to the driver, who stopped the car and leaned out of the window, turning to face Kerwell. There was a flash of light, followed by a rapid cracking sound and Kerwell ducked behind his dashboard as a whole series of bangs followed in quick succession.

Then he heard the BMW's engine rev and then accelerate away. A moment later, Kerwell, shaking with shock, looked up to see the BMW disappearing around a corner. He climbed out and saw half-a-dozen bullet holes in his bonnet and radiator and called the police.

The shooter, we would later find out, was Gary Nelson.

# CHAPTER TWENTY-SIX

# CRIMINOMICS

Today, we know that crack addicts need to make about (conservatively speaking) £100 a day to pay for their drugs, so have to find £30–40k a year to fund their habit. Many do this through street robbery and burglary.

Heroin is a slow-release drug. The 'hit' – which puts most users into a stupor – lasts for several hours and so addicts only have to 'work' once or twice a day to find the cash they need for their next fix. Many heroin addicts rely on burglary, which takes time. You have to find a suitable property, wait until the right moment and then, once you have the goods, you have to find someone to sell them to, or find a dealer prepared to accept stolen goods in return for drugs.

Crack is far more addictive than heroin and the effects wear off after just a few minutes, so the addiction demands that users earn their cash quickly. With the rise in crack use, we were seeing a corresponding rise in street muggings and cashpoint robberies (where victims were robbed once they'd entered their pin, or were even escorted at knifepoint to a cash machine to withdraw cash,), which could be committed quickly, with instantaneous cash results.

Some crack addicts don't have the bottle for street robbery and prefer the non-confrontational act of burglary. This requires far more work. Brand new items can be sold for about one-third of their market value. Used items go for about one-fifth. So the average addict (who relies on burglary to fund their addiction) has to steal at least £150,000 worth of goods every year.

It's hard to know just how many heroin/crack addicts there are in the UK but according to Statistics for drug treatment in England 2013–14 from the National Drug Treatment Monitoring System (NDTMS), around 200,000 crack/heroin users sought treatment that year. Even if only half of these people had previously funded their addiction through crime – it's probably more – how many crack addicts do you know that can maintain a job, let alone a career while feeding their habit?-, then each year they're stealing enough goods to repay the national debt.

Going after burglars is time consuming and expensive. But, even though the underlying cause behind the rise in burglary might have been the rise of crack, we couldn't simply put all our resources into taking out drug dealers and let burglars get away with their crimes in the meantime.

Informants had led us to target one such crack-addicted burglar called Henry. Henry, who was white and in his mid-twenties, had perfected his own unique system. He didn't confine his targets to one area, or anywhere local, but struck anywhere he found a likely looking house during one of his scouting missions, usually somewhere on the outskirts of London, but within the M25.

We started watching his home address to build up a basic idea of his movements. Henry, who lived in a bedsit not far from Battersea High Street, was out every other night (no doubt on burgling missions) and spent the rest of the time in his flat taking crack. It soon became clear to us that Henry was an organised fellow. Every time he embarked on a fresh crack binge, he prepared by taking a trip to the local supermarket where he stocked up on various items, usually bottled water, juices, vodka, biscuits, bread and burgers. He also bought a lot of cleaning fluid. It turned out, as we watched Henry, that he liked nothing more than to clean his bedsit when he was high. We saw him marching vigorously back and forth with his Hoover in regular and ever decreasing circles.

On the nights he went to 'work', he emerged from his bedsit at about 11pm, a ghostly pale thin figure. It was a good time to go unnoticed; the pubs were closing and the streets and tubes were busy enough so that he didn't stand out.

After a few days watching, we were cleared to follow Henry to try and catch him in the act. I tried this with Mark at first but were foiled when Henry doubled back shortly after leaving his bedsit, walking back upon himself, scrutinising every face in the street. I was about fifty metres behind Henry and near a side street, so I immediately ducked down it, while Mark, who was in an unmarked car facing in the other direction and watching via the mirrors, drove away.

We soon found out that Henry performed this criminal's version of "What's-the-Time-Mr-Wolf?" several times in the early stages of his journey. Mark and I kept well back and we made it as far as Stockwell Underground Station before Henry caught us out by ducking back out of the train carriage at the last moment, so we left with the train, leaving Henry safe to carry on with his night's work.

We returned with reinforcements in the form of Foxy and Trist and between the four of us we followed him to Bromley train station's car park. Foxy was eyes-on, with Mark and I close by in support, and she watched as Henry, constantly check-ing around him, searched the car park until he found a vehicle he liked the look of, which in this case was an old Ford estate, jammed a key into the door and popped it open. Moments later, Henry drove away, but Foxy radioed Trist, who was trained in surveillance driving, and who'd chased the train to Bromley in an unmarked Astra. The three of us jumped in the Astra as Trist began to follow Henry. He held as far back as he dared, letting Henry take turnings far ahead of us before racing to catch up, to make sure he hadn't slipped away, all the time conscious of the fact that Henry might have parked up somewhere to try and catch out anyone following him.

"I've never known anyone so paranoid," Trist said. "Better contact the station Mike," he added. "We're letting Henry commit criminal acts right under our nose."

We needed permission from a senior officer to allow Henry to continue to drive the stolen car; otherwise we were duty bound to arrest him. Permission duly given, we followed Henry to Orpington, where he checked out a number of detached houses before driving home, parking the Ford a few streets away from his bedsit.

The following night he returned to the car and, after he'd driven around in circles a few times – yet more efforts at counter surveillance – we followed him back to Orpington, to one of the houses he'd checked out the previous night. It was a large house without an alarm and with original bay windows, so no double glazing. The front door was also original, with four glass panels in the top half. Henry approached the door, cut four lines, making a square, fixed a suction cup, tapped the glass and removing a fist-sized section. He then reached inside and opened the door, which was only secured by its Yale lock, and not the mortise – many people don't bother with this deadlock at night- and stepped into the house.

Presumably, Henry could also have cut through the bay windows, but these had window locks, although these could be forced with a 'shaved' key. Henry had used a shaved key on the old Ford, which had a basic key system, as opposed to more modern vehicles. You file down a certain key type and then, with a bit of jiggling and a firm hand it's possible to force certain lock types.

Henry vanished into the house and set about removing cash, jewellery, antiques and electronic goods, loading the car until it's suspension sagged. Soon, he was ready to leave.

We'd spent this time arguing amongst ourselves.

"We should follow him to where he takes the goods," I said.

"Better not Mike," Trist warned. "If we lose him then the homeowners might never see their possessions again."

"But if we lose him we could pick him up at home," Foxy said.

"It's much easier to prove in court if we catch him bang to rights, here and now," Trist said. "I'm confident we'll be able to get him to talk once his cravings kick in."

When Henry tried to leave he found the driveway blocked by our unmarked Astra. Henry immediately leapt out of the Ford and turned to run back towards the house but Trist was already behind him.

"I don't think so, old boy," he said. "Better come quietly, don't you think?"

Realising he was well and truly busted, Henry sagged and did as he was told.

Henry wasn't a 'bad' man in the sense that he didn't want to hurt anyone, knew what he was doing was wrong and even went as far as saying he felt sorry for his victims. His life was a long hard luck story and his descent into crack addiction was as rapid as it was catastrophic. He'd been with his girlfriend, Sarah, for seven years and they had a child, a son, aged three when the crack took hold.

"We were deadly skint," Henry told us, "Just a jar of no frills peanut butter with the merest smidgen left inside. That was all the food we had. But I'd done some painting work, painting the outside of a house, cash-in-hand job and was due to get paid. So I swore to them I'd be back with the money. Sarah made it clear that this was absolutely my last chance, point of no return because I'd done this sort of thing before, disappeared with my pay on a binge, but now we were at the point where we literally had not a bean to rub together. Starvation was nigh. So I was absolutely determined that under no circumstances whatsoever was I going to fuck up and not bring home the bacon. But that was before Chippie, who'd done the painting job with me, showed up to get paid and came armed with a rock, which he offered to share. I thought was mighty generous, and so we smoked it right there and then at the house. I mean why not? It wasn't costing me or my family anything but then I thought I'd better get some, so that it's fair for Chippie, after all a £10 bag out of £300 I'd earned for the house-painting is nothing, right? Plus, yes, I'd get a bit more high. So we went and got some and had a hit of another £10 rock and the next thing I know I'm standing in the flat, an unwashed, trembling, gurning mess in the throes of a painful comedown, Sarah and boy are gone and I'm looking at an empty jar of peanut butter sitting on the crumb-less kitchen worktop crying my eyes out. I wanted to go to rehab but the only thing that works for me is more of that stuff. That's when I decided to change my life but not for the good, just for the crack. Set it up. Do the burglaries, sell the gear, buy the crack and so on. I thought if I was careful I wouldn't get caught. That's the only reason people get caught at this game, because they're careless, isn't it? So what gave me away?"

"Your greed," Foxy said simply.

"If you help us," Trist said, "Then maybe we can make it clear that you did all you could to help clear up your own crimes, regret what you did and you would be prepared to enter into a court-ordered drugs rehabilitation programme with the full and honest intention of kicking your habit."

We drove around with Henry to all the burgled addresses we had in our files.

"All you have to do is nod if you see one of yours," I told him.

Henry nodded over 100 times.

We then interviewed Henry in detail, asking him how he did each one, what was taken and lots of other details, in order to avoid the accusation we'd somehow coerced him or buttered him up into admitting to crimes he hadn't committed.

When we were on one of these trips, Henry told us he stole so much he couldn't sell everything, so he used a friend's empty lock up to store the stolen gear. It was underneath a railway bridge, in an arches lockup. Henry produced a key from behind a drainpipe and let us in.

It was an Aladdin's cave. TVs of every make, size and shape were stacked against one wall, along with leaning towers of microwaves, hi-fis and speakers. There were DVD players, VHS recorders, CDs, records, various ornaments, a couple of chiming clocks and even some cutlery.

"Thought the cutlery was silver," Henry said, "Turned out to be stainless steel."

When Mark walked in he said: "Mate, I think you're addicted to burglary as well!"

"You could be right there," Henry said. "I think I got one of them addictive personalities."

"I think you might have three or four," Mark replied.

In court, we argued against a long prison sentence and recommended that Henry receive treatment for his addictions. Our reasoning was that it was better to cure him of his addictions rather than risk him continuing his life of crime once he was free.

"Considering the number of the crimes," the judge said, "This would be an extraordinarily unusual move, would it not?"

"In this case, your honour," our CPS lawyer said. "We think both Henry and society will benefit from treatment. He wants to come clean. He's been nothing but honest and cooperative since his arrest and has helped us solve over a hundred crimes and recover an extraordinary amount of stolen property."

"All of which he stole."

In the end, the judge went for it and so, after a short spell in prison, Henry entered into a drug treatment programme. Now that was good police work. Loads of crimes solved, property returned and a criminal treated fairly by the system and ready to go straight.

Sadly, Henry was the exception. In December that same year, a Brixton teenager was jailed for ten years after he admitted committing over 1,000 crimes to fund his £300-a-day drug habit. Duane Daniels, 19, spent three weeks with CID detectives travelling across London for more than 12 hours a day, pointing out the scenes of his crimes which included 600 burglaries, 130 muggings and 220 car break-ins, nearly all of which took place in south London. It sounded like there'd been a mistake when, in court, Daniels admitted nine charges of aggravated burglary, robbery and car break-ins and then asked for 950 other offences to be 'taken into consideration.' This was a record for the Old Bailey.

Daniels was the leader of Posse 28, which operated in Brixton, Clapham and Lewisham. Part of the gang's initiation rites included violent random assaults on strangers and, earlier that year, his posse had raided the offices of a Clapham building contractor one evening and smashed a bottle over the head of John Metcalf, who was working late and the only person there. They also robbed his credit card, tied him up and after forcing him to reveal his PIN number, Daniels stabbed Metcalf in the leg, saying: "I'm going to let you bleed to death."

Unable to free his hands, Metcalf's only chance was to throw himself through a window to escape the building and get the medical help he needed to save his life.

Daniels daily dose of drugs included:

Twenty rocks of crack cocaine
Half an ounce of cannabis
Ten cans of strong lager
A quarter-bottle of spirits
Two doses of LSD
Fourteen milligrams of tranquilliser

Cases like this were starting to appear with startling regularity. And we were seeing more and more fighting in Battersea, especially with knives, and between gangs that had become well-established. The So Solid Crew, the Junction Boys (later the Stick 'em up Kids, aka SUK) from Battersea were at war with gangs from other side of the borough's borders, including Daniels's gang, Posse 28 and the Peckham Young Boys. Some of these gangs had terrifying initiation ceremonies – terrifying for the public, as they involved random attacks on complete strangers. We were entering a new and frightening era of criminality.

# CHAPTER TWENTY-SEVEN

# KILLER IN THE NIGHT

9 pm October 20, 1993

William 'Kwame' Danso, 31-years-old, father of four (he was separated from their mother), was watching football on TV with a friend when there was a loud knock at the window of his ground floor flat in Cato Road, a short, quiet street in Clapham. The flats, converted Victorian housing blocks, had survived (and would eventually outlast) the modern estates that had grown up around them. They had also managed to preserve their community feel. The neighbours knew one another; they met in the children's playground to discuss local issues and held an annual street party sponsored by the council.

Danso, a huge and cheerful Ghanian who worked as a club doorman and security guard, hurried to answer the front door. He was keen to get back to the match. All thoughts of football vanished from Danso's mind when he saw three men standing in front of him. One was holding a baseball bat. The other two were carrying handguns – a Browning 9mm semi-automatic and a rarely-seen Tanfoglio self-loading pistol. The men stepped into the hallway, raising their weapons; Danso started to run back down the hallway.

***

By the time Gary Nelson was 24-years-old he had everything he wanted: a fortune in cash, a luxury apartment, access to a selection of top-of-the-range cars; walk-in wardrobes lined with designer suits opposite a row of coordinated shirts and ties; dozens of limited edition trainers, all neatly stored in line; a jewellery collection that rivalled any platinum-selling recording artist and finally, most importantly, there were his guns. It was Nelson's willingness to use his 'special thing(s)' as he called his guns that provided him with all of the above.

Nelson lived exactly the life he wanted, the life of a powerful outlaw. He could order people to have his enemies beaten, shot or even killed. And he had no shortage of enemies – nearly all of whom were frightened of Nelson and, in his world, fear = respect. Respect was the commodity Nelson prized above all else. Guns helped him get that respect.

It wasn't just the guns, however. Anyone can create fear by pointing a gun. Nelson wanted people to remember him and so he did all he could to foster a 'legend'.

Everyone is scared of the unknown and to this end, Nelson revealed little about himself. People's imaginations filled in the gaps; the few stories featuring Nelson that were known were repeated over and over and embellished until they became urban legends. If a local bad lad left town, the word on the street was that Nelson was responsible – no matter what the real reason was.

Nelson's granite-cold stare would have made Tyson himself blink. He wasn't sensitive or kind but he knew how to win anyone over – male or female – with a sudden smile or a moment of mutual respect. When he spoke, he chose his few words carefully. Silence helped to intimidate others into talking or into looking away. When Nelson did business, he didn't smile, he never blinked, fidgeted, flinched, fiddled or repeated himself. He always looked disgusted. All of this was calculated to make 'weaker' people want to please him, to fill in the gaps, to help him, so that they might win his favour. If people knew you were a friend of Nelson's then you were treated with respect.

Nelson also looked the part. He trained as a boxer and took it seriously; people knew he could fight and the word was that he always welcomed the chance to try out his boxing skills bare-knuckle-style. He dressed well in loose-fitting clothes, wearing layers to enhance his size and the smoothness of his movements.

When there was trouble, he always went with backup, usually Chen and Lips, his two chief henchmen. Chen lacked Nelson's brains but most people could not even imagine trying to take him on in a fight. He had a large, square head that sat on neckless shoulders. If you were to hit him with a baseball bat, he wouldn't even blink – and that's if you were lucky enough to find a way to get past his enormous arms. Lips was a hot-headed psycho who had 'The Stare' down to a tee and always looked like he was searching for someone to stab, with his hand half-in and half-out of his coat.

With backup like this, there was never any misunderstanding. And people knew. If Nelson came calling, he would come prepared for trouble and then some.

To this end, Nelson always held a grudge – and if he held it, then Chen and Lips held it too. If they wanted revenge, they got it. They *never* backed down, no matter who it was or how many friends they thought they had. To do so would have been fatal to Nelson's legend. No apology, no matter how grovelling was ever going to rescue you once you pissed off Nelson.

And when he did show his face in public, usually at a night-club, people whispered his name to one another: "That's him! Nelson, the guy I was telling you about, you know?" and Nelson made sure he was even harder in person that he was in legend.

People ate it up. It got to the stage where Nelson just had to say what he wanted and it would be delivered on a silver platter; he became intimidating without even trying. It seemed as though everyone was ready to embrace Nelson's 'legend'.

Everyone, except for William Danso.

***

October 16 1993

Nelson and Chen marched to the front of queue of the Brixton Academy nightclub only to find, to their surprise and displeasure, that doorman William Danso was blocking their way.

Danso, who found himself standing nose-to-nose with Chen, was used to queue-jumpers trying to intimidate him.

"What do you think you're doing?" Chen demanded.

"You can't come in here."

"You know who I am," Nelson said.

"Yeah, and for that reason you can't come in."

Danso knew that Nelson had recently shot a man in a nightclub and was likely to be armed. He couldn't rest easy with the knowledge that Nelson would be inside a club he was supposed to be securing.

Nelson remained expressionless. He wasn't going to repeat himself and, as Danso clearly wasn't about to budge, he calmly turned around and walked away. Perhaps he wasn't prepared to risk fighting this tough bouncer in public (having a large audience can work both ways, in terms of establishing one's reputation).

***

5pm October 20 1993

Danso was at work in his other job, as a security guard at Street Communications, a mobile phone shop on the busy Leigh

Court Road in Streatham Hill. His boss was fellow Ghanian Eugene Djaba, 26, who was up to his ears in a counterfeit cigarette smuggling racket. As well as working as a security guard, Danso also dealt small amounts of cannabis on the side. In the cut-and-thrust streets of South London, it was every man and woman for themselves. There was, as the saying goes, more than one way to skin a cat – and in South London this usually involved the subterranean economy, where anything could be bought and sold, from sex to cigarettes, from bushmeat to DVDs, from drugs to knocked-off perfumes. Men squeegeed car windows to raise money for cheap beer smuggled from France and cannabis grown in houses under lamps (a process managed by teenagers, paid in cash). Women sold their bodies to make a living or to pay for their addictions. Children worked cash in hand as lookouts for the dealers, or delivering leaflets, drugs or doing housework.

It wasn't legal, nor was it right, but it worked. After all, most people were all after the same thing (money or cheap services/goods) they were united in their pursuits so, most of the time they obeyed the first and only rule of the economic underground: Don't Make Waves.

Unfortunately for Danso, at 5pm on October 20 1993, two men had decided to make waves at the entrance of Street Communications. Their argument – over the sale of a stolen mobile phone – was on the verge of turning nasty when Danso stepped in and broke it up, calmly and efficiently. One of the men was Tony Francis, aka Lips. The other man was known only as 'Blue', who had some 'friends' with him to back him up. Lips felt as though he'd been disrespected by Blue and called Nelson.

Djaba knew Nelson and Lips. He told Danso to be careful. Nelson had come into his shop the day before and pulled a gun from inside his jacket. Nelson waved it around, boasting he was going to put a bullet in someone's belly. When Djaba asked why, he received a one-word answer: "Disrespect."

Nelson arrived at the shop entrance about five minutes later and together they squared up to Blue. Danso ended up physically parting Nelson and Lips from Blue and then holding the two men back while urging Blue – and his friends, who had just rolled up – to leave. They took his advice, at which point Danso released Nelson and Lips.

Danso had now disrespected Nelson *and* Lips. Worst of all he had stood up to Nelson and opposed his authority; rejected his righteousness – in front of a large audience outside a nightclub. Nelson had no choice but to turn to his gun. As Nelson himself once put it: "The gun is might and might is right."

***

9pm October 20, 1993

As Danso ran back down the hallway, the men started to shoot. They fired a total of twelve shots, hitting Danso six times as he ran down his hallway. As Danso crumpled in a heap, Nelson, his bloodlust satisfied and respect restored, strode away laughing.

***

A domestic. That was all it was. A routine call. The kind of thing that 44-year-old PC Patrick Dunne had dealt with more times than he could remember since he had joined the police four years earlier.

A broad 6ft 3in, Pat was a gentle giant who lived on his own – his fiancée had been killed in a car crash some years earlier. He was close to his two brothers, Stephen and Ivan. He had given up his job as maths teacher and head of department at a Bolton high school after fifteen years to be closer to his mother after his father died.

This move also gave him the chance to fulfil his long-held ambition of joining the police. Pat wanted to help others. He loved the life of a community officer, much like myself, except Pat liked to cycle everywhere on his beat. He became known as 'the cycling cop'. Apart from dealing with day-to-day crimes, he performed many roles in his neighbourhood, from talking to schoolchildren to playing piano and leading sing-songs at old people's centres (Pat loved classical music and had learned to play the piano when he was in his 20s). His police file was full of grateful letters from local people.

Pat was due to go off shift when the call came in. A colleague volunteered to go in his place.

"No, it's my beat," Pat said, "And I should go."

The disturbance was at 31 Cato Street, the home of a man called Mario Ceria. Minutes after Pat arrived, the argument was forgotten when a series of sudden cracks echoed across the road. Pat, who had cycled to the disturbance, was wearing a hi-vis vest as usual, and, unarmed (save for his wooden truncheon), he went to investigate, calling in "possible gunshots," over his radio.

Mario, along with his friend, Henry Woods, followed Pat into the street. Unfortunately, the sound of gunfire was not that unusual anymore in Clapham at night. Cato road was narrow, with just enough room for a single vehicle to squeeze between the rows of cars parked on either side and Pat could clearly see the faces of each of the three men who were no more than ten yards away. He could see the cruel smiles on their faces and the weapons still in their hands. Pat would have known Nelson's face. I have some inkling as to how much of a shock that must have been to Pat, having accidentally confronted Nelson and Chen at Battersea Market. But Pat didn't buckle when the men turned to see Pat, clearly visible in his fluorescent jacket; instead Pat yelled at Ceria and Woods to get back inside and pushed them away.

Nelson made a calculation – a cop witness to the murder of Danso would put him and his friends bang to rights – and raised the Tanfoglio, firing twice over the parked cars at the beat bobby.

The first bullet missed, the second hit Pat's hand. It ricocheted off a bone in his wrist and into his chest, collapsing his lungs and severing his aorta.

Pat was dead by the time his body hit the pavement.

The three men were heard laughing as they swaggered away. One of them fired his gun into the air, a sick celebration. They walked 200 yards to the end of Cato Street and into Bedford Road, out of the sight of terrified residents who gradually emerged from their homes to find a police constable lying dead on the ground.

# CHAPTER TWENTY-EIGHT

# A TERRIBLE HISTORY

**1**9 October 1993, 5pm

I'd come a long way since arriving at Kings Cross just over five years earlier as fresh-faced and extremely naïve Yorkshire lad. Now I lived in the concrete jungle and fought drug-wielding criminals in the name of law and order and loved it.

I wanted even more action and finally made up my mind to apply to the Territorial Support Group, whom I'd admired from afar when they'd dived headlong into crack dens. I was delighted when my application was accepted but, at the same time, I had mixed feelings. I loved life at Battersea; my colleagues were my family, and I treasured the community I policed – but the pull of the professional excitement of the TSG was strong.

On my last day at Battersea, I went to clear out my locker; I was especially keen to get a box containing all my records of known robbers, dealers, gang members, etc., including photos, maps and notes on who knew whom and any other associates, legal or otherwise. Every TSG van was in effect a mobile intelligence vehicle as the officers within had been drawn from many different areas in London, so whoever happened to be the local expert often informally briefed their colleagues en route.

It had already been an emotional day and when I saw someone had left a giant hand-drawn 'goodbye' card in my locker, I felt a lump in my throat. It featured a caricature of yours truly in uniform and running, with the word 'Supercop' drawn in big cartoon letters over the top. Everyone had signed it. I still have it.

That night they took me out for a Chinese at Wong Kei's in Leicester Square. I'd never had Chinese food before. I loved it but was at first taken aback by the waiters' rudeness, before it was explained to me that this was, apparently, part of the restaurant's charm. The experience brought home to me how much I loved my band of brothers and sisters. We'd be friends for life.

The following evening I was in front of the TV, tea in hand, watching the 10 'o'clock news.

"A policeman has been shot dead in Cato Road in Clapham."

I dropped my mug. Oh god, oh god, who the hell was it? As the report continued, they described a car that had been seen driving away from Bedford Road, around the corner from the shooting, and the first half of its registration.

I recognised it.

Not long after I'd seen Nelson at New Covent Garden Market, I'd spotted him sitting at the wheel of a grey 7-Series BMW, waiting at a set of traffic lights. I remembered it because the car looked just like the kind of car a gangster would aspire to own. I even nodded a 'Hello' and, for once, Nelson looked relaxed, although he didn't acknowledge me. I automatically clocked the registration number, memorised it, and passed it onto Pete.

The TV news gave out a hotline number. I called it immediately and spoke to a Detective Sergeant.

"I know who did this. I took that registration number down just a couple of weeks ago."

He thanked me and hung up.

I called the station and got through to Pete.

"Who is it Pete?"

"Pat Dunne from Clapham," Pete replied.

"Oh good god."

I didn't know what else to say. I was in complete and total shock. I knew Pat. We often dropped by Clapham for tea in their canteen. He'd been four years into the job. We all called him Dixon of Dock Green because he was such a gentle lad and looked somewhat antiquated on his bicycle.

"He was called to a domestic when he heard gunshots," Pete said. "He radioed it in and ran over to see what was going on. Shot with a single bullet, hit his wrist and it bounced up into his chest. Died on the street."

"Any witnesses?"

"I think so, but it's early yet."

"You know who did this don't you?"

\*\*\*

This was the moment that William Danso died. 10.05pm. He'd been hit by six bullets but, amazingly, was still conscious when the first police officers arrived. Danso told them he was having trouble breathing but not who had shot him. By the time the ambulance arrived, it was too late. One of the bullets had severed a major artery and Danso bled out into his abdomen.

\*\*\*

After I'd finished talking to Pete, my phone rang.

"This is Detective Superintendent John Jones."

John, a chain-smoking police legend who would marry MP Edwina Currie in 2001, and would go on to become the head of Operation Trident, the police squad that dealt with black-on-black shootings. He was just about to tuck into a steak dinner in a Surrey restaurant when he was alerted to the shooting and raced off in his Reliant Scimitar SS1 sports car arriving at the scene 15minutes later in a haze of overheated brakes.

Jones's one lucky early break had come from a woman who'd seen a car racing away from the scene just after the murder. It had nearly collided with another car and she had glanced at the number plate as it blasted away, remembering the half that I was able to complete.

"How well do you know Gary Nelson?" he asked.

"I've put together a dossier on him, and a former girlfriend was an informant of mine. I've even got his mobile number, he was still using it as of a week ago."

"Where are you working now Mike?"

"I've just left Battersea for the TSG."

"Forget the TSG. I'll talk to them. I need you on my Murder Squad, to familiarise my officers with the local scene, the faces. Bring me everything you've got on Nelson first thing tomorrow morning."

The Murder Squad's office was above the TSG's base in Thornton Heath. The TSG sergeant who'd interviewed me came over. He looked at my suit. This was not what one wore on one's first day with the TSG.

"Oooh get you," he said. "What do you think you're doing?"

"Hasn't John Jones called you?"

"I just got here myself son," he replied, so I explained.

The sarge nodded, serious. "Well, I'm sorry to lose you Mike, but you're clearly needed elsewhere. Come back when you're done. In the meantime, good luck, son."

I stepped into the office. Inside there were forty of the best detectives in the Met. And me. Not yet three years out of probation and only just had my first Chinese dinner. The energy in that room was intense. Noses were to the grindstone, no one spoke an unnecessary word, or made a joke (all police squads usually rely on dry humour) and although we didn't need any reminding about how important it was that we caught the killers as quickly as possible, the office was brought to a brief standstill when Commissioner Paul Condon arrived: "There's nowhere we don't go, no one we don't talk to, no stone left unturned," he said. "You don't kill a copper in cold blood and get away with it. Pull out every stop."

John Jones, unlit fag in mouth, welcomed me to the unit and got me settled in. "You're going to help us nail those bastards, Mike. Witnesses said they were laughing as they walked away. These men think that killing two men in cold blood is funny. We can't let them walk free. I've got the best men and women working here, the cream of the Met," he said, "But we won't get anywhere without intelligence and insider knowledge and that's where you'll come in. Any new suspects or associates come up and you know them, you make sure we know everything you do."

"Got it guv."

I was pleased to be of help but suddenly felt well and truly out of my depth. I was a community police officer, not a detective. At the same time it was eye-opening and I got to learn about a side of policing that even most police constables didn't know about. I was amazed to learn, for example, that various secret police units had been set up to pursue criminals like Nelson for some years, ever since the Yardies and crack cocaine had arrived in London.

But it hadn't been going well.

A confidential report published by the National Criminal Intelligence Service (NCIS) earlier that year revealed that drug-related murders had taken place all over the UK and concluded, when talking about the crack dealers: "By the very nature of their stranglehold on the crack cocaine market, they are a threat to the security and stability of the nation." Despite this, an internal report from the Met stated that there was "an almost complete breakdown" in operations mounted against the Yardies and the associated rise of UK-born crack dealers. Part of the reason for this was the lack of enthusiasm for specialist drug squads within each London borough, or a London-wide drugs squad. After all, if you didn't have a drugs squad, then you didn't have a drugs problem and the more drug users and dealers you arrested, the higher your drug crime stats rose. So the Met's initial response to the crack dealers (starting in 1987) was haphazard, a period of denial was followed by the belated recognition that crack was a real phenomenon after crack flooded into housing estates, leading to the sorts of spikes we'd seen in associated crime in Battersea, street robbery and burglary in particular. And then came the increased use of knives and then guns, including machine guns, which became increasingly casual – the number of offences involving firearms rose 50 per cent between 1988 and 1991.

Then, in March 1988, came Operation Lucy led by Commander Roy Ramm, which clocked up an impressive 400 arrests and 50 deportations by the middle of 1989. Ramm's squad produced a report warning that the Yardies had "in [Ramm's] view, found a gap in the force's structures." The only answer, Ramm felt, was for a squad permanently dedicated to the termination of the Yardies' operations. Unfortunately the Met leadership instead terminated Operation Lucy for fear of being accused of racism. Stop and Search had great success in targeting Yardies but had angered some local people and community leaders who constantly saw 'institutionally racist' police targeting young black men. As the Met gave an inch, the Yardies took a mile. They filled planes from Jamaica with mules carrying crack in their bellies, one dying every now and again when one of the packages burst, or dissolved in stomach acid. The crimes grew more and more outrageous; enemies were shot and tortured, a senior official from the US Embassy's visa section was murdered, strangled to death to prevent her from revealing a fake visa scam. Extortion and prostitution rackets were run alongside major crack dealing operations worth millions of pounds.

It wasn't until 1990 that a new 'Yardie squad' was formed, composed of Customs officers and police detectives but it collapsed, a result of infighting, by the late summer of the year of its creation.

Around this time John Jones was dealing with at least three shootings every fortnight on his Lambeth manor. He'd also noticed that officers were often called out to scenes of reported gunshots but that they generally found nothing and presumed that the callers had simply heard a car backfiring. Jones decided to send specialist officers to these scenes whenever they were reported to search for bullet fragments, which they duly found. The sites of these shootings were eventually linked to specific criminal groups from across the whole of London, creating a spider's web of evidential patterns, linking shootings to turf wars.

Jones, who was due to retire, went to Scotland Yard with his evidence and asked the senior management to finance the creation of an intelligence-led operational unit (this would be the first police unit in the Met to combine operational and intelligence units under one roof). When he told them how much it would cost (£50,000 for the first three months) they said no.

"Fair enough," Jones replied, "I don't need to be here," and got up and left. A senior officer caught up with him before he'd left the Yard and told him he'd get his 50k. Operation Dalehouse (an early version of today's Operation Trident) was run from an office in Barnes, southwest London, and had immediate success. Jones's team made 274 arrests and destroyed more than £1 million in crack. Yardies quickly grew to know and fear 'Mr Dalehouse' and sent out shooting parties to try and find him. Operation Dalehouse, which also attracted the praise of the FBI, lasted for three months, until November 1992 when it was put to sleep – for no good reason – by the Met's senior management. The official explanation was that there had been a sudden and huge drop in shootings, so the operation was no longer necessary. Jones, somewhat exasperated, replied that Dalehouse was why shootings had almost stopped. Ultimately, Jones believed that because most of the victims of Yardie crimes were black, the success of Operation Dalehouse received almost no press coverage, and so Scotland Yard policy-makers looked for more media-friendly operations. The week after Dalehouse was shut down there were two crack-related murders.

In early 1993, Detective Chief Superintendent Roy Clark (who was later promoted to Deputy Assistant Commissioner) produced a confidential report which revealed just how poor the leadership's response had been to the crack problem, stating that local beat teams could only pick up the pieces each time the Yardies and crack dealers dished out some mayhem. The only concerted effort by the Met was a secret team set up by half-a-dozen detectives and immigration officers whose makeshift office was the bar of a small Southwark pub, which they nicknamed 'The Annexe' and where they installed a fax machine, which the landlord kept falling over. The immigration officers reported how the Yardie gangs in Jamaica had friends in the police and the government, some of whom had stolen tens of millions of dollars of US aid money and had given it to the Yardies. Criminals travelled between Jamaica and London on easily acquired false visas and passports. If they were unlucky enough to be caught and booted out of the country, they simply travelled back using new false papers. One Yardie assassin called Tuffy simply shoved UK immigration officials aside when they tried to stop him entering the UK and escaped into Birmingham airport. Tuffy was shot dead in London a short time later.

When two Drug Liaison Officers at the British High Commission in Jamaica begged the Foreign Office for money for a Polaroid camera so that they could fax pictures of suspected Yardies to London and have them stopped at the airport, they were told that the money simply wasn't there.

As Clark said, the Yardies saw London as a soft target compared to most other countries. UK police officers weren't routinely armed and no dedicated unit had been set up to challenge the Yardies. Unfortunately, Clark lost what little support he might have gained from the Met's leadership when he came up with the idea of using an informer, a man called Eaton Green to spy on the Yardies in Jamaica. Clark couldn't have known but Green, who was based in Brixton, already had his police handlers twisted around his little finger. Two days after Green submitted his reports, on July 8 1993, Green was arrested by Nottingham detectives and charged with committing the biggest armed robbery in Nottingham since Robin Hood. Clark's 35 recommendations to deal with the crack/Yardie problem were largely ignored, although one squad was formed in August 1993: the Drug-Related Violence Intelligence Unit based in Scotland Yard's intelligence department, SO11. Sounds great – except for the fact that the man in charge was a constable from Brixton. PC Steve Barker, much like myself and my colleagues in Battersea, had discovered the Yardie problem while on his beat. Barker was now expected to work with almost no supervision or support, save for a man called Brian Fotheringham, an immigration enforcement officer. Between them they had no equipment, not so much as an interview room and no budget, so they resorted to illegal 'squeal deals,' and in a matter of weeks they were up to their eyeballs in trouble. They turned arrested Yardies into informants in return for their continued freedom but these Yardies went on committing serious crimes. One such informant, Delroy "Epsi" Denton, aged 35, raped a 15-year-old school girl in south London and followed this by raping and murdering a young mother of two children. Other examples include a Yardie murderer who conned the Met out of £30,000, providing them with zero intelligence in return – the police even helped the killer to bypass immigration at Heathrow; a Yardie who lived illegally in the UK for ten years with the help of the police and made a living from crime before the Flying Squad nicked him for an armed robbery in south London, and a man who confessed – among many others things – to eleven murders.

Even when SO11 managed to get some intelligence, they were unable to put it to good use. Those few boroughs with Area Drugs Squads were too busy trying to stay on top of their own operations and problems and didn't have time or resources to make arrests for SO11.

And then, in October 1993, Pat Dunne – a white bobby on a bicycle nicknamed Dixon of Dock green – was murdered. Suddenly, the Yardies and crack were front-page news, the lead story on the News at Ten. *The Sunday Telegraph* raised the question of the death penalty in a half-page editorial: "It is surely time to consider practically whether the death penalty would reduce ... crime and restore respect to the law," before adding that Home Secretary Michael Howard should lead "the best minds in public service to turn to the subject." *The Times* complained of "the general lawlessness that is increasingly dividing [Britain] into a nation of predators and victims." It asked for a revision of the drug laws, tougher penalties and a more comprehensive arming of the police.

Meanwhile, a mountain of floral tributes appeared in Cato Road; children left poems at the scene; a police officer standing guard at the crime scene was filmed with tears in his eyes. Unable to bear the stress, Pat's mother suffered a heart attack and Diana, Princess of Wales, sent her flowers to her in hospital.

Extra hearses were brought in for Pat's funeral so they could carry all the wreaths. Thousands of people squeezed onto the streets and stood with heads bowed, many weeping, as the cortege passed slowly by.

After the funeral, Prime Minister John Major said that everything would be done to bring the killers to justice, and to end the scourge of crack.

If anyone was going to do the job and do it right, I thought, it was John Jones. He had some success with the Yardies and the crack dealers, he knew exactly what we were up against. He said he was "quite amazed" by the chaos of the 'squeal deals' but understood that working with informants sometimes required bending the rules (not that he'd ever done it himself). With the eyes of the nation upon him, this job was going to have to be done by the book and if there was one thing I could be certain of, it was that Nelson wasn't going to make it easy.

# CHAPTER TWENTY-NINE

# TO CATCH A KILLER

The Job binds us together, especially those who patrol the streets. Only a fellow cop can ever understand what life as police officer is like. It is this cop empathy that binds us together, that makes it possible for us to hold the line against crime in what can sometimes be extraordinarily difficult circumstances.

No matter how we're feeling, or what's going on in our personal lives, or how dangerous a situation is, every single police officer in the UK will come running to help the victims and catch the bad guys. It's a role we love, obviously, and it is perhaps for this reason that we make 'lousy' victims. We're not used to it. We solve problems, lock up criminals and try to restore some sense of normality to the lives of innocent civilians, so when we lose a colleague, it's like losing a family member, and we struggle to cope. We all want to catch the people responsible but we have to get on with holding the line and let those who are assigned to the case to crack it. This knowledge does nothing to help remove the sense of helplessness and associated stress that comes with the knowledge that the killer is still free, walking the streets you are responsible for policing.

I returned to Battersea nick for a visit shortly after I was seconded to the Murder Squad. When Patters spotted me, he dragged me off to the canteen where we were soon joined by Mark, Foxy, Trist, Pete, Darren and Timbo.

"So what news Pannett?" Patters asked.

"Not much you don't already know," I said. "Fingerprints and footprints in the hallway but they're not on any records, not Nelson's, and all we've got from witnesses so far is that the three men were West Indian, in their 20s and 30s, and were wearing dark clothing."

"Fuck all then," Stevie sad bitterly.

"They're going to get them," I said. "It's just a matter of time."

"We need that gun," Mark said.

"Bound to have tossed it," Timbo added.

"Maybe not, you know how he loves his guns," I said. "Plus, he's so arrogant he thinks he's untouchable."

"So it's all hands to the pump then," Foxy said. "As in, pump everyone we know for information."

This was our best bet. Although it seemed as though everyone was scared of Nelson, there was always a chance someone would inform on him. After all, he had broken the underworld's first rule: Don't Make Waves.

Now we were about to turn over the underworld, some criminals might be prepared to speak out before their operations were discovered and they themselves were arrested. The unfortunate reality was that the murder of Danso did not make the same kind of headlines as the murder of a police officer. In the UK, the murder of a police officer signifies societal breakdown and the ensuing media fall-out and police 'leave-no-stone-unturned' response was bad for criminals' business.

"Well, we have some good news for you at least," Trist said.

"Yeah, Foxy caught your serial rapist, a fine collar," Pete said.

"Fantastic!" I exclaimed. "How did you get him?"

"Just walking the beat one evening a few days' back," Foxy said with a shrug. "Recognised Corkhall's hideous mug and took off after him. There was no way I was going to let him outrun me."

"You're being a bit modest there Foxy," Timbo said before turning back to me. "She scoured the streets for that bastard."

"Early indications are Corkhall's bang to rights on DNA," Stevie said. "He'll be going down for at least five rapes. Collar of the year that one, Foxy."

"Hopefully the judge will see enough sense to throw away the key," Pete said to strong murmurs of agreement.

I can still see that poor woman curled up beside the entrance to the tower block, the blood and then those deep, deep cuts to her hands.[5]

"And that's why we're going to get Nelson and his motley crew," Patters said. "That murder squad's all very well; they're fine detectives I'm sure, but we know these streets. We know the people. And they are going to want to help us. This nutter is shooting civilians and cops. It can't be allowed to stand."

"Nelson's made waves," Pete said. "No one's going to be loyal to him now."

"So we get out there and talk about Pat, about William," Patters said. "Remind them that their brother, sister, son, uncle or aunt could be next, until someone gives us the information we need and those bastards are off our streets for good."

At that moment I wanted to be with them, back on my beat, talking to everyone I'd met over the past two years. I felt certain I'd be able to get something useful. It was frustrating but I knew that the Murder Squad wouldn't have taken me on if I wasn't going to be of significant help and so I focussed on that.

---

5 The serial rapist would indeed eventually go down for five rapes, all of which involved sickening violence, and was sentenced to life.

***

"Nelson is a major-league, organised criminal who is into extortion, drug smuggling and armed robbery and will use extreme violence in pursuit of his aims," John Jones said in his briefing to the team. "He is never to be underestimated. Many people fear him and a number of potential witnesses have refused to give statements as a result. He has few friends and, as he's previously admitted, they're all criminals. He likes guns, cars, designer clothes, computer games and porn and has visions of fantastical movies being made about his life. Needless to say, he has an ego the size of a planet. His mobile's greeting message says 'I'm too sexy for my phone.' He has power, and can make people do things for him; he's admitted having a prisoner beaten up for having the "wrong attitude." To Nelson, as we know, respect is everything.

"He's a wealthy man, not only from dishonesty but legitimate operations funded by his ill-gotten gains and we know he's trying to make serious moves into the nightclub business. He's clever and knows all the rules. That is why he has risen to the highest echelons of organised crime. South London born and bred, Nelson started young, his was charged with his first offence at 15 and his tally now runs to 21 offences – robbery, theft, assault, possession of firearms – and now two murders. He carries a 9mm Browning pistol and a Tanfoglio self-loading pistol he calls 'my special thing,' and wears the best body armour money can buy; he even wears it in bed, so he's ready to fight to the death. You do not approach this man ever, unless SO19 are in front of you and have him trussed up on the ground. We are here to find that evidence that will convict him. When the time comes to make the arrest, we will do it with overwhelming odds, to make it absolutely clear he has no chance of fighting his way out and therefore, will see sense, surrender and take his chances in court.

"SO11 have lumped his latest vehicle (lumped = installed tracking and listening devices) and will continue to bug any other vehicle he's seen in. We will follow him everywhere but he does employ counter-surveillance, so it won't be easy."

\*\*\*

The police motorcyclist was in plainclothes on an unmarked Honda, doing his best to keep up with Nelson, who was driving his car through London's West End at high speeds, racing the wrong way down one-way streets.

Nelson had fled to Jamaica after the shootings, but with seemingly little progress in terms of investigation and, thinking he was in the clear, even though he knew he was chief among suspects and that he would be followed day and night, Nelson was arrogant and greedy enough to return to London to carry on his criminal enterprises. He had spent too much on his reputation to throw it all away by hiding abroad.

The motorcyclist surveillance officer had been radioed by his colleagues, who'd told him that Nelson had turned into Air Street from Piccadilly, and was racing towards Golden Square. Trying to catch up, the motorcyclist took a short cut across Regent Street into Brewer Street but, as he crossed Regent Street, he was sideswiped by a black cab and killed. Yet another life lost thanks to Nelson.

A few days later, I was with John Jones listening to live radio reports from the surveillance teams following Nelson. Nelson, who was driving with Richard Watts, aka Chen, in the passenger seat, was confident that he'd given us the slip and continued on his mission. Behind him in another car was Anthony Francis, aka Lips and another man called Donville Gibson. The surveillance officers still had both cars in full view however, and watched them enter a pub in Highbury where an informant was already positioned. He called to alert the officers that Nelson and his crew had just picked up their 'shooters'. The assumption was that they were tooling-up in preparation to rob a crack house they'd been watching.

"We have to nick them right now before they hurt anyone," Jones said.

The problem was, after the motorcyclist's accident, the surveillance teams had been ordered to hand in their guns, if only for a few days. Their colleague's death had left the team shaken, and made their mission to get Nelson behind bars personal. Carrying guns while in this state of mind was seen as potentially risky.

With this in mind, I immediately called in SO19 who would arrest the gang using a 'hard-stop', the most aggressive form of arrest that would see the car disabled and the men dragged from the vehicle at gunpoint.

Then the surveillance officers reported that Nelson had gone off on his own in a separate car while Chen and Lips continued in the original vehicle. Before SO19 were near the scene, a pair of eagle-eyed local police officers in a marked car had latched onto Chen and Lips, thinking they looked 'dodgy' and announced over the airwaves that they were about to pull them over. John and I desperately tried to call the officers off, but it was too late.

Before the uniformed officers got close enough to stop them, Chen pulled over and climbed out of the car armed with a shotgun; he levelled it at the police officers and fired before legging it with the gun into some nearby gardens. The officers (who were lucky to escape unhurt, having heard the bullets whistle past their ears) ran for cover, and were then stunned to see SO19 screaming in from all directions in unmarked vehicles, charging after Chen, who was already clambering over the garden walls of the great and the good – this was the then future PM Tony Blair's neighbourhood.

Meanwhile, Nelson stepped out of the drivers' side of his car and walked calmly away. He quietly surrendered when SO19 caught up with him down the road, assuming the so-called 'crucifix position', kneeling on the floor, hands behind head and then out to the sides, ready to be cuffed. A gun was found in a front garden a short distance away.

Armed officers looking for Chen noticed a woman at a back window pointing urgently towards her shed. SO19 surrounded the shed, slowly closing in until they spotted Chen and yelled at him to surrender. Thankfully, he did just that. All four men were arrested and put in cells close to one another that were wired for sound, and I was one of the officers who worked twelve-hour shifts eavesdropping on them. Nelson was too smart to be caught out that way. He only spoke once, when I happened to be listening.

"Say nothing," he said to his crew. "They've got fuck all."

Anthony Francis, Donville Gibson and Richard Watts were given between eight and twelve years for possessing firearms with intent to endanger life. Gary Nelson walked free because we couldn't prove that any of the guns were his. None of them had his prints on them and he'd been smart enough to walk away at the right moment.

Nelson's one and only slip came when his temper got the better of him during a filmed interview at Islington police station, when he suddenly said: "Watch yourself sergeant, watch yourself Mr Sergeant, watch yourself... You will cop it like the other fucker copped it."

Shortly after Chen and Lips had been taken off the streets, John Jones finally caught the break he'd been hoping for. He was going over all crime reports relating to Nelson and had, via his intelligence network, been told that Nelson was the one who'd shot Mohammed Massaquoi. Massaquoi was by this time in prison on remand for murdering his own brother and when

Jones's team visited him, Massaquoi told them how he'd been arrested for bilking (running away from a taxi without paying) in Harlesden. When the police officers searched Massaquoi, they recovered a small plastic bottle filled with cotton wool containing three pieces of squashed metal. When asked what this was, Massaquoi replied: "Oh, that's nothing, I was shot a while back and the doctor who took out the bullets said I should keep them as a souvenir."

When asked what happened to the bullets, Massaquoi shrugged. "Those cops took them." Members of Jones's team rushed to Harlesden and, after a frantic search of the evidence room, the unlogged bullets were found sitting on a shelf. The officers who had confiscated the bullets hadn't bothered to follow up Massaquoi's shooting story to see if any investigations were still live, which goes to show just how important every piece of evidence is, for these bullets were eventually matched to a gun owned by Nelson.

Both Massaquoi and Gary Kewell were finally persuaded to give evidence against Nelson. He was charged with attempted murder, possessing a firearm with intent to endanger life and of possessing a firearm in a public place. During the trial, held at the Old Bailey and Southwark Crown Court, Nelson did a poor job of protesting his innocence, turning up to court wearing gold worth tens of thousands of pounds (he said his profession was 'security guard') and telling the judge: "I walk heavy. I am a serious person." Nelson was acquitted of attempted murder but, after four hours of deliberations, in February 1994, the jury found him guilty of the remaining charges and the judge sentenced him to eight years. Nelson appeared unfazed and simply winked at his supporters watching from the public gallery.

Massaquoi was found dead, hanged, in his cell the very evening after he gave evidence. The judge said the cause of Massaquoi's death wasn't known but that it was "likely" to be suicide (and this was indeed the official verdict). He had given his evidence clearly and confidently at the Old Bailey and we couldn't understand why he would take his own life, unless it was perhaps out of some terrible fear of what Nelson might do to him in revenge. There was no evidence of foul play but this terrible event only served to strengthen Nelson's legend – the implication being that witnesses who spoke out against him would face a very different kind of justice from the kind one found in court.

Ten days after starting his sentence at Belmarsh high security jail, in south-east London, Nelson charged from his cell, naked, his skin made slippery with oil. He attacked prison officers with a snooker cue, injuring several before they got him under control. This earned him another six months.

With Nelson and his main henchmen in prison, we had a great chance to break the case, to get people to talk while Nelson couldn't get to them, to get the evidence that would keep him in prison for the rest of his life. I spent my time with the squad going through my files, helping detectives track down Nelson's known associates, looking for that one person who could make the case for us.

And then the unthinkable happened.

## CHAPTER THIRTY

# MURDER IN THE MORNING

The robbers broke into the empty flat above the post office at 99 Calley Down Crescent, new Addington, South London on the evening of February 8, 1994.

At 8am the following morning, post office manager Albert Britton stepped through the front door only to be grabbed from behind by a masked man who clamped his hand over Britton's mouth, while one of the other men, all of whom were wearing full-face ski-masks, waved a knife in his face, warning him not to make a sound. Once they had Britton's keys, they emptied a coin safe of £2,750. Britton couldn't open the main safe, which was on a time lock, until 9am. It contained £31,000, so the three robbers sat down to wait.

Then the phone rang.

"It's my wife," Britton said. "I'd better answer otherwise she'll just keep calling and get suspicious."

The robbers agreed but Britton's wife heard that something wasn't right in her husband's voice and called the police.

Constable Stephen Wilson and Sergeant Derek Robertson arrived a few minutes later. All was quiet at the front of the building so they decided to check out the back, where they became unsure which section of the jumbled row of buildings belonged to the post office. Derek waited at the back while Stephen returned to check out the front, where he met Constable Robert Brown. Together they took a closer look at the premises and checked the door, by pulling it, to see that it was secure.

Hearing the sudden noise, one of the robbers grabbed Britton from behind and put a knife to his throat.

"Open the back door!" he demanded.

Britton did so, only to be confronted by Derek, who reported over his radio that three men armed with a knife were robbing the post office and had a hostage.

Two of the robbers ran back into the post office, leaving the knifeman in a standoff with Derek, and tried to leave by the front door, where they ran into Stephen and Robert. The men were arrested and once cuffed, the constables ran to the back to help their sergeant.

Derek was lying on the ground; he had been repeatedly stabbed while trying to arrest the third robber. Despite desperate attempts by Stephen and Robert to stop the bleeding, Derek died at the scene, shortly after the paramedics had arrived.

The murderer, Robert Eades, 32, was caught after a brief man-hunt and was jailed for life. The Old Bailey judge ordered him to serve at least 25 years. Eades's two accomplices, brothers Christopher and Terence Snelling, were both found guilty of manslaughter and were sentenced to 12 years.

A few months later nine-year-old Fraser and Sacha, aged six, collected the Queen's Gallantry Award from HRH Queen Elizabeth II in a private ceremony at Buckingham Palace, as their mum, Derek's widow, looked on.

And then, in March 1994, the unthinkable happened yet again.

Constable James Seymour, 31, and his colleague, Constable Simon Carroll, 23 approached a man outside a Brixton pub in Acre Lane.

The man was Leroy Smith, 26, who had links with Yardie drug gangs. Smith organised couriers to bring crack cocaine from Jamaica into the UK. He had been convicted of gun charges the previous year but escaped from three prison officers in April 1993 by holding one at knifepoint during a prison transfer. Smith adored his 9mm firearm, to which he had attached an infrared gunsight. He'd boasted that police would never catch him, because if anyone got in his way he would shoot them.

Before the constables could even get close to Smith, James heard a bang and then the sound of Simon screaming. When he turned to help his colleague Smith shot James in the back. James could still hear Simon screaming and tried to get to him but his own wounds were too severe, and he collapsed, hearing more shots as he fell, and he tried to take cover behind a parked car. James, unable to move, shaking from the shock and from his injuries, waited for the gunman to come and finish him off. But the next thing he heard was the sound of a motorbike roaring away. The bullet that hit James entered his back and exited through his side, just missing vital internal organs. Simon had been shot in the leg, the bullet narrowly passed by major arteries.

Smith fled to Jamaica then America after the shootings. John Jones was at home one day when he received a call from an American police officer in Connecticut.

"You're after a Leon Smith, right?" the officer said.

"Yeah," Jones replied but before he could say any more he heard the officer scream: "Armed police! Assume the position!" The officer had been watching Smith along with another suspect and just then arrested them, recovering two Mac10 machine guns in the process (these weapons, known as 'spray and pays' can fire up to thousand rounds a minute).

Smith had been running a drug smuggling operation between Jamaica and Bridgeport, a large town in Connecticut, sending teenage Jamaican girls who'd swallowed greased condoms full of drugs in Jamaica on flights to New York. While in Connecticut, Smith caught one of these girls stealing some of his cocaine. Smith tied her up, left her for a day and the following night he put her in the boot of his car, telling the other girls that they were never going to see her again. He drove off and later opened the boot on a quiet side street, untied the girl and told her: "You disobeyed me but I'm going to give you a chance, so run!" As she fled down the street, Smith fired his 9mm but missed and the girl made it to a police station.

Before his arrest, Smith was overheard telling his girlfriend: "The buzzards [the police officers] deserved it…I should've got them good and proper." Jones flew out to interview Smith about the police shootings only to find him begging for extradition. He was the only Jamaican guy in the county jail and was being beaten up by every other gang in the prison. Jones extracted a confession and Smith was duly deported to the UK where he was jailed for two years for the escape, eighteen years for a firearms offence, and five years for robbery. He was given a 25-year sentence for attempting to murder James and eighteen years for wounding Simon. The sentences were ordered to run consecutively. As Judge Richard Lowry told him: "Dreadful crimes must attract dreadful sentences." Even after he'd been handed this record-breaking set of sentences, Smith showed no sign of remorse or respect. He instead made a mock gun with his hands and pretended to fire at constables James and Simon as he was led away to his cell.

These terrible crimes all generated headlines and the debate about what was happening in South London was turned into a debate about whether the Met should be armed as so many criminals seemed to be arming themselves. There was suddenly much talk of Yardies and guns but little about the drugs and what could be done to stem the flow of crack into the UK.

As a result of these murders and shootings, British policing was changed forever in May 1994, when Commissioner Paul

Condon announced that Met police would be able to openly carry guns and would not need a senior officer's authority to draw them. The Commissioner said that this would hopefully 'postpone the necessity to routinely arm police officers,' adding that all police officers in Brixton had been issued with bullet-proof vests and that our old wooden truncheons were being replaced by new, longer, lighter plastic versions.

"I think we all value the traditional image of the British bobby but we have to police the real world and the equipment and training must have some link with the real world," the Commissioner said.

Previously, officers based in the armed response vehicles (ARVs) or Trojan units on 24-hour mobile patrol around London needed authority from a high-ranking officer before removing guns from a secure metal box inside the vehicle. The Commissioner also increased the number of ARVs from five to twelve.

The reason we had such a problem with guns and guns being used so indiscriminately was that we had failed to act when we should have. What did work were the patrols that targeted robbers, which operated alongside those officers who worked with local people to break through the wall of silence protecting London's worst criminals.

In Nelson's case, the wall of silence was broken thanks to a huge joint effort by murder squad detectives and local police constables alike.

Nelson's aunt, Rose, had managed to find out that Nelson had buried the murder weapons somewhere in Earlsfield cemetery, close to where he lived at that time. A secret midnight expedition to find them proved fruitless (the cemetery was huge) and it took another four months of relentless campaigning and investigation before we received an anonymous phone call from a friend of one of Nelson's relatives to say that if we followed the lipstick crosses on gravestones in the cemetery, then we would find the guns.

Detectives found them in plastic bags buried in a patch of rough, overgrown grass beside a grave. Inside were both the Browning and the Tanfoglio and more than forty bullets.

Specialist fingerprint officers examined the guns and found a fingerprint belonging to Nelson's mother on the plastic bag. Ballistic officers from the Forensic Science Laboratory were able to match the residue from the guns to residue recovered from clothing taken from the suspects' homes. Bullets fired by both guns matched those at the scene of the murder as well as those found in William Danso's body. The bullet recovered from Pat's chest came from the Tanfoglio, which was traced to a crooked Essex-based gun dealer called Sidney Wink.

Nelson, Chen and Lips were all charged with the Clapham murders.

It seemed as though we were on the way to securing their convictions for murder, but there were some major problems, foremost of which was the firearms residue. This was an issue that had long been a problem for the police in terms of proving when and where the firearms residue was deposited on the clothing. It is not enough to claim that suspect's clothing contains traces of gunpowder. Defence barristers will argue that the gun was fired on a different date, or that it was from a different gun, or even , as has been successfully argued on several other occasions, that gun residue had come from the armed officers who made the arrest.

It was thought that gun dealer Sidney Wink would provide a key piece of testimony by linking the guns to Nelson and his crew. Wink was a former Met Police officer who had a reputation for providing reliable and untraceable firearms – he was thought to have supplied the guns used in the Brinks Mat gold bullion robbery – and Jones's team had been led to him in the Dunne case thanks to a tip off from someone close to the Nelson family. Probably unable to bear the thought of prison, while on bail in

August 1994, Wink turned one of his guns on himself, putting a bullet in his brain.

And it was for these reasons that the Crown Prosecution Service (CPS) decided to drop the case against the three men. This came as a complete shock to us all. John Jones was utterly devastated. "I was very, very angry with the advice we received from the QC (Queen's Counsel) advising the Crown Prosecution Service," John said afterwards. "He felt that our chances of conviction at that time were not as high as he felt they ought to be ... I feel personally that had we gone ahead ... the chances of conviction would have been pretty good and the Danso family and the Dunne family would not have gone through this trauma ..."

I remember when Jones got the news; I could see him through the door window throwing stuff around in his office in a fury. We just couldn't believe it. As well as everything described above, we had supergrasses, witnesses (including the woman who'd seen Nelson's car close to the scene minutes after the shooting) and bullets that could be linked to Nelson (bullets from one of firearms used in the murders matched those recovered from the club shooting of Massaquoi; another bullet had been found in Chen's ashtray; the bullet fired in sick celebration into the air after the murder had been found by chance in Wandsworth, one-and-a-half miles away and was matched to one of the guns recovered from the cemetery).

The families were no less shocked. Ivan Dunne, Pat's younger brother said: "What justice is this? It is insane to think the man who detectives think killed my brother will not face a jury."

And then, on 30 September 1996, John Jones's team, already much reduced from thirty to six detectives, was disbanded. I'd already left by this point, and had restarted my career with the TSG. The investigation wasn't closed but had been dramatically scaled down.

Nelson, who spent his time in jail intimidating some of the country's most hardened criminals (including IRA terrorists) into handing over phone credits so he could ring his many girlfriends, was released in 1999, after serving only half of his sentence.

# CHAPTER THIRTY-ONE

# THE PRICE OF JUSTICE

**"T**here is not a police officer in Britain who does not want to see PC Dunne's killer brought to justice." These were the words of Detective Superintendent Brian Tomkins, who took over the murder investigation in the years after the killings. As true as this was, we were under fire in the media for failing to bring William and Pat's killers to justice. Even Home Secretary Michael Howard had hinted strongly at his disappointment.

It wasn't for lack of trying. In just over 1,000 days since the murders, we'd spoken to 6,700 people and had taken more than 11,000 statements. Detectives had gone back to the CPS to try and persuade them to go ahead with a prosecution against Nelson but for three years they repeated the same answer: there simply wasn't enough evidence and they weren't prepared to risk a long and expensive trial when they felt there wasn't a realistic prospect of conviction. What we needed, they said, were witnesses and/or some solid physical evidence that tied Nelson to the killings, otherwise Nelson would end up in the clear and we'd never get another chance.

These were the days when a defendant could not be tried for the same offence twice, often called 'double jeopardy.' The idea was to prevent scenarios where an innocent person could be retried multiple times until the police, or prosecution, got the result they wanted. It was also a way of making the courts more efficient, so that the police and CPS were fully prepared and wouldn't clog up the courts repeating cases whenever some new evidence was found, or new witnesses came forward. Of course, the terrible thing about double jeopardy was that the accused could be acquitted only for new evidence to be found that proved their guilt. Someone could, this way, get away with murder. Such was the case with the racist murder of teenager Stephen Lawrence in 1996 where two men – Gary Dobson and David Norris – were acquitted following a private prosecution brought by Stephen's parents. Even when new evidence was found (thanks to developing technology) there was no chance of ever bringing the men back to court.

This remained the case until the double jeopardy rule was abolished under the Criminal Justice Act 2003, which came into effect in April 2005. It is now possible to be tried for the same offence twice (and you only get one more attempt), although second trials are given the most stringent of examinations by the director of public prosecutions, who will only allow them to proceed if it is in the public interest and there is "new and compelling evidence." Stephen's murderers were retried and jailed in 2012.

At the time, we had one chance and one chance only and, although the police thought they had enough evidence, the CPS refused to budge. So the Murder Squad had no choice but to continue to investigate but, with no leads and no one prepared to come forward, there came a day in 1999 when Nelson, labelled by both police and press as "the most dangerous man to walk the streets of Britain," stepped out of the prison gates and into the streets of London a free man.

He was soon back in business and celebrated his growing success with a trip to Florida with his new girlfriend and fellow criminal Roger Vincent; we now know that while in Florida, Nelson bought a silencer and a laser sight for his beloved Browning 9mm.

Roger Vincent, white and in his early thirties, was one of the UK's most violent and successful criminals who funded his lavish lifestyle by laundering his fellow criminals' ill-gotten cash. Like Nelson, Vincent had no qualms about killing his enemies. He would eventually be jailed for a minimum of 30 years in 2005 – reduced to 25 on appeal – for the gangland killing of Dave King, a minder who'd protected, among many other celebs, Nigel Benn and Robbie Williams. King, a father of two, had been charged by Customs with attempting to import 14kilos of heroin into the UK. But the charges were unexpectedly dropped and King's criminal buddies suspected that he'd been 'turned,' i.e., had become an informer for Customs. Vincent shot King with a Kalashnikov AK-47 automatic assault rifle in the leafy suburban town of Hoddesdon in Hertfordshire. King was hit by five of the 26 bullets fired by the AK47, famous for being wildly inaccurate – known as a 'pay and spray' in the underworld because they're expensive and spray their bullets every which way except for where they're supposed to go.

The Assets Recovery Agency (ARA) later froze most of Vincent's assets, worth £948,000 – a villa in Malaga, land in Cyprus, a £500,000 house, cash squirrelled away in various bank accounts and a BMW X5, which Vincent had admitted paying for with the proceeds of crime. The ARA said Vincent had made his fortune from "drug trafficking, fraud, extortion, contract killings and money laundering."

Although the investigation into William and Pat's murders never stopped – unlike other countries, UK police never 'close' unsolved murder investigations- other, newer murders needed to be cracked and so the heat on Nelson eased up somewhat as resources were diverted elsewhere. Then, in 2001, Pat's brothers kick-started a new campaign which reawakened the nation's memories, and the investigation was re-launched in a blaze of publicity, thanks also to a six-and-a-half minute reconstruction on BBC's Crimewatch, after which it was announced that a national newspaper, with the Met Police, was offering an unprecedented £100,000 reward for information that would lead to the conviction of William and Pat's killers.

Detective Chief Inspector Steve Richardson, from the SCD1 Homicide South team, who was appointed to take over the investigation in 2001, believed that a combination of new DNA techniques and 'shifted allegiances' in South London's underworld might give them the break they so desperately needed. He also said that any witnesses who were fearful of what might happen if they testified in court would be given the chance to change their identities and start a new life in a foreign country.

It started to work. The woman who'd been prompted by her Christian faith to lead detectives to Nelson's guns in 1994 came forward and told police that she was prepared to speak up in court.

Eugene Djaba, the manager of Street Communications, the shop where Danso had worked, had gone on the run in 1996 before he could be tried for a £3m cigarette fraud. Djaba got the surprise of his life when Met detectives showed up in his hometown in Ghana and persuaded him – after reassuring him that they weren't interested in his fraud conviction – to testify via live video link.

The Crimewatch appeal prompted a fellow inmate of Nelson's to come forward. 'Alf Davies' (not his real name) said that while they were in Wormwood Scrubs in 1994, Nelson told him: "I shot that copper, the one on the bike." Davies said he was willing to testify for the reward.

Meanwhile, specialist surveillance officers were tasked to follow Nelson and bugged his car. They listened as he boasted to a group of fellow gangsters about how it was only a matter of time before he'd carry out his own "St Valentine's Day Massacre" to eliminate his rivals. He also told of how he'd gone to the opening of a nightclub armed with a machine gun.

If Nelson was arrested and it could be proven that any guns in the vicinity were indeed his, then, under the so-called two-strikes rule – based on his previous firearms convictions–the maximum sentence was life.

A chance finally came in 2003 when the surveillance officers heard the distinctive double-click of a gun being 'racked', i.e., being readied for use. There was never going to be a better time. With authorisation given, a team of armed officers from SO19 raced to Nelson's flat in Woolwich, south east London and, after blowing the door off its hinges, the master criminal was caught with his pants down – watching a porn film.

A search of his spare bedroom revealed his 'hitman's kit' including the Browning, laser sight and silencer in a small zip-up bag. The police also noted Nelson's trademark suits, shirts and ties all neatly arranged in wardrobes, and thirty pairs of trainers lined up along the bedroom floor.

He was charged with ownership of the Browning with intent to endanger life, having a stun gun capable of sending out half a million volts, being in possession of various types of ammunition and handling three luxury stolen cars worth nearly £100,000.

I was at home in Yorkshire when I got the call, the same call anyone connected to the case received and as soon as I heard the opening words: "We got him, Mike," I knew exactly what they were talking about.

Nelson was found guilty and sentenced to life in January 2004.

Nelson's conviction was a major victory but we still wanted justice for William and Pat and so detectives continued to build a case against Nelson for murder. Two months after Nelson's conviction, it was announced that the Specialist Crime Directorate building of the Metropolitan Police at Sutton, Surrey would officially be known as Patrick Dunne House. Five murder investigation units were based at the centre at the time, including the team investigating William and Pat's murders.

Armed with the fact that they had two new witnesses, detectives went back to the CPS and although they had not fulfilled the

CPS's wishes, in that there was no definitive forensic evidence and no witness had picked Nelson out at an identity parade, the detectives argued that they had more than a dozen pieces of circumstantial evidence that put Nelson in Cato Road with the Tanfoglio in his hand. Plus, Nelson had two convictions for owning and using weapons and, thanks to a change in the law, they would be able to inform the jury of this. Finally, at the end of 2005, the CPS had the go ahead and Nelson was charged with both murders.

Early in 2006, almost thirteen years after William and Pat's murder, Nelson appeared in Woolwich Crown Court via video link from Belmarsh Prison. Wearing a black, white and blue tracksuit, Nelson entered a plea of Not Guilty.

Richard Horwell QC, prosecuting, made it clear that there was no shortage of people that placed Nelson at the scene; that he had motive to kill William Danso and that Nelson had in fact confessed to the murders, not once, not twice but three times; twice during police interviews and once more to Alf Davies, the thief he shared a cell with in Wormwood Scrubs. After his arrest in Islington, he told a custody sergeant he would "cop it like the other one," following this the next day by telling two other officers: "I will take one of you out again," and then told his cellmate: "I shot the copper, the one on the bike."

Djaba kept his promise and testified via video link about seeing Nelson pull the Tanfoglio – he recognised the gun- from his jacket and threaten to put a "bullet in the belly" of another man, adding that Nelson had told him that if Danso had tried to stop him then he "would have shot him in the belly."

"He showed me the gun, told me how many bullets the gun carried," Djaba said. "It was fully loaded."

Much was made of Nelson's attitude, that he thought he was too clever for the police and untouchable but as Horwell said: "Arrogance and notions of invincibility sometimes go before a fall."

William Danso's widow Deborah and his sister Gifty burst into tears after the jury announced its verdict: guilty.

Mr Justice Wilkie, sentencing Nelson on February 22, 2006 to another life term with a minimum tariff of 35 years said: "His utter disregard for any civilised behaviour is reflected in the fact that they were so pleased by what they had done they were heard by a number of witnesses laughing... These killings were callous as they were brutal and as they were senseless."

Nelson refused to come out of his cell below the court for the final week of the trial. Wilkie made a point of highlighting this. "Nelson, who is so jealous of the respect which he thinks he should be accorded, has amply demonstrated the same moral cowardice in which he, mob handed and armed, killed these two unarmed men."

Superintendent John Jones, who for the last thirteen years had joined Pat Dunne's family for lunch on the anniversary of his murder, was in court to hear the verdict but, although delighted, he told the press that he thought we could have achieved a conviction twelve years earlier, and I had to agree.

William's family said they had forgiven the killers and, talking about the time it had taken to convict Nelson, Pat's brother, Steve said: "In all that time we never gave up hope – and we never stopped forgiving... Forgiveness is the other side of justice's coin."

Pat's other brother, Ivan, speaking to the press outside the court said: "He [Nelson] loved the gun and lived by the gun but he did not have the moral courage to face us when he was being sentenced. I do not forgive him and never will."

Of course, this wasn't the end of the story.

As DCI Richardson said, Nelson's accomplices could expect to be arrested. "It has taken a great deal of work both by my team and the original inquiry team to arrive at this point... Our work is not yet complete and we will continue to investigate this case to bring the remaining perpetrators to justice. They must expect that one day there will be a knock on the door."

That knock is yet to come.

# EPILOGUE

13 December 1995

Five minutes ago I was drinking tea in the station canteen. Now I'm kitted up in riot gear – visored NATO helmet, see-thru shield, baton, steel toecaps, stab vest, shin and elbow guards. It's heavy stuff but I don't feel the weight, thanks to the adrenaline. There are fifty of us holding the line at Brixton Road and more than a hundred rioters are ahead. They are chanting "Killers! Killers! Killers!"

A man has just died in police custody.

Twenty-five-year-old Wayne Douglas, who was black, was suspected of robbing a young couple at knifepoint when he was arrested. The officers had a tough job controlling him and had held Wayne facedown with his hands cuffed behind his back on four separate occasions. He was in an interview room, sitting down and being questioned about the robbery, when he collapsed and died.

An inquest will reveal that Wayne had a heart condition. The jurors will decide by eight-to-one that the arresting officers cannot be blamed for his death: it was a tragic accident.

The local people who had protested peacefully outside of the police station earlier this evening have long gone. As I look at the young men ahead, chanting angrily at us, the TSG, I know that they are not 'Brixton', they are the enemy, the few people in society who seek out crime and destruction, who want to fight. Well, now they've got one.

***

To me, it felt as though the era of the bobby on the beat had died with Pat. We were in a new age now; with the rise or crack and the associated gun crime, policing our communities had become much more dangerous and more community beat officers would lose their lives as a result.

On 18 April PC Phillip Walter and PC Derek Shepherd were called to what they thought was a routine domestic in Ilford, East London. Instead, they walked into a flat where three Yardies were beating up a fourth man. One of the Yardies, a 28-year-old Jamaican illegal immigrant known as 'Ray Lee' (one of three names found on fake passports in his possession) pulled out a Smith & Wesson revolver from his jacket and started to shoot.

Action beats reaction. Derek dived towards the gun as Ray Lee fired; the bullet hit Phillip in the chest; Ray Lee fired again, the bullet grazed Derek's shoulder a moment before he was able to jam his finger in front of the gun's hammer. Ray Lee released the gun and ran.

Phillip, 28-years-old, died where he fell. He had been in the police for just one year.

Ray Lee was jailed for eighteen years for manslaughter and possession of a firearm.

The Gary Nelson case taught me many things, but foremost, it had shown me that it was always better to do something than nothing at all. All it had taken was for some members of the Met's leadership to ignore the rising tide of crack and Yardie-related crime.

As Dave, one of the managers of the Providence House Community Centre in Battersea had said, young people are full of energy. If we can't get them to direct that energy in a construc-tive way then there's always the chance they'll be drawn into crime.

People need to belong. I belong to the police. It helped me find myself; it gave me a sense of purpose. When you belong, you care about the world in which you live. If you don't belong, you don't care. Dave, backed up by much evidence, had seen smart kids who were growing up in poverty – many without fathers – fail at school simply because they were ill-prepared for a system that frustrated and then alienated them. From that day, they looked for an outlet for their energy and for some, a minority perhaps, but a significant minority nonetheless, per-haps those whose brains had been wired a certain way by early experiences, and were susceptible to the influence of the Yardies (or were inspired by them), and who saw young white people getting rich and finding happiness in Margaret Thatcher's every-man-for-himself system, gradually grew into Nelson-types whose eventual cost to society was incalculable in terms of the misery and pain, generated by violence and the spread of drugs.

When I joined the TSG, young UK-born criminals were starting to surpass the Yardies for sheer savagery. Gary Nelson may have been one of the worst criminals we'd ever seen in London but the young wannabe gangsters coming up behind him were just as bad, if not worse.

Remember Duane Daniels, the nineteen-year-old gang-leader who committed more than a thousand crimes and was jailed for ten years in 1993? He went straight back to his old ways after he was released in 1998.

In 2000, Daniels' friend, Spencer Sheppard, was "boil-ing with indignation" when bouncer George Napier ejected him from the Paradise Club in New Cross, southeast London. Sheppard retuned to the club with some friends – including

Daniels – and his American pit-bull dog, Colonel, who immediately started to attack one of Napier's colleagues. Sheppard then started punching Napier (according to local people, Napier was, like William Danso, a 'gentle giant') before Daniels stepped in and stabbed Napier in the heart, killing him. Daniels, who was later found guilty of a series of post office and building society raids in which he'd held people hostage and tortured them with his knife, received six life sentences in 2002.

There were many other Nelsons out there, on the rise. We had been left with a Herculean task if we were going to defeat the UK's most violent criminals. For my part, I'd gone to the other extreme, from beat cop to the TSG. I was now called in to restore order to communities that had broken down and, as my new colleagues told me, we'd never been so busy.

Mark, meanwhile, was on his way to becoming a detective and would soon be investigating serious crimes. Trist had become a sergeant, Darren aka Dr Death was still a PC, as were Timbo and Foxy (who received a commendation for the capture of the serial rapist), while Jonny was just a few months away from achieving his dream of driving the area car. Pete was facing the horror of total computerisation of the Met's records and was fiercely defending his paper archive from the advance of the evil microchip. Thanks to many cock-ups with new IT systems, Pete was able to keep it running for quite a few years before the geeks finally took over the asylum. Sergeant Phil had retired as did Stevie, who claimed he took early retirement 'to spend more time with my family,' which no one believed and while I never did see Patters' Puck, I did bump into the wily sergeant a short time later to find he'd risen to the rank of Inspector after Hugh left to join the TSG as a Superintendent.

Whatever happened, wherever we went and whatever we did, we would always be family. We would always be united in our battle to keep our communities safe, whatever the danger.

***

The battle lines are drawn. Brixton and Stockwell tube stations are closed. A police helicopter beats the air above our heads. Cars are on fire. The Dogstar Pub in Coldharbour Lane is also in flames, its windows smashed. Formerly the Atlantic, a predominantly black pub, it is – was, now – a symbol of gentrification, a playground for the wealthy outsiders who were snapping up Brixton properties as investments, a stepping stone on the property ladder.

The sudden sound of a gunshot makes everyone duck, even the TV cameramen, normally unflappable observers.

A police motorcyclist makes the mistake of trying to race past the mob, god knows why. Bottles, cans and bricks rain down on him; he slows and swerves and ten men run from the mob and are on him, he breaks his shoulder as he falls to the ground, his ribs crack as boots fly. We don't wait for the order; we charge, ignoring the bricks, letting them bounce off our shields as we run towards our injured colleague.

To be continued ...

8166959R00169

Printed in Germany
by Amazon Distribution
GmbH, Leipzig